Move! A Minimalist Theory of Construal

Generative Syntax
General Editor: David Lightfoot

Recent work in generative syntax has viewed the language faculty as a system of principles and parameters, which permit children to acquire productive grammars triggered by normal childhood experiences. The books in this series serve as an introduction to particular aspects or modules of this theory. They presuppose some minimal background in generative syntax, but meet the tutorial needs of intermediate and advanced students. Written by leading figures in the field, the books also contain sufficient fresh material to appeal to the highest level.

Move! A Minimalist Theory of Construal

Norbert Hornstein

First published 2001

2 4 6 8 10 9 7 5 3 1

Blackwell Publishers Inc.
350 Main Street
Malden, Massachusetts 02148
USA

Blackwell Publishers Ltd
108 Cowley Road
Oxford OX4 1JF
UK

Library of Congress Cataloging-in-Publication Data
Hornstein, Norbert.
    Move! : a minimalist theory of construal / Norbert Hornstein.
      p. cm. — (Generative syntax ; 5)
    Includes bibliographical references and index.
    ISBN 0–631–22360–6 (alk. paper) — ISBN 0–631–22361–4 (pbk. : alk. paper)
    1. Minimalist theory (Linguistics). 2. Grammar, Comparative and general—
Syntax. I. Title: Minimalist theory of construal. II. Title. III. Series.

P158.28.H67 2000
415—dc21
                                00–031017

British Library Cataloguing in Publication Data
A CIP catalogue record for this book is available from the British Library.

Typeset in 10/12 pt Palatino
by Graphicraft Limited, Hong Kong
Printed in Great Britain by MPG Books, Bodmin, Cornwall

This book is printed on acid-free paper.

Contents

Preface

This book has an immodest goal: to eliminate construal processes from UG. The ambitions are minimalist in motivation though, no doubt, idiosyncratically so. In place of construal processes I suggest that we generalize movement so that it replace construal operations in control theory, the binding theory and the licensing of 0-operators. The result is a rather homogeneous looking UG, bereft of many of the modules characteristic of GB inspired proposals for the structure of Universal Grammar.

The hope that this is a feasible goal has been nurtured by the successful work of others. I am particularly indebted to recent work on these topics pursued within the minimalist framework. Let me name some names.

The general way that I conceive of the issues to be pursued owes everything to Chomsky's writings on Minimalist syntax, especially Chomsky (1993, 1995, 1998). Though the analyses presented here deviate in most details from those Chomsky explores, the book would not have been possible but for the methodological setting these papers urge.

I have also benefited greatly from various published and unpublished papers by Jairo Nunes. The fingerprints of Nunes (1995) are all over chapter 3. However, the influence of this work on this book are more pervasive. Nunes (1995) explores the possibility of extending movement operations to cover general licensing conditions that were heretofore thought to require construal operations. The success of Nunes' efforts in showing that what appeared to be enormous problems with this approach could be circumvented in such an elegant manner inspired me to consider extending this approach in every direction. As note, chapter 3 buys into his analysis of parasitic gap formation as involving sidewards movement. I have shamelessly borrowed (stolen?) what I could and was disheartened when I could not use more.

Nunes (1995) owes an intellectual debt to Uriagereka (1998). I owe a more personal one to Uriagereka himself. We have been arguing about various issues in minimalism, both general and specific, since Chomsky (1993) was first made available back in 1992. We ran joint study groups, conferences, seminars, grants and more. I sat in his office for many hours pumping him for insights and having him fumigate whatever bees happened to be in my bonnet at any particular time. Though I suspect that Juan does not endorse much of what you read below, at least not in the way that I present it, I could not have even begun to think about these topics without his help and generosity.

All of the material presented here has been vetted by two linguistics depart-
ments; the one at the University of Maryland, College Park and the one at the
University of Southern California. It is rare to have such a bi-coastal opportunity. However, for about the last three years I have been able to present my
work at USC during the spring semester (usually when the weather in Maryland
is less than ideal) to a well informed supportive yet skeptical audience. This
audience was always kind enough to laugh at my jokes, gently inform me
when my arguments went nowhere and generous enough to offer remedies.
Particular thanks go to Joseph Aoun, Hagit Borer, Mary Kato (visiting), Audrey
Li, Barry Schein, Tim Stowell (UCLA carpetbagger), Jean Roger Vergnaud, and
Maria Luisa Zubizarreta.

This material has also been presented over the years in seminars at the
University of Maryland, College Park. The participants in these seminars have
greatly influenced the directions taken. Thanks in particular to Mark Arnold,
Juan Carlos Castillo, John Drury, Kleanthes Grohmann, Kwang Sup Kim,
Akeemi Matsuya, Roger Martin, Nobue Mori, Jairo Nunes, Paul Pietroski, Juan
Uriagereka, and Jiangxin Wu.

Earlier versions of the book were read and commented on by Joseph Aoun,
David Lightfoot, Jairo Nunes, Paul Pietroski and Juan Uriagereka. Their comments were *all* incorporated into subsequent drafts.

Thanks to Kleanthes Grohmann for compiling the bibliography and doing
the index.

I also acknowledge support from the National Science Foundation (NSF) in
the form of two NSF grants awarded to Norbert Hornstein and Juan Uriagereka:
SBR9601559 and BCS9817569.

One last point. This book does *not* go where no one has gone before. Many
of the analyses I present have the flavor of re-invented wheels. I have tried to
site preceding analyses where I knew of them. However, I am not particularly
good at keeping track of these things and I am sure that I have failed to
acknowledge work that has gone in essentially the same direction years (if not
decades) before. One such piece of work is John Bowers' thesis *Grammatical
Relations* (1973) (reprinted in the Garland series (1985)) and his *The Theory of
Grammatical Relations* (1981). He argues for a movement treatment of control
that I reargue the merits of in chapters 2 and 3. I am sorry that I did not cite
Bowers' work in earlier published papers that form the bases of chapter 2. I
have little doubt that this case of neglect on my part is not unique. I apologize
in advance to those whose work is relevant that I do not mention.

1

The Minimalist Program

Introduction

It is my opinion that the implications of the Minimalist Program (MP) are more radical than generally supposed. I do not believe that the main thrust of MP is technical; whether to move features or categories for example. MP suggests that UG has a very different look from the standard picture offered by GB-based theories. This book tries to make good on this claim by outlining an approach to grammar based on *one* version of MP. I stress at the outset the qualifier "version." Minimalism is not a theory but a program animated by certain kinds of methodological and substantive regulative ideals. These ideals are reflected in more concrete principles which are in turn used in minimalist models to analyze specific empirical phenomena. What follows is but one way of articulating the MP credo. I hope to convince you that this version spawns grammatical accounts that have a theoretically interesting structure and a fair degree of empirical support.

The task, however, is doubly difficult. First, it is unclear what the content of these precepts is. Second, there is a non-negligible distance between the content of such precepts and its formal realization in specific grammatical principles and analyses. The immediate task is to approach the first hurdle and report what I take the precepts and principles of MP to be.[1]

1 Principles-Parameters and Minimalism

MP is many things to many researchers. To my mind it grows out of the perceived success of the principles and parameters (P&P) approach to grammatical competence. Here's the story.

The central problem for grammatical theory is how it is that kids are able to acquire grammatical competence despite the impoverished nature of the data that is input to this process. No sane person doubts that the attainment of grammatical competence is influenced by the nature of the primary linguistic data (PLD); children raised in Paris learn French and those raised in Brooklyn speak English.[2] However, it is also clear that the knowledge attained vastly exceeds the information available in the PLD.[3] This, in essence, is what Chomsky (1986b) dubbed "Plato's Problem," the problem of the poverty of the stimulus. The greatest virtue of P&P accounts is that they provide a way of addressing Plato's problem in the domain of language.

The idea is simple. Kids come biologically equipped with a set of principles of grammar construction, i.e. Universal Grammar (UG). The principles of UG have open parameters. Specific grammars arise once these parameter values are specified. Parameter values are determined on the basis of the PLD. A language specific grammar, on this view, is simply a vector specifying the values that the principles of Universal Grammar leave open.[4] This picture of the acquisition process is sensitive to the details of the environmental input (as well as the level of development of the child's other cognitive capacities) as it is the PLD that provides the parameter values. However, the shape of the knowledge attained is not restricted to whatever information can be gleaned from the PLD since the latter exercises its influence against the background of rich principles that UG makes available.

In retrospect, syntactic research since the mid-1970s can be seen as largely aimed at elaborating this sort of picture and demonstrating its viability. Government-Binding theory (GB) is the best known version of a P&P theory of UG. It has several distinctive features.

First, GB is modular. The grammar is divided into various subcomponents sensitive to different kinds of well-formedness requirements. There are modules for case, binding, phrase structure, movement, control, theta-structure, and trace identification. These modules are tuned to different kinds of grammatical information (e.g. case versus antecedence), exploit different kinds of rules (e.g. construal versus movement) and locality principles (e.g. binding domains versus government configurations). GB modules, in short, are structurally and informationally distinct.

One of modularity's primary virtues is that it radically simplifies the kinds of rules that grammars exploit. In place of construction specific rules (such as Passive, Raising, WH movement, and Relativization), the grammar is pictured as having very general highly articulated modules whose interactions yield the properties observed in specific constructions. The modules factor out features common to different structures and allow principle based grammars to replace rule based ones.[5] Thus, in place of grammars with rather complex rules (i.e. rules stated in terms of complicated structural descriptions and structural changes), GB contains very simple rules whose overgeneration is curtailed by the combined filtering effects of the general principles constitutive of the various modules.

Second, GB contains a very general transformational component. It contains movement rules and construal rules which index nominal expressions to one another. As a by-product of its modular design, GB has been able to adopt a very simple movement rule: 'Move alpha'. 'Move alpha' allows any category to move anywhere at any time. The modules function to circumscribe the massive overgeneration that this very general rule inevitably leads to.

'Move alpha' incorporates a version of the trace theory of movement, viz. movement always leaves a trace – a lexically empty XP of the same category – in the position from which movement originates. For example, every application of NP-movement leaves an '$[_{NP}$ e]' in the launching site. Traces must be licensed. The module concerned with licensing traces is the ECP. Trace theory in concert with the ECP severely constrains the movement which a 'Move alpha' based theory permits. A central feature of GB theories is the exploitation of traces both for purposes of interpretation and to constrain the overgeneration of 'Move alpha'.

Third, a GB grammar has four critical levels at which various conditions are applied to filter out illicit phrase markers. The levels are D-structure (DS), S-structure (SS), LF and PF. The latter two are "interface" levels and constitute the grammatical contributions to semantic and phonetic interpretation respectively. DS and SS are "internal" levels and only interact with other parts of the language faculty.

DS has several distinctive properties: (i) it interfaces with the lexicon (ii) it is the level where the thematic information specific morphemes carry is integrated into the grammatical structures that transformations subsequently manipulate (iii) it is the locus of recursion in the grammar (iv) it is input to the transformational component and (v) it is the output of the phrase structure component.

SS is the point in a derivation at which the grammatical information required by the phonology splits off from the information required for meaning. Thus, LF and PF are blind to each other and only relate in virtue of being derived from a common SS phrase marker. SS is also the locus of a variety of filters from the Binding, ECP, Subjacency and Case modules. Observe that DS and (especially) SS are the most abstract levels in UG. They are the most remote from "experience" in the sense that they are furthest removed from a sentence's observable properties, its sound and meaning.

Fourth, the central grammatical relation in GB is government. This relation is ubiquitous and appears in every module of the grammar. Government lends conceptual unity to otherwise rather diverse components. Thus, though the modules themselves may be structurally very different, using different notions of locality and different kinds of rules, still they share a degree of unity in that they all exploit the same basic relation. Theta-roles and structural cases are assigned under government, binding domains are defined in terms of government, the ECP licenses traces that are in certain government configurations with their antecedents or heads, the subjacency condition on movement is defined in terms of barriers, which are in turn defined in terms of government. In short, though the modules "worry" about different kinds of information, and use different rules and locality domains they are nonetheless organized in terms of the same basic structural primitive.

GB has been very successful in illuminating the structure of grammatical competence. Given the emphasis on Plato's problem, research has focused on finding constraints of the right sort. By "right sort" I mean constraints tight enough to allow grammars to be acquired on the basis of PLD yet flexible enough to allow for the observed variation across languages. In short, finding a suitable answer to Plato's problem has been the primary research engine and GB proposals have largely been evaluated in terms of whether they satisfactorily meet its demands. This does not mean to say that other methodological standards have been irrelevant. Simplicity, and naturalness have also played a role. However, in practice, these yardsticks of theory evaluation have been quite weak and have been swamped by the requirements of outlining principles with a reasonable hope of addressing the poverty of stimulus problem.

Let me put this point another way. The issue of explanatory adequacy has been the 800 pound gorilla of grammatical inquiry and it has largely overshadowed the more standard benchmarks of theory evaluation. This is now changing for the following reason. As GB research has succeeded, a consensus has developed that P&P accounts answer Plato's problem in the domain of language. This consensus has served to cage the gorilla allowing other sorts of measures of success to drive theory construction, measures such as simplicity, elegance, parsimony, and naturalness. To put matters more starkly and tendentiously than is warranted: given that P&P models solve Plato's problem the issue now becomes which of the various conceivable P&P models is best and this issue is resolved using conventional criteria of theory evaluation. In other words, once explanatory adequacy is bracketed, as happens when P&P proposals alone are considered, an opening is created for simplicity, elegance and naturalness to emerge as the critical measures of theoretical adequacy. This reorientation, however, prompts a question: how to concretize these heretofore subordinate evaluative notions in the specific research setting that currently obtains. It is here that minimalism aims to make a contribution. I turn to this next.

2   Economies in Theory Evaluation

To ask for the simplest most elegant theory based on the most natural sorts of principles often asks for very little. These notions are generally too obscure or subjective to have much practical purchase. To give them life we need to flesh out the problems against which theories are expected to measure up. Only then (and perhaps not even then) can we develop rough measures of theoretical beauty and parsimony. What then is the appropriate backdrop for linguistic theory? One way into this question is to recruit those facts about language, the "big facts," that any conceivable theory must address to be worthy of consideration. A second way is to develop simple parsimonious grammars that exploit "natural" thematically unified principles. Chomsky (1993) suggests ways of moving in both these directions.

MP exploits three kinds of considerations. First, it takes certain very general facts to be self evident and requires any theory of grammar to accommodate them. As noted in section 1, MP endorses the assumption that UG has a principles and parameters architecture. Other indubitable features of natural language (NL) include the following: (i) sentences are the basic linguistic units, (ii) sentences are pairings of sounds and meaning, (iii) there is no upper bound to the number of sentences in any given NL, (iv) sentences show displacement properties in the sense that expressions pronounced in one position are interpreted in another, and (v) sentences are composed of words organized into larger units with hierarchical structure, i.e. phrases. Together, these six facts serve as very general *minimal* conditions of adequacy on any theory of UG.

In addition MP deploys two types of economy considerations. The first type are the familiar methodological benchmarks such as simplicity and parsimony, i.e. standard Ockham's razor sort of considerations: *ceteris paribus*, two primitive relations are worse than one, two levels are better than four, four modules are better than five, more is worse, fewer is better. Let's call such principles measures of *methodological economy*.

The reason that simplicity and parsimony are methodologically valuable is that they enhance the empirical exposure of one's underlying assumptions. To illustrate: if one can derive a body of data D using three assumptions, then D can be interpreted as lending empirical support to each of these assumptions. Each one carries part of the explanatory load and each is grounded to the degree that it is required to account for D. Note that if we reduce the required set of assumptions to two then this should, all things being equal, enhance the empirical support that D lends to each given that D is now spread over two assumptions rather than three.

Of course evaluation of alternatives is never this straightforward as things are never equal. There are trade offs that are hard to quantify between naturalness, parsimony and simplicity. However, the point remains that there are good epistemological reasons for adopting Ockham's strictures and trying to shave one's set of basic assumptions down to a minimum.

There is a second set of minimalist measures. Let's dub these *substantive economy*. Here a premium is placed on least effort notions as thematic sources for grammatical principles. The idea is that locality conditions and well-formedness filters are reflections of the fact that grammars are organized frugally to maximize resources. Short steps preclude long strides, derivations where fewer rules apply are preferred to those where more do, movement only applies when it must, no expressions occur idly in grammatical representations (i.e. full interpretation holds). These substantive economy notions generalize themes that have consistently arisen in grammatical research. Just think of the A-over-A condition (Chomsky 1964), the Principle of Minimal Distance (Rosenbaum 1970), the Superiority Condition (Chomsky 1973), the Minimality Condition (Rizzi 1990) and the Minimal Binding Requirement (Aoun and Li 1993a). It is natural to reconceptualize these in least effort terms. Minimalism proposes to conceptually unify all grammatical operations along these lines.[6]

These three sorts of considerations promote a specific research strategy: look for the simplest theory whose operations have a least effort flavor and that accommodate the six big facts about grammar noted above. This recommendation actually has considerable content. For example, the fact that sentences pair sounds and meanings and the fact that the number of sentences is essentially infinite requires both that grammars exist and that they interface with systems responsible for the articulatory/phonetic (AP) and conceptual/intentional (CI) properties that sentences display. Given this, there is a premium on grammatical principles that originate in this fact, e.g. if some sorts of grammatical objects are uninterpretable by the CI or AP interfaces, then phrase markers that contain these will be ill-formed unless these wayward objects are dispatched before interpretation. Given least effort criteria, the favored accounts will contain the simplest grammatical products that meet these interface requirements. This could mean the simplest to produce, in which case economy of derivational resources are key, or simplest to interpret, in which case economy of representational resources (i.e. full interpretation notions) are highlighted.

Consider another set of questions minimalist considerations lead to. What are the basic primitives of the system; the basic relations, objects and operations? If phrases exist (i.e. (v) above) then a set of relations is provided if phrases are organized in roughly X' terms, as standardly assumed. In X'-theory, phrases have (at least) three parts – heads, complements and specifiers – and invoke two relations – head/complement and specifier/head. Given the obvious fact that NLs contain phrases, UG requires these objects and relations whatever else it needs. Therefore, parsimony counsels that at most these objects and relations should be part of UG. This implies, for example, that sentences be analyzed as types of phrases rather than as having an idiosyncratic structure. This is essentially the conclusion GB has already drawn. Labeling sentences as IPs, TPs and CPs embodies this consensus.[7]

The recognition that phrases are a minimally necessary part of any theory of grammar further suggests that we reexamine whether we need government among the inventory of basic grammatical relations. Methodological simplicity urges doing without this extra notion given that we already have two others. All things being equal, we should adopt government only if the X'-theoretic relations we already have prove empirically inadequate.[8]

The same reasoning extends to the inventory of rules in UG. It is self evident that natural languages manifest "displacement" in the sense that expressions in a sentence are heard in one position yet interpreted from another. Thus, grammars must have means of representing this. In GB, the basic means of accommodating this fact is via movement processes. MP requires that we treat this fact in the most parsimonious way possible. Grammars should therefore treat all instances of "displacement" in a unified manner. In GB, movement operations are dislinguished from construal processes. Construal rules are different in kind from movement rules and are used to analyze some instances of displacement. For example, control structures involve an expression pronounced in one place yet related to another position that contributes to its thematic interpretation. All things being equal, one set of rules is preferable. Thus, optimally, either movement is construal or construal is movement.

Assume, for sake of argument, that only movement rules exist. We can then ask how much of the GB theory of movement is motivated on minimalist grounds. Are traces, for example, conceptually required? In part perhaps, insofar as they simply model displacement (one of the big facts noted above) and provide a mechanism for coding the fact that expressions can be interpreted as if in positions distinct from the ones they overtly appear in. Does the simple fact of displacement motivate the GB view that traces are indexed categories without lexical contents, i.e. '$[_{XP}$ e$]_i$'? Or does the existence of displacement phenomena suffice to ground the claim that traces are subject to special licensing conditions that do not apply to lexical items more generally? This is far less clear. Traces in GB are grammar internal constructs with very special requirements that regulate their distribution. Historically, the main motivation for traces was their role in constraining overgeneration in the context of a theory where movement was free, not in providing vehicles for interpretation.

The primary service traces and the conditions on them provided was to filter unwanted derivations that resulted from a grammar based on a rule like 'Move alpha'. Why assume that such entities exist, especially in the context of a minimalist theory in which it is assumed that movement is not free (as it is in GB) but only occurs if it must? Methodologically we should resist postulating traces as grammatical formatives unless strong empirical reasons force this conclusion. On conceptual grounds traces are of dubious standing.[9]

What could replace traces? Well, we independently need words and phrases. Why not assume that they are used by the grammar to accommodate displacement? In other words, assume that traces are not new kinds of expressions but they are copies of expressions that are already conceptually required.[10] This seems simpler than postulating a novel construct if one's main goal is to accommodate displacement. In short, GB traces must earn their keep empirically and all things being equal a copy theory of traces is preferable.[11]

What holds for traces holds for other grammar internal formatives as well; PRO, 0-operators and chains to name three more. It also brings into question the value of modules like the ECP, control theory and predication whose purpose is to monitor and regulate the distribution of these null (grammar internal) expressions. None of this means that the best theory of UG won't contain such entities or principles. However, minimalist reasoning suggests that they be adopted only if there is strong empirical motivation for doing so. On conceptual grounds, the burden of proof is on those who propose them. At the very least, minimalist scruples force us to reconsider the empirical basis of these constructs and to judge whether their empirical payoffs are worth the methodological price.

These sorts of abstract considerations can be easily amplified. The six facts MP takes as obvious make serious demands on GB style theories once issues of parsimony, naturalness and substantive elegance are taken as important measures of theory success. Both methodological and substantive economy lead to qualms about the adequacy of GB style theories. These in turn suggest grammars that have a different "look" from their GB precursors. Let's sample a few concrete MP arguments to see how these considerations are deployed.

3   Minimalism in Action

GB assumes that a grammar has four distinctive levels – DS, SS, PF and LF. PF and LF are conceptually necessary as they simply mirror the fact that sentences are pairings of sound and meaning. Thus, if there are grammatical levels at all, there will at least be a level that interfaces with the AP system and a level that contributes linguistic information to the CI systems. The other two levels, DS and SS, have a different status. If required at all, they are motivated on narrower empirical grounds.

Note that parsimony considerations favor the simpler two level theory unless there are good empirical reasons for postulating the more complex four level grammar. One minimalist project is to show that the two levels that are conceptually required – LF and PF – are also empirically sufficient. Chomsky (1993) argues for this conclusion. Consider the reasoning. Let's begin with S-structure.

SS is useful in GB in at least three ways.

First, it is exploited in distinguishing languages like English from those like French with regard to verb movement and English from Chinese with regard to WH movement. English verbs do covertly (after SS) what French verbs do overtly (before SS) and Chinese WH words do covertly what English WH elements do overtly. SS, then, marks the divide between overt and covert syntax which, it appears, is useful in describing both the differences and commonalities among language specific grammars.

Second, SS is where case theory applies. Case is relevant both phonetically and semantically in GB. Phonetically, pronouns with different cases sound different; 'he' versus 'him'. Semantically, case marking is critical in that the Visibility Condition assumes that only case marked nominals are theta active at LF. Assigning case at SS meets both PF and LF requirements.

Third, the binding theory can apply at SS as well as LF in certain versions of GB to filter out unwanted derivations.

Chomsky (1993) argues that the first two problems can be accommodated without postulating an SS level if one assumes that movement is driven by a feature checking requirement and that features come in two flavors; weak and strong. Strong features must be checked prior to the point at which a derivation splits into separate LF and PF branches. Weak features, in contrast, can be discharged at LF. Using this technology, English verbs can be treated as bearing weak features checked at LF while French verbs bear strong features that require checking in overt syntax.

WH movement can be treated in a similar fashion.[12] So can case. For example, if accusative case is a weak feature, then it can be checked in covert syntax after the grammar branches. If nominative case is strong then overt movement is required to check it.[13] Note that we have replaced the GB idiom of "assignment" with the terminology of "checking." Expressions enter syntactic derivations clothed with their features. These features get discharged/licensed via checking through the course of the derivation. As should be evident, this approach, in particular the combination of weak/strong features plus checking, eliminates the need for SS in theories of case as well as cross linguistic accounts of verb raising and WH movement. The new technology renders SS superfluous.[14]

This technology has a further interesting feature. It reflects the least effort themes of substantive economy. Movement is never gratuitous. It serves to license otherwise unacceptable items. Strong features are uninterpretable at either the PF (Chomsky 1993) or the LF interface (Chomsky 1995). Thus, these features would violate full interpretation were they to survive to the interface. Movement serves to "eliminate" such features by allowing them to be checked. In this sense, movement is recast in least effort terms as the way in which uninterpretable features get checked.

Movement in MP is a last resort operation in the sense of being illicit if it fails to result in some form of feature checking. Standard versions of MP incorporate this idea in the principle that movement must be "greedy": if A moves to K then either some feature of A or K is checked as a result. Greed, in effect, defines movement in the sense that non-greedy moves are simply not moves at all. Greed is the quintessential expression of substantive economy. Virtually all minimalist models exploit it in some form and thereby incorporate a least effort conception of grammatical operations.

The above illustrates the interplay of methodological and substantive economy considerations in MP. SS is suspect on methodological grounds. Thus, its utility must lie in its empirical virtues. But, the empirical motivations for SS fade if substantive economy notions are cast in terms of feature checking processes which reflect the least effort themes of MP. Interestingly, recasting grammatical processes as feature checking operations appears to be no less empirically adequate than prior approaches that exploited SS filters. Thus, there is less empirical motivation for SS than GB originally supposed. This supports the MP position, arrived at on general methodological grounds, that grammars have at most two levels, LF and PF.[15]

This conclusion invites further minimalist projects. Dumping SS requires reanalyzing all the phenomena that appear to exploit it. Chomsky's (1993) reanalyses provide important first steps and indicate that the minimalist program has plausibility. However, there are additional phenomena whose standard accounts exploit SS in crucial ways, for example: parasitic gap licensing, predication, 0-operator licensing and island effects. Without SS, processes that have been described as holding at SS cannot be literally correct. Standard accounts of island effects, obligatory control phenomena, and 0-operator constructions such as 'purpose'-clauses, tough constructions, relative clauses, and parasitic gaps rely on SS centered processes and so call for reanalysis. The succeeding chapters discuss possible ways of rethinking these phenomena in service of retaining the minimalist conclusion that UG has no SS level.

Chomsky (1993) also provides arguments for dispensing with D-structure. He argues that there can be no phrase marker that divides lexical insertion from the transformational component once 'tough'-constructions are considered. The standard GB analysis of these constructions requires the interleaving of these two processes once mildly complex cases are considered. If so, DS, with the properties GB assigns it, cannot exist.

The argument Chomsky presents goes as follows. Chomsky, following standard GB practice, assumes that *John* is not base generated in the post verbal position of *please*, despite its thematic dependence on this post verbal position, but is directly inserted into the matrix subject position.[16] This leaves 'tough'-constructions with a property inconsistent with the GB notion of DS in that the syntactic subject is not base generated in a theta-position. (1b) indicates that the matrix subject has no thematic function as it can be filled by an expletive. The problem is how 'John' is inserted into the derivation while respecting the assumption that lexical insertion precedes movement.

(1) a. John is easy to please
     b. It is easy to please John

Chomsky (1981) recognizes the problem posed by 'tough'-constructions and weakens the DS thematic requirements in response. The idea was to allow simple NPs to be exempt from this requirement. Assume, for example, that 'John' can be inserted at DS without a theta-role so long as it gets one by LF. This allows lexical insertion to precede transformational rules in (1a) though at the cost of weakening the GB conception of DS as the place where grammatical functions and thematic roles meet. 'John' can be inserted in (1a) without a theta-role as it receives one via predication by LF. To repeat, this maneuver has two substantial costs. First, it weakens the DS requirement that insertion be exclusively to theta-positions. In addition, it complicates the grammar by adding a new kind of rule: predication. Predication fills the thematic gap that generating expressions in non-theta-positions opens up. This process, though distinct from the DS process of theta-marking, also serves to assign a theta-role to an expression. As such, a predication rule is a necessary complement to any attempt to retain the services of DS given the standard analysis of 'tough'-constructions. These complications seem to allow GB to preserve DS as the border between lexical insertion and other kinds of transformations.

However, it does not work once slightly more complex samples of the 'tough'-construction are considered. The amendment to the GB theory of DS aims to allow DS to mark the border between insertion and other transformations. However, it is possible to find subjects of 'tough'-constructions that are transformationally formed. For example, a relative clause formed from a 'tough'-construction.

(2)   A man who is easy to please is easy to please

It appears that the subject here is formed via the application of rules such as relativization and 'tough' movement. Thus, it seems that the strict separation of movement from insertion transformations cannot be maintained. In sum, the GB version of DS as the level which is the output of lexical insertion, the input to the transformational component and "purely" represents thematic structure cannot be retained.[17]

This conclusion can lead to two different kinds of conclusions. One calls for reapportioning the tasks of DS to other parts of the grammar. Recall that it is uncontested that NLs are infinite. Thus, any theory of UG must have a mechanism for recursion to be adequate. In GB, recursion is lodged in DS, in the phrase structure rules of the grammar. MP substitutes generalized transformations for these phrase structure rules and makes them the recursive engine of the grammar.

Similarly, Chomsky (1995) relocates parts of theta theory to the transformational component. The GB hypothesis that DS is the domain in which thematic functions get defined is analyzed in MP as a condition on phrase formation. It is assumed that only trivial chains can assign or receive theta-roles, i.e. technically, theta-roles are assigned under Merge not Move. This has the effect of leaving theta-role assignment sensitive to base (i.e. pre-movement) configurations but without adverting to any level akin to DS. In short, as was the case with SS, Chomsky shows that garnering the services of DS conditions does not require postulating a DS level. Once again, the MP conclusion is that DS, like SS, is not required and so can be dispensed with as it is without empirical or conceptual warrant.

There is a second kind of conclusion one can draw. One can begin to question whether the conditions generally assumed to apply are really required at all. Note that this is different from assuming that the generalizations are correct but do not necessitate the technology heretofore deployed. This sort of conclusion has a more radical tinge in that it asks that the generalizations that have been taken as established be reevaluated. For example, Chomsky (1995) retains a central feature of DS in the idea that trivial chains are the only proper vehicles for theta role assignment or reception. His reasoning relies on analyzing theta-roles as very different from morphological features such as case and phi-feature agreement (c.f. chapter 2 for discussion). How good are the empirical and conceptual arguments for this distinction? I argue that there are advantages in rejecting it. The payoff is a more general conception of movement and a simpler picture of universal grammar. More specifically, the logic of MP invites the following line of investigation.

Jettisoning the vestiges of the GB conception of DS has two potentially positive consequences. First, it allows for the elimination of PRO from the inventory of empty categories. Second, it allows for the elimination of the PRO module from UG. Each consequence is attractive on methodological grounds if empirically sustainable. The conceptual superiority of fewer levels extends to modules too; one less is better than one more! As for PRO, it is a theory internal abstract entity whose worth must be supported on empirical grounds. All things being equal, it is no better to have grammar internal abstract entities than it is to have grammar internal interfaces.

This line of inquiry has another consequence. It suggests an extremely general approach to movement, one in which it is completely unrestricted. GB permits movement from theta to non-theta-positions and from non-theta to non-theta-positions. However, it forbids movement from one theta-position to another or from a non-theta-position to a theta-position. These restrictions follow from the role that DS plays in theta-role assignment in a GB theory and from the analogue of this restriction concerning trivial chains that Chomsky's version of MP incorporates.[18] All things being equal, however, these restrictions are undesirable as they stand in the way of the most general approach to movement; anything can move from anywhere to anywhere. Any restrictions require strong empirical support as, *ceteris paribus*, they complicate the operations of MERGE and MOVE.

This general conception of movement is in turn part of a larger project: to use movement as the primary vehicle for establishing grammatical coupling, e.g. for coding internominal dependencies intrasententially. Assume that core grammar only contains the simple operations of MERGE, COPY and DELETE.[19] Movement, let us assume, is COPY+MERGE.[20] The applications of MERGE and COPY result in various kinds of feature checking. I argue in the following chapters that almost all core grammatical relations can be analyzed in terms of these processes if they are completely generalized, in particular, if one drops the thematic restrictions on movement. Expressions check and gain features via movement and they establish anaphoric relations by movement. If this is correct, there is no control module or binding module and grammars contain no analogues of rules of construal in the GB sense.

One could go further still. The possibility arises that strictly speaking UG is *not* composed of separate modules with specific organizing principles and constraints. Rather, the main grammatical operations – MERGE, COPY, DELETE – apply to all features. Different applications of MERGE and MOVE (COPY+ MERGE) may check different features – case, agreement or theta-features for example – but the way in which all these features are checked is essentially the same. If this is correct, the GB picture of interacting modules placing different kinds of well formedness conditions on phrase markers, exploiting different domains of application and different sorts of rules is replaced by a theory in which grammars check features by merging and copying expressions in the same way for every feature. As the operations involved are the same, the locality domains and restrictions should hold indifferently across the various types of checking operations. Just as modules in GB allow the elimination of construction specific rules, the proposal here is that there are no morpheme specific processes either; no grammatical rules that specifically target PROs or anaphors or pronouns.

This is the picture. I believe that this conception is implicit in one version of MP. It arises from considering how various aspects of the program have been articulated and considering to what extent GB fits in both with these details and with the larger methodological and substantive economy issues noted earlier. Let me expand on this a bit.

For concreteness consider the GB Binding module. It is suspect in several ways from a minimalist perspective. First, it exploits different kinds of rules from those found elsewhere in the grammar. Rules of construal are indexing procedures additional to the one that 'Move alpha' already embodies. GB thereby contains two kinds of indexing operations. Parsimony urges UG to make do with just one, all things being equal.[21] So, either we eliminate movement processes or construal rules.

The reduction of movement to construal was investigated in earlier GB work by Koster among others.[22] This is achieved by treating traces as lexical items that are base generated. Subsequent rules of construal provide the relevant relations via indexing algorithms of various kinds. However, this requires treating traces as *lexical* expressions with distinctive needs. This is a high price to pay if one aims to eliminate morpheme specific processes. Moreover, the advantage of so recasting movement is quite unclear. These approaches generally postulate two kinds of indexing processes, those subject to the locality conditions characteristic of movement and those not subject to these restrictions. We thus end up with the same reduplication of procedures embodied in the earlier GB accounts (c.f. Chomsky 1981).

Note that the presence of displacement phenomena is uncontroversial. The only question is what rules the grammar exploits in accommodating it. The standard assumption has been that movement processes in some form are ineliminable. Thus, if there is to be a reduction it plausibly goes in the direction of analysing construal as movement rather than the reverse.

Some GB work has examined this alternative in the domain of anaphora. Chomsky (1986b), building on work of Lebeaux (1983), proposes that 'self'-anaphors move covertly at LF to positions close to their antecedents. Anaphor movement does not replace Principle A of the binding theory in Chomsky (1986b). However, once operative, Principle A appears to be redundant in that the antecedence relation that it establishes can just as easily be treated as the by-product of the movement alone. This, in fact, has been tacitly concluded by the field. GB, then, began the move towards reducing Binding Principle A to (A-) movement, at least in cases of local anaphora.

Observe that this "reduction" serves to make unnecessary the locality restrictions on reflexives induced by the binding theoretic notion 'domain'. From a minimalist perspective, this is a very positive result. Consider why.

Binding domains are defined in terms of government.

(3)   D is a domain for β iff D is the least complete functional complex containing β and a governor for β

MP considers the government relation methodologically suspect on grounds of parsimony. The world would be a better more elegant place if government were not a primitive relation required by UG. Reducing anaphora to movement allows Principle A of the binding theory to be dispensed with and thereby removes one reason for retaining government as a primitive grammatical relation.

In short, reducing anaphora to movement serves to simplify things in several respects. First, it would be a step towards eliminating construal rules as separate grammatical operations thereby allowing the inventory of rule types to be reduced. Second, it would be a step towards removing 'domain' as a theoretical construct. As the locality properties of anaphors would reduce to those of movement, there would be no need for binding domains to circumscribe their distribution. Last of all, removing domains from UG also aids in removing government as a basic primitive relation of the theory. As this notion is independently suspect, any move towards its elimination is welcome.

Reducing Principle A to movement, should it prove successful, immediately adds another item to the research agenda: how to eliminate Principle B. Assume for the sake of argument that the distribution of anaphors can indeed be reduced to the theory of movement. This would then place Principle B in a very odd light. Why should there be a principle of grammar whose main concern is the distribution of pronouns? What makes them so special? Moreover, even if the grammar does care about pronouns why should it devise *sui generis* relations (i.e. government), operations (i.e. construal rules) and locality restrictions (i.e. domains) to determine their distribution? Without anaphors, domains serve exclusively as vehicles to specify the distribution of pronouns. This further enhances the *ad hoc* status of the notion and renders it (and the notion of government that defines it) yet more suspect.

The problem is not just a theoretical one. Once the distribution of anaphors is reduced to movement, an empirical puzzle emerges: why is it that pronouns and anaphors are generally in complementary distribution? The GB approach to binding accounts for this observation, which, though not perfect, is surprisingly robust.

The near complementary distribution of (local) anaphors and pronouns follows in GB given the nature of principles A and B of the binding theory.

(4)   A: an anaphor must be bound in its domain
      B: a pronoun must be free (i.e. not bound) in its domain

Principles A and B make opposite demands on anaphors and pronouns. If one assumes that domains for anaphors/pronouns are defined as in (3) this results in anaphors being licensed by Principle A if and only if (bound) pronouns are forbidden by Principle B. Thus, one important empirical consequence of the GB binding theory is that anaphors and pronouns should be in complementary distribution. This seems to be a largely correct description of the facts.[23]

However, once one abandons Principle A and makes the distribution of anaphors the province of the theory of movement (as has been standard practice since Chomsky (1986b)) the above GB account evaporates. There is no obvious reason why (near) complementarity should exist between pronouns and anaphors if they are regulated by entirely different modules of the grammar. As should be evident, there are good reasons for finding the GB Binding theory wanting. The MP concerns simply bring its inadequacies into sharper focus.

The foregoing is meant to illustrate a general feature of MP. Once one starts to pull on part of the theory, the economy considerations that drive the program quickly lead to a general unravelling of the theory as a whole. It is in this sense that MP is potentially so far reaching and radical.[24] No part of the theory is very remote from any other part and changes in one domain naturally lead to questions about others when global evaluations of simplicity, parsimony and elegance drive theory choice.

A second important point to note is that methodological concerns such as parsimony get their bite when pairs of possibilities are played off against one another. Theories are neither simple nor complex, neither parsimonious nor profligate simpliciter. They must be as complex and intricate as required. Thus, when accounts are considered singly evaluations of methodological economy are moot. It is only in the context of theory *comparison* that such notions find a foothold. As such, it always pays to have a competing companion account for purposes of comparison. Absent this, methodological considerations quickly lose their grip and utility.

GB accounts admirably fit the role of straight man to the minimalist kibbitzer. One way of fruitfully launching a minimalist research program is to simplify, naturalize and economize earlier GB accounts. These are always good places to begin and provide solid benchmarks against which to measure putative progress. I adopt this comparative strategy in what follows.

4   Some Specific Principles

The earlier sections have tried to instill a feel for the global ambitions of MP by illustrating the types of principles assumed and how they are invoked to generate questions and projects. Now it is time to outline some specific grammatical principles that will serve as fixed points in the chapters that follow. These (hopefully) reflect the larger themes outlined above. However, they are more specific and constitute particular ways of concretizing these minimalist sentiments. There are surely other ways of pursuing the broad outlines of the program. Some of the analyses that follow argue for the specific principles outlined below in being required if these analyses are to succeed. More often, however, the chosen implementation is just one of many ways of setting the stage and other arrangements could serve as well. For concreteness, I list the relevant principles.

4.1   *There are only Two Grammatical Levels, LF and PF*

For all practical purposes, only LF has grammatical standing as PF is too unstructured. Thus, whatever filters apply, do so at LF. This does not mean to say that there are no bare output conditions imposed by PF. For example, the Linear Correspondence Axiom (LCA), the algorithm that takes a hierarchical structure and produces a linearization of its constituents, is a plausible requirement on phrase markers imposed by the PF requirement that expressions be pronounced in a particular serial order. This follows Chomsky's (1995) interpretation of the LCA.[25] Chomsky notes that it is natural to think of linearization as a PF requirement given that phonological operations are sensitive to the linear properties of strings. As such, the LCA can be seen as part of the contribution the grammar makes to the interpretive requirements of the PF interface.

In the best case, filters reflect "bare output conditions," i.e. conditions imposed on LF (or PF) from the fact that it is a level that interfaces with the conceptual/intentional systems (CI) (or the articulatory/phonetic (AP) systems) whose intrinsic properties impose conditions on LF (or PF) phrase markers. The above interpretation of the LCA is one example of this. Consider an example on the LF side.

It is reasonable to accept Full Interpretation (FI) as a condition imposed by CI on LF phrase markers. FI requires all features that pass across the interface to receive an interpretation. On this conception, FI is a bare output condition that filters out sentences containing expressions that have unchecked uninterpretable features, e.g. unchecked case features. In effect, on this view, the case filter simply reflects the requirements of the CI interface. It is not a specifically language internal requirement.[26]

There are other LF filters that plausibly have similar interpretations, e.g. the recoverability of deletion, parts of the theta-criterion, viz. the requirement that theta-roles of a predicate be expressed and the requirement that all DPs have theta-roles. On the other hand there are many requirements that fit less well, e.g. the various locality conditions on anaphors and pronouns imposed by standard versions of the binding theory and the requirement that DPs have at most one theta-role. There seems nothing inherent in the notion pronoun or anaphor that brings with it the requirement that it meet its antecedence conditions within fixed domains nor with the notion argument that restricts it to having but one role. This contrasts with the requirement that an anaphor have an antecedent or that a pronoun can be bound. These conditions do plausibly follow from the inherent interpretive properties of such expressions.

4.2   There is a Fundamental Distinction Between Case and Theta Theory

This is executed in various ways within MP. For example, Chomsky (1995) takes case to be a feature checked in functional domains. Thus, for example, an expression bearing case can check this feature by moving to the Spec of a phrase headed by a functional expression that bears such a feature, e.g. the Spec of TP for nominative case and the Spec of AgrOP or the Spec of vP for accusative case. Theta-roles, in contrast, are *not* features and are (typically) assigned within lexical domains, i.e. phrases headed by lexical expressions, to trivial chains and by trivial chains.[27]

An interesting consequence of this bifurcation is that it implies some version of the predicate internal subject hypothesis, the idea that theta-marked subjects get their roles within the predicate phrase, (e.g. VP) rather than in Spec IP.[28] In the context of MP this has a further attractive implication. MP aims to pare down the required grammatical operations to a minimum. The predicate-internal subject hypothesis allows for the elimination of operations like "predication" as follows. If subjects are generated in Spec IP then they must be assigned theta-roles via a rule of predication. This rule is different from standard forms of theta marking in which roles are simply assigned by heads within their local phrasal domains. If rules like predication are dispensed with then subjects must receive their roles in some other way. Thematically marking subjects within lexical shells and raising them to Spec IP dispenses with the need for predication in such cases.

In the chapters to come, I follow Chomsky partway. I assume that the domains of case and theta theory are distinct; the former being a relation between a D/NP (or its features) and a functional head (e.g. the Tense or Agreement), the latter (typically) a relation with a lexical head (e.g. V or N). However, I drop the other two assumptions.

In particular, I treat theta-roles as features in at least one important sense: like all other features they are able to license movement. This contrasts with Chomsky (1995, 1998) where it is assumed that only morphological feature checking can license movement. Concretely, I assume that theta-roles are assigned by heads (mostly verbs are examined) to D/NPs that merge with them. This allows any instance of MERGE to be a potential theta discharge configuration. Thus, movement can result in theta-marking and is not limited to non-trivial chains.[29]

4.3 Features are Checked in Configurations Licensed by Phrasal Structure

As noted in section 2, the theory of phrase structure requires at least two kinds of relations – head/complement and specifier/head. Chomsky (1995) assumes that the former is the most basic configuration with Spec/head being the residue of the head/complement configuration. Thus, spec/head relations encompass the standard cases of spec/head configurations as well as head/head relations formed via head movement. Both 'ZP' and 'Z$^{0\prime}$' in (5) are in spec/head relations with 'X$^{0\prime}$'.

(5) a. [ZP [X^0 YP]]
     b. [[Z^0 [X^0]] YP]

Case features are checked in spec/head relations.[30] Internal theta roles are checked in head/complement configurations while non-internal roles are checked in spec/head structures.

The assumptions in section 4.2 and section 4.3 constitute one important difference between GB and MP. GB aimed to unify the configurations of case and theta assignment under government. MP questions this goal. Rather, it unifies what it sees as disparate instances of case assignment by treating all instances as the reflex of a spec/head relation between a nominal and a functional head. Given that theta-roles are assigned in lexical domains, this requires that nominals move to check case in MP. The movement is necessarily to some non-complement position, i.e. it results in a spec/head configuration.

The conclusion that case is checked in derived positions is one of the most interesting claims in MP and it is worth pausing to consider the theoretical and empirical reasons behind it. The GB theory of case tries to unify case assignment under the government relation. Government is defined so that verbs govern their canonical objects, inflections govern subjects and ECM verbs govern the subjects of their sentential IP or small clause complements, c.f. (6).

(6) a. [$_{VP}$ V D/NP]
     b. [$_{IP}$ D/NP [$_{I'}$ Infl . . .
     c. [$_{VP}$ V [$_{IP/SC}$ D/NP . . .

From a minimalist perspective, this unification of the circumstances of case assignment seems rather contrived. (6a) is an instance of a head/complement relation, (6b) a spec/head relation and (6c) neither of these. The last is clearly incompatible with a phrasal source for basic grammatical relations. However, even the difference between (6a) and (6b) suggests that the GB approach to case is not conceptually unified.

The lack of structural homogeneity in the three instances of case assignment suggest that a revision is in order. (6) indicates that case cannot be unified under the head/complement relation. The only alternative (given MP) is the spec/head relation. In short, the MP theory of case requires taking (6b) as the canonical case configuration. The nominals in (6a,c) must move to configurations analogous to (6b). Chomsky (1993) takes the target of this movement to be Spec AgrO while Chomsky (1995) assumes it is the outer Spec of vP. In any case, this means that objects and ECM subjects have moved out of their VPs or clauses to higher Spec positions to check case.

This reasoning gets interesting support from binding data. Lasnik and Saito (1993), resurrecting earlier observations of Postal (1974), argue that ECM subjects appear to have wider scopes than their overt positions would support. For example, the ECM subject in (7a) appears able to bind the reciprocal in the matrix adjunct, in contrast to the embedded subject in (7b).

(7)   a.   The DA proved [the defendants$_i$ guilty] during each other's$_i$ trials
      b.   *The DA proved that [the defendants$_i$ were guilty] during each other's$_i$ trials

The contrast follows on the assumption that 'the defendants' moves (perhaps at LF) to the matrix clause to check (exceptional) accusative case while it remains in the embedded clause when checking nominative. On this assumption, 'each other' is in the scope of the ECM subject but outside the scope of the nominative.

4.4   Movement is Greedy

Earlier sections outlined show this fits in with the general precepts of MP. For present purposes I interpret this requirement as mandating that movement is only licensed if the resulting structure allows for the checking of some feature. In current parlance, I assume that greed is "enlightened."[31]

(8)   MOVE allows A to target K only if a feature of A or K is checked by the operation

Other versions of greed require a "moved" expression to check one of its own features. (8) allows either the moved expression A or an expression in the target K that comes into relation with A to check some feature. This is now a common way of understanding greed.

4.5   Movement is Actually the Combination of Copy and Merge

This view is proposed in Chomsky (1993) and defended extensively in Nunes (1995). Chomsky indicates how making this assumption allows one to dispense with certain binding arguments for SS. However, the issue is more general.

Analyzing movement as a complex of two simpler operations – COPY and MERGE – allows one to dispense with traces as primitive grammatical formatives, as noted above. Lexical copies can replace traces for marking the positions from which movement takes place.

Moreover, viewing movement as composed of Copy and Merge may allow one to account for other postulated properties of MP grammars. For example, Chomsky (1995) proposes that Merge is a more economical operation than Move in order to account for the unacceptability of sentences like (9).

(9)   a.   *There seems a man to be here
      b.   There seems to be a man here

The explanation proceeds as follows. On building the phrase marker for (9) one starts with a lexical array of items and progressively builds the sentence by Merging and Moving expressions. Consider the point at which (10) has been formed.

(10)   Infl^0 be [$_{SC}$ a man here]

At this point, it is possible to move *a man* to the Spec of Infl or to Merge *there* from the array into this same position. If Merge is less costly than Move then the latter option is preferred. This allows for the derivation of (9b) but not (9a).

This proposal requires that Move be more costly than Merge. Treating Move as the combination of Copy and Merge has this as a trivial consequence given that the operations that underlie Move properly include Merge. Hence, the number of operations required to extend the derivation using Merge is less than those using Move.

So treating Move has other desirable consequences. Chomsky (1998) uses it to account for reconstruction effects in the grammar.[32] It further permits the formulation of a simple generalization: all features are checked via MERGE. This generalization is methodologically desirable. Consider why.

If MOVE is a totally different operation from MERGE then feature checking could be licensed either by merging two categories or by moving a category from one position to another. Economy considerations dictate that there be only one way of checking features. Given that MERGE is a virtually conceptually necessary operation (it follows from section 4.5 above which states that atoms (i.e. words) can combine to form more complex structure) it would seem that MOVE should be related to it rather than postulated as an entirely distinct kind of process. Resolving MOVE into the pair of operations COPY and MERGE does just that. Thus, the reason that both MERGE and MOVE lead to feature checking is that both involve a common MERGE component.

Note one last point. This suggests that what makes MOVE expensive is the fact that it involves copies. Making copies costs! Copies are tolerated only if they promote convergence by eliminating uninterpretable features. This reasoning rationalizes the link between MOVE and greed which is part of the standard MP package of assumptions.

4.6   *Overt Instances of MERGE and MOVE Adhere to the Extension Condition (Chomsky 1993)*

The Extension Condition is the requirement that grammatical operations enlarge the tree in the sense that the phrase marker that results from the operation contain as a sub-constituent the phrase marker that was input to the operation. (11) illustrates the condition.

(11)   a.   [A .. [B ... [C ...]]]
     b.   [D [A ... [B ... [C ...]]]]
     c.   [A .. [B ... [C . D ..]]]

Assume that (11a) is the input to the relevant operation. Then "adding" D as in (11b) obeys extension in that the phrase marker in (11a) remains as a proper subpart of (11b). (11c) is not a licit phrase marker for it "thickens" rather than extends the phrase marker. Note that the phrase marker (11a) is no longer a constituent of (11c).

A consequence of the Extension Condition is that overt syntax adheres to the strict cycle and also prohibits lowering operations from applying in overt syntax. Chomsky (1998) suggests (following Epstein (1999), Epstein, Groat, Kawashima and Kitahara (1998), and Kawashima and Kitahara (1996)) that the restriction of the Extension Condition to overt movement might be reduced to the LCA by assuming that command is a derivationally determined relation. I here assume that extension applies to overt syntactic operations whether or not the Extension Condition can be derived from more general principles. I follow Nunes (1995) in assuming that the Extension Condition also applies to adjunction. These issues are discussed in further detail in chapter 3.

All of these assumptions are standard though some of the implications I draw from them are not. They are more or less drawn from Chomsky (1997). However, there are a host of standard assumptions that are rejected in what follows. I list some of them below and return to justify these departures from the current consensus in the relevant chapters.

4.7   *Theta-Roles Are Not Features*

This assumption is rejected in order to reduce parts of the theory of control to the theory of movement. The details are outlined in chapter 2. Note, the assumption that theta-roles are features does not imply that they are identical in all respects to morphological features like case. I continue to crucially assume that the domains within which case features and theta-features operate are distinct. However, for the purposes of MOVE and greed theta-roles are no less able to license operations than case features are.

4.8   *The Binding Theory Applies at LF*

Section 3 has argued that there are minimalist reasons for questioning the status of the Binding Theory in MP. This is investigated more fully in chapter 7.

4.9   *The Theta-Criterion Does Not Hold*

This is crucial for the analyses in chapters 2 and 3. For example, chapter 2 argues that control can be reduced to movement. A necessary assumption for this sort of analysis to work is that a DP be permitted to move into more than one theta-position. This, however, requires dispensing with the theta-criterion which is intended to prevent such movement.

4.10   *Movement is Actually Attraction*

This is proposed in Chomsky (1998) and (1999). Chapter 4 argues against the Attract based conception of displacement.

5   Conclusion

The proof of the pudding is in the eating. The ingredients for the MP pudding I propose to make here have been outlined above. I have also attempted to outline the broader MP concerns and show how they interact to motivate various moves in the minimalist research program. This prolegomenon will hopefully serve to guide the reader through the thickets of the remaining arguments.

One last point. Let me reiterate what I said at the outset. Minimalism is a program, not a theory. The program, if successful, will prompt the creation of various minimalist models of grammar each of which gains inspiration from the sorts of considerations outlined above. These models will differ in (at least) (i) what they take the broader issues that motivate minimalism to be (ii) how they weight these broader concerns (iii) how they implement them in particular analyses and (iv) other things I haven't thought of. As such, when in what follows I lapse into talking as if the particular combination of assumptions I am exploring is the "one and only true path," I implore the reader to have a good chuckle at my expense, forgive the slip, and move on.

Notes

1   The discussion here stresses the epistemological underpinnings of minimalism. There are alternative minimalist visions that articulate the program from the perspective of a metaphysics of complexity. What I say below is compatible with this

view but does not presuppose it. For discussion of this alternative see, for example, Uriagereka (1999) and Martin and Uriagereka (2000).

2   It appears that many doubt Chomsky's sanity as they appear to believe that he and his followers deny this trivial point. See, for example, Bates and Elman (1996).

3   This has recently been challenged in Cowie 1999. For a critical review of Cowie that I personally find completely decisive see Crain and Pietroski (1999).

4   This is a vastly simplified picture. However, little is gained in going into the complexities here. For some discussion see Chomsky (1986b), Dresher (1998), Dresher and Kaye (1990), Hornstein and Lightfoot (1981), and Lightfoot (1982, 1999).

5   For discussion see Chomsky (1983).

6   The history of physics demonstrates the power of pursuing thematically consistent theories. The search for inverse square laws gave way to the pursuit of conservation principles which in turn was replaced by an interest in field equations which itself yielded to theories based on symmetry principles. For discussion of how these themes drove research see Weinberg (1988).

7   This conclusion was based on work by Stowell (1981), Chomsky (1986), and Koopman (1984) among others.

8   Chomsky (1995) argues that X′ properties of phrases follow from very modest conceptual assumptions. If his Bare Phrase Structure hypothesis is correct it further strengthens the point made here that X′ relations have conceptual priority over notions like government.

9   Nunes (1995) forcefully makes this point. Chomsky (1998) has recently endorsed the same conclusion.

10   Chapter 6 argues that copies are conceptually required objects within grammars that postulate a distinction between the lexicon and the computational system. If so, copies are conceptually costless. See chapter 6 for discussion.

11   In GB, traces are part of the definition of Move. This suggests that within MP, movement be defined as involving Copy as a suboperation. In other words, there is a very short conceptual distance within minimalism between eliminating traces as undesired grammatical entities and adopting the copy theory of movement. See below for further discussion of the copy theory of movement.

12   Though this is not the route taken in Chomsky (1995: ch. 3). He follows Watanabe (1992) and Aoun and Li (1993b) in assuming that WH movement always takes place in overt syntax even in languages like Japanese and Chinese.

13   Chomsky (1995) assumes that both nominative and accusative are weak but that another feature, the EPP feature, is strong and forces nominatives to raise overtly. For present purposes these details are irrelevant.

14   There is nothing particularly "minimalist" about feature checking, nor is it especially interesting to check rather than assign features. What is interesting is Chomsky's (1993) claim that adding features to standard GB operations eliminates the need for SS conditions. In other words, what we find is that a rather trivial technical change of implementation eliminates one of the strongest arguments for what we took to be one of its striking features, viz. the existence of a level of S-structure.

15   See Chomsky (1995: ch. 3) for a discussion of how to eliminate the Binding Theory from applying at SS.

16   See Chomsky (1981) for the standard GB analysis of such constructions.

17   To be honest, it is not clear why 'tough'-constructions are required to make this argument. It appears that the nub of the argument relies on the proper treatment of relativization. The assumption seems to be that relative clauses are formed by movement and until formed, they cannot be merged. However, if so, then a sentence

like (i) could just as easily have been used to make the case. The detour through 'tough'-constructions is irrelevant.

(i)   John met the man who I like

Proponents of GB, however, might well resist the conclusion that movement is required for having an NP sufficient for insertion. After all, phrase marker rules were developed to generate relative structures. What movement then does is relate the head to a theta-position internal to the relative. It is unclear why this is illicit.

   This said, 'tough'-movement structures do introduce serious complications into the GB view of DS, as noted in the text, and these suffice by themselves to cast doubt on its value. See chapter 3 for a possible reanalysis of these constructions.

18   Parts of the theta-criterion are plausibly part of the Bare Output Conditions that characterize the interpretive properties of the CI interface. However, one feature is clearly grammatical: the requirement that DPs and theta roles be bi-uniquely related. There is little conceptual reason for prohibiting a DP from having more than a single theta-role. See chapters 2 and 6 for more discussion.

19   See chapter 6 for some discussion of DELETE.

20   This view of movement is first examined in detail in Nunes (1995). It is adopted and elaborated below.

21   I do not intend to treat indexing as a "real" process. Rather it stands surrogate for real relations among expressions. GB conceives of at least two distinct ways of doing this; via movement and via rules of construal.

22   See Brody (1995) for a version of Koster's (1978) program with a minimalist accent.

23   For a recent discussion of this complementarity see Safir (1997).

24   It also indicates that GB must have a rather interesting theoretical structure if pulling on one part leads so quickly to reconsideration of so many other aspects of the theory.

25   Kayne (1994) first proposes the LCA. However, he takes it as a condition on all phrase markers, including those at LF. Chomsky (1995) notes that Kayne's arguments do not accomplish what is desired nor are they necessary. In chapter 3, I suggest a reinterpretation of Kayne's original idea so that something analogous to the LCA holds at LF.

26   Note, the requirement that expressions bear morphological features *is* an internal requirement of the language system! Why this is required is unclear. However, there is strong evidence that it is. Note, moreover, that case is linked to the fact that displacement exists in NLs. Just what the conceptual relation is between these two facts, however, is still unclear. Chapter 6 offers an account for why uninterpretable features might be part of an optimally designed system.

27   I say *typically* as the external theta-role is assigned in the Spec of vP in Chomsky (1995). This small *v* has a standing in between the lexical and the functional.

28   See Kuroda (1988), Koopman and Sportiche (1991).

29   This is also examined by Bosković (1994), Boskovic and Takahashi (1998), and Lasnik (1995b).

30   At least in languages like English. There is nothing in MP that forbids checking case in head/complement configurations and there is some research that indicates that this indeed happens in some languages. In what follows, I put this possibility to one side.

31   C.f. Lasnik (1995b).

32   See Aoun, Choueiri and Hornstein (1999), Fox (1999), and Kim (1998) among others for other examples that tie reconstruction to movement.

2

Movement and Control[1]

Introduction

From the earliest work in generative grammar, control structures have been treated as theoretically *sui generis*. Rosenbaum (1967) distinguishes control from raising, assigning the former to the category of deletion processes while relegating the latter to movement. This partition survives the move from the standard theory to GB, albeit with a change in technical garb. In control configurations, deletion under identity yields to construal of a base generated empty category PRO. PRO is a contentless unindexed NP, *viz.* $[_{NP}$ e], a base generated denizen of D-structure whose antecedent is determined at LF by the control module. This treatment differentiates PRO from NP-t(race) in two ways. First PRO is base generated whereas NP-t is a transformational by-product. Second, an NP-t's indexation is fixed under applications of MOVE while that of PRO is a function of the construal rules in the control module. This said, at LF, raising and control structures are rather similar, in that both involve the binding of structurally identical empty categories. Where the two structures differ is that control is an inter-chain relation (i.e. between two chains) while raising is an intra-chain relation (i.e. between two parts of a single chain). This in turn is the theoretical reflex of the central empirical distinction between raising and control, viz. that the binder of NP-t is not independently q-marked while the antecedent of PRO is. (1) illustrates these points.

1   Introduction: PRO, the problem

(1) a.   John$_i$ seemed $[[_{NP}$ e]$_i$ to kiss a koala]
     b.   John$_i$ hoped $[[_{NP}$ e]$_i$ to kiss a koala]

In (1a), 'John' is interpreted as a "koala-kisser" while in (1b) it has this role in addition to having the "hoper" role. 'John' and the empty category in (1a) form two "links" of a single chain. 'John' and the empty category in (1b), in contrast, each constitute their own chains and the indicated indexation relates them anaphorically.

This theoretical distinction between raising and control accounts for additional grammatical differences. Consider two.

First, raising predicates host idioms and expletives in their subject positions, in contrast to control predicates.

(2) a.   There seems [t to be a dog in the barn]
     b.   It seems [t to be raining]
     c.   The shit seems [t to have hit the fan]
     d.   All hell seems [t to have broken loose]

(3) a.   *There hopes [PRO to be a dog in the barn]
     b.   *It hopes [PRO to be raining]
     c.   *The shit hopes [PRO to have hit the fan]
     d.   *All hell hopes [PRO to have broken loose]

Second, passivization under raising predicates leaves interpretation unchanged, in contrast to control predicates. This "voice transparency" is reflected in the 'expect' versus 'persuade' paradigm. (4a,b) are essentially paraphrases of one another. Not so (5a,b). The different interpretive behavior of these predicates follows from the fact that 'persuade', but not 'expect' is a control predicate.

(4) a.   John expects the doctor to examine Mary
     b.   John expects Mary to be examined by the doctor

(5) a.   John persuaded the doctor [PRO to examine Mary]
     b.   John persuaded Mary [PRO to be examined by the doctor]

In sum, the standard assumption that chains are the bearers of θ-roles and that PRO heads a chain explains the observed facts. Raising structures involve a single chain and hence only one theta-role. Control configurations involve multiple chains and multiple theta-roles. This accounts for the multiple roles 'John' is interpreted as having in (1b). Similarly, it explains why sentences like (3) are unacceptable. Idioms and expletives do not bear standard theta-roles, if they bear any at all. Thus, 'there' cannot be a hoper nor can expletive 'it' or idiomatic 'all hell'. The unacceptability of the examples in (3) thereby follows.

Similar reasoning extends to (4)–(5). In (4a,b) neither 'Mary' nor 'the doctor' are arguments of 'expect'. The latter assigns no θ-role to either. This contrasts with (5a,b) where 'persuade', being a control predicate, assigns a θ-role to each.[2] Consequently, (5a and b) differ in that 'the doctor' is the persuadee in the former while 'Mary' is in the latter. The thematic structures of (4a,b), in contrast, remain constant under passivization.

Empirically, then, there is ample reason for distinguishing raising from control structures. The theoretical basis within GB for distinguishing the two constructions relies on contrasting traces and PROs: PROs head chains, traces do not. D-structure implements this difference. In fact, the classical distinction between raising and control follows seamlessly from the assumption that D-structure exists. Consider the reasoning.

D-structure has two distinctive properties: it is input to the transformational component and the locus of all thematic discharge; a representation of "pure GF-θ."[3] Thus, prior to "displacement" operations (i.e. transformations) that rearrange phrase markers, words/morphemes are assembled into D-structure phrase markers by being lexically inserted into the available theta-positions. After lexical insertion, transformations apply to map D-structure phrase markers into others.

Given the requirements of D-structure, transformations cannot relate theta-positions (via movement) as all theta-positions have been filled by lexical insertion in forming the D-structure phrase marker. Consequently, movement between θ-positions is impossible and so control relations (which involve multiple theta-roles) cannot be the observed manifestations of movement operations.

Furthermore, if D-structure has *only* θ-positions filled (in addition to all such positions being filled), then raising structures must be products of movement as only movement will be able to relate a theta to a non-theta position. In sum, the classical vision of D-structure as the representation of pure GF-θ, i.e. the phrase marker where all and only thematic information is grammatically rendered, forces the theoretical distinction between raising and control.

The Theta-Criterion further buttresses this view of D-structure, in particular the idea that all thematic information is discharged via lexical insertion. The relevant feature of the Theta-Criterion is the demand that there be a bi-unique relation between θ-roles and chains, in particular that every chain bear at most one θ-role. This effectively prohibits all movement from one θ-position to another. But if movement into θ-positions is forbidden, yet all θ-roles must be discharged, then the only alternative is to fill each θ-position via lexical insertion. The step from the Theta-Criterion to the postulation of PRO in control structures is a short one.

This picture of control survives essentially intact to the present day. Chomsky (1995, 1998), for example, maintains that only trivial chains (i.e. 1-member chains) can receive or assign θ-roles. In effect, theta-roles can only be discharged via MERGE not MOVE. This restricts theta-role assignment to simple 1-member chains, or, to put this negatively, prohibits the assignment of theta-roles to chains of more than one member. This is functionally equivalent to the Standard Theory/GB requirement that θ-roles only be discharged at DS via lexical insertion.

Without D-structure, this prohibition against moving into θ-positions is ensconced in two assumptions.

(6)   a.   θ-roles are not features
      b.   movement must be greedy

(6) is interpreted as requiring that movement result in a configuration in which some yet unchecked feature becomes checked. However, if θ-roles are not features, then movement into a θ-position cannot be greedy. Thus, we derive the conclusion that θ-discharge can only result from MERGE, an operation which in Chomsky (1995) is not governed by GREED.

Chomsky (1995: 300–1) buttresses this position in its definition of chains in which intermediate "links" of chains effectively disappear at LF, leaving only heads and tails of chains visible for interpretation. This serves to bar movement into θ-positions on the standard assumption that heads of chains (generally) reside in case positions. To see this, consider what a simple control structure would look like were movement involved.

(7) a. John hopes to win the race
     b. John [John [hopes [John to [John win the race]]]]

(7b) displays the structure of (7a). Note that given the VP internal subject hypothesis, the thematic positions for 'John' are the specifiers of the verbs 'win' and 'hope'.[4] If (7b) were formed by movement, then the chain would consist of the set of copies of 'John'. Note that the θ-positions consist of the copy in the tail of the chain in the embedded Spec VP of 'win' and the intermediate copy in the Spec VP of 'hope'. If intermediate links delete, as Chomsky (1995) proposes, then the information that 'John' has the "hoper" role is lost. This is clearly undesirable. The conclusion is that this sort of derivation is illicit and movement cannot underlie control configurations.

All of this suggests that the minimalist abandonment of D-structure as a level (Chomsky 1993) is less radical than often perceived. Chomsky's argument does not lead to a general repudiation of the core characteristics of D-structure. Rather, D-structure's earlier properties are packed into restrictions on the computational operations. In fact, the only feature of D-structure that is forsworn is the principle that *all* lexical insertion precede the application of *all* other transformations, i.e. the rule SATISFY has been dumped (Chomsky 1993). All the other features of D-structure have been retained.

This chapter submits these other assumptions to minimalist scrutiny; how well motivated are they? Why assume that chains are bi-uniquely related to θ-roles? What goes wrong if one moves from one θ-position to another? Why distinguish trace from PRO? As is generally the case with minimalist meditations, I assume that the burden of proof is on those that wish to promote these assumptions and invoke these distinctions. What is not at issue is that control sentences manifest different properties from raising constructions.[5] The minimalist question is whether these differences require the theoretical and technical apparatus standardly invoked in distinguishing them.

In the particular case of control, methodological skepticism is fully warranted. The distinction between raising and control multiplies the inventory of empty categories. Furthermore, the distinction massively complicates the grammar. PRO brings with it two big theoretical complications: (i) a control module whose job it is to specify how PRO is interpreted and (ii) theoretical modifications to account for PRO's distribution. The next several sections review the GB approach to these issues and some recent minimalist modifications. I then outline and explore the consequences of an alternative approach based on the idea that (a subset of) control structures are derived by movement.

The chapter is organized as follows. Section 2 and section 3 review what empirical ends are served by a theory of PRO and control. Section 4 and section 5 argue that the general properties of Obligatory Control (OC) structures can be reduced to movement if we abandon the residues of D-structure still extant within the Minimalist Program and abandon the θ-Criterion based prohibition against moving into θ-positions. Section 6 discusses adjunct control. Section 7 reviews further empirical properties of control structures discussed in Burzio (1986). Section 8 addresses the distribution of non-obligatory control structures (NOC). Section 9 provides some additional empirical support for the analysis using floated quantifiers. Section 10 is a brief conclusion.

2   The Issues and Some History

Control structures come in two varieties; local and long distance.

(8)   a.   John hopes to win
       b.   John hopes that winning will be fun

In the earliest treatments, two distinct rules were involved in the derivation of (8a,b). Equi NP Deletion applied in (8a) while Super Equi was responsible for (8b). Equi interacted closely with the Minimal Distance Principle in determining the antecedent of the controlled clause, 'John' in (8a).

   GB has adopted essentially the same distinction. Williams (1980) argues for a distinction between obligatory and non-obligatory control configurations. The former conform to the earlier Equi structures while the latter shadow Super Equi configurations. This distinction is adopted in much subsequent work including Koster (1984), Lebeaux (1984–5), and Manzini (1983) among others. The relevant GB structures of (8) are provided in (9).

(9)   a.   John hopes [PRO to win]
       b.   John hopes [that [[PRO winning] will be fun]]

   Obligatory and non-obligatory control configurations differ in several important ways. Note, for example, that (9b) has at least two interpretations; one paraphraseable as 'John hopes that his own winning will be fun' and one as 'John hopes that one's winning will be fun'. This ambiguity is absent in (9a) with the second "arbitrary" reading missing. We return to a full description of the interpretive differences between obligatory and non-obligatory control structures below.

   In light of (9), control structures pose two questions: (i) where can PRO appear and (ii) how is PRO interpreted. The GB answer to the first question is that PRO appears in ungoverned positions, in effect, the subject position of non-finite clauses. In (9a) we find 'PRO' in the subject position of an infinitive clause and in (9b) it appears in the subject of a clause initial gerund. PRO seems unable to appear anywhere else.

(10)   a.   *John hopes (that) PRO will win
     b.   *John saw PRO
     c.   *John talked to PRO

It is reasonable to assume that in the examples in (10) PRO is governed by various lexical heads. In (10a) it is the finite morpheme in Infl, in (10b) the verb 'saw' and in (10c) the preposition 'to'. If one further assumes that non-finite clauses do not contain lexical heads (at least of the relevant sort), then the presence of PRO in (9a,b) correlates with the absence of head government (henceforth simply 'government') of these Spec IP positions. Thus, the distribution of PRO conforms to the descriptive generalization (11).

(11)   PRO can only appear in ungoverned positions

Note that (11) need not prohibit generating PRO in a governed position. This is fortunate as PRO can be base generated in object position so long as it moves to an ungoverned position by S-structure. (11) is a generalization that holds at S-structure or later.

(12)   John hopes [PRO$_i$ to be recognized t$_i$]

Is (11) an axiom or does it follow from more basic principles? There are several GB attempts to reduce (11) to other grammatical principles. Bouchard (1984), for example, proposes reducing the distribution of PRO to case theory (see also Wyngaerd (1994) for a related approach based on agreement). He observes that the contexts that disallow PRO are generally also contexts in which case marking applies. This point is clearly illustrated in the examples in (10).

Lasnik (1992) notes a problem for the proposal that case can fully account for the distribution of PRO. There are several non-case marking contexts where PRO is nonetheless disallowed.[6]

(13)   a.   *John believes sincerely Mary/PRO to be clever
     b.   *it is likely [John/PRO to solve the problem]
     c.   *My belief [Harry/PRO to be intelligent]

It would appear then, that a case theoretic approach to the distribution of PRO is too weak.

A second approach, the one that became the GB standard, links the distribution of PRO to the binding theory. Chomsky (1981) proposes that PRO is a pronominal anaphor, i.e. [+P,+A], subject to both principles A and B of the binding theory. Principle A requires an anaphor to be bound in its domain, Principle B that a pronoun be free (i.e. not bound). Given that a single expression cannot be both bound and free in its domain, this entails that PRO never has a domain. A way for PRO to fail to have a domain is if it is ungoverned given the definition of domain in (14).

(14)   δ is the domain for an expression E iff δ is the smallest phrase in which
       E is governed and δ has a subject

Note that if PROs are pronominal anaphors subject simultaneously to principles A and B of the binding theory then we have derived the descriptive
generalization (11) from more general principles. Note too, that given that the
binding theory applies at S-structure or later, then we have also derived the
fact that (11) is a generalization that holds later than D-structure.

   This reasoning brings with it an additional bonus. It accounts for why PRO
is phonetically null. In GB D/NPs are assigned case by a case marking head
that governs the D/NP. Since PROs cannot be governed they cannot be case
marked. If phonetically full D/NPs must be case marked, then the absence of
a governor for PRO forbids its having phonetic content. In sum, the PRO
theorem and case theory combine to provide an account both of PRO's distribution and its phonetic status.

   Nonetheless, there are problems with the PRO theorem approach to the
distribution of PRO.

   First, as noted by Bouchard (1984), it appears that if we advert to subjects in
the definition of domains, then we need not invoke government. Consider, for
example, an alternative definition of domain.[7]

(15)   δ is the domain for an expression E iff δ is the smallest domain in which
       δ has an accessible subject.

(16)   β is an accessible subject for E iff β is a SUBJECT and β is distinct from E

(17)   SUBJECTs are [NP,IP], [NP,NP] and Agr

(15)–(17) in conjunction with standard clauses of the Binding Theory handle
the standard binding data.

(18)   a.   An anaphor must be bound in its domain
       b.   A Pronoun must be free in its domain

   These definitions cover at least as much empirical territory as Chomsky
(1986). However, they do so without adverting to the notion 'governor'. As
such, it is unclear that adding this notion to the definition of domain is truly
necessary. But if it isn't, the PRO theorem exploits a feature of the binding
theory that is unnecessary except for deriving the distribution of PRO. This
leaves the PRO theorem on the same conceptual footing as the bare assertion
that (11) obtains.

   A second problem is that it is not always the case that pronouns and anaphors
are in complementary distribution. This means that they do not always have
identical domains. Consider examples such as (19).

(19)   a.   The men saw their mothers
       b.   The men saw each other's mothers

Here we appear to have a pronoun ('their') and an anaphor ('each other') both licit in the same Spec NP/DP position. By the logic of the binding theory one might expect PRO to be licit here as it could be free in its guise as a pronoun yet bound in its anaphoric aspect. Nonetheless PRO is prohibited here.[8]

(20)   *The men saw PRO mothers

Chomsky (1986) provides a technical escape for cases such as this. The remedy is to require that an expression have a unique domain. The reasoning from (19) to (20) first evaluates PRO qua pronoun with respect to Principle B and then evaluates PRO qua anaphor to see if it respects Principle A.[9] The domain relevant for the Principle B evaluation is different from the domain exploited to determine if Principle A is met. Chomsky (1986) proposes that we disallow this domain shifting when the binding status of a single expression is being considered. In effect he proposes that a single expression E must have a unique domain, as in (14) above. Thus a PRO cannot be evaluated with respect to two different domains as (20) does. Chomsky's proposal allows the binding theory to block (20) while preserving the assumption that PRO is a pronominal anaphor. However, the solution circumvents a problem unique to PRO. Thus, this fix to the PRO theorem once again challenges the claim that the distribution of PRO actually derives from independently motivated principles of the binding theory.

A third problem with the PRO theorem is evident when one considers the interpretation of obligatory and non-obligatory control structures. The PRO theorem relies on the assumption that every PRO is *simultaneously* +P and +A. However, obligatory control and non-obligatory control PROs differ rather dramatically in their interpretive properties. Furthermore, these differences make sense if obligatory control PROs are anaphors while non-obligatory control PROs are pronouns. In short, the interpretive data point to the conclusion that PRO is ambiguous. A PRO theorem approach to PRO's distribution cannot accept this ambiguity thesis. To handle the interpretive differences evident in obligatory and non-obligatory control structures requires a rather complex control module.

The following data illustrate the complexity of the problem. Williams (1980) distinguishes obligatory control (OC) from non-obligatory control (NOC) structures on the basis of several interpretive phenomena. Consider the following OC paradigm.[10]

(21)   a.   *It was expected PRO to shave himself
     b.   *John thinks that it was expected PRO to shave himself
     c.   *John's campaign expects PRO to shave himself
     d.   John expects PRO to win and Bill does too (=Bill win)
     e.   *John$_i$ told Mary$_j$ PRO$_{i+j}$ to leave together
     f.   The unfortunate expects PRO to get a medal
     g.   Only Churchill remembers PRO giving the BST speech

(21a) shows that an OC PRO must have an antecedent. (21b) indicates that this antecedent must be local and (21c) indicates that it must c-command the PRO. (21d) shows that OC PRO only has the sloppy reading under ellipsis. (21e) shows that OC PRO cannot have split antecedents. PRO in (21f) only has the 'de se' interpretation in that the unfortunate believes *of himself* that he will be a medal recipient. (21g) has the paraphrase (22a) not (22b). On this reading only Churchill could have this memory for Churchill alone gave the speech. The two different readings follow on the assumption that OC PRO must have a c-commanding antecedent. This requires 'only Churchill' to be the binder. The absent reading requires 'Churchill' as the antecedent.

(22)   a.   Only Churchill remembers himself giving the BST speech
       b.   Only Churchill remembers that he gave the BST speech

These properties of OC are not shared by PRO in non-OC (NOC) environments. In fact, the latter contrast in every respect with the OC cases.

(23)   a.   It was believed that PRO shaving was important
       b.   John$_i$ thinks that it is believed that PRO$_i$ shaving himself is important
       c.   Clinton's$_i$ campaign believes that PRO$_i$ keeping his sex life under control is necessary for electoral success
       d.   John thinks that PRO getting his resume in order is crucial and Bill does too
       e.   John$_i$ told Mary$_j$ that PRO$_{i+j}$ washing each other would be fun
       f.   The unfortunate believes that PRO getting a medal would be boring
       g.   Only Churchill remembers that PRO giving the BST speech was momentous

(23a) indicates that NOC PRO does not require an antecedent. (23b) demonstrates that if it does have an antecedent it need not be local. (23c) shows that the antecedent need not c-command the NOC PRO. (23d) contrasts with (21d) in permitting a strict reading of the elided VP, i.e. the reading in which it is John's resume which is at issue. (23e) supports split antecedents. (23f) can have a non 'de se' interpretation and (23g) is consistent with many people other than Churchill recalling that the BST speech was a big deal. The NOC readings contrast on every property with those available in the OC examples in (21).[11]

The cases in (21) and (23) contrast in one further interesting way; the former can be paraphrased with PRO replaced by a reflexive while the interpretive doubles of (23) replace PRO with pronouns. (24) illustrates this with the counterparts of (21c) and (23c).[12]

(24)   a.   *John's$_i$ campaign expects himself$_i$ to shave himself
       b.   Clinton's$_i$ campaign believes that his$_i$ keeping his sex life under control is crucial for electoral success

The sentences in (22) also illustrate this. The different readings available in (21g) and (23g) are similarly available in (22a,b) when pronouns and anaphors are used. (22b) where the pronoun appears is ambiguous and can take either 'only Churchill' or 'Churchill' as antecedent. (22a) only has the reading parallel to (21g).[13]

In short, the differences in OC and NOC structures duplicate, where applicable, what one finds with locally bound anaphors versus pronouns. This makes sense if PRO is actually ambiguous – an anaphoric expression in OC configurations and pronominal in NOC structures – rather than simultaneously a pronoun and an anaphor as the PRO theorem requires. This, then, speaks against reducing the distribution of PRO to the binding theory by way of the PRO theorem.

This conclusion is quite welcome given minimalist sensibilities as the PRO theorem approach to the distribution of PRO is theoretically unappealing relying as it does on government. Chomsky and Lasnik (1993) (Chomsky 1995: ch. 1) have further argued against this approach to PRO on empirical grounds. Consider the sentences in (25).

(25)   a.   We never expected/hoped [PRO to be found t]
       b.   *We never expected/hoped [PRO to appear to t [that Bill left]]

If movement is a last resort operation and PRO must be ungoverned then the threat of being governed suffices to force PRO's movement in (25a). But if being governed suffices to license movement in (25a) why is it insufficient in (25b)? Chomsky and Lasnik argue that both examples are accommodated if we assume that PRO has a case that must be checked. Movement in (25a) is then a typical case of last resort movement under passive. (25b)'s unacceptability stems from a violation of greed; PP being a domain for case checking makes movement to Spec IP unnecessary and so prohibited. This essentially assimilates the unacceptability of (25b) to that of (26).

(26)   *We never expect that Bill will appear to t that . . .

In (26), 'Bill' raises to Spec IP to check case. However, it has moved from within PP which is also a case checking domain. As case is checked inside the PP, further movement is prohibited by greed. Chomsky and Lasnik propose treating (25b) in exactly analogous fashion. They assume that the embedded Spec IP in (25b) is a case position. PRO checks its case here. Movement of PRO from within the PP to Spec IP, therefore, violates greed.[14]

Chomsky and Lasnik also trace the absence of lexical D/NPs in this Spec IP position to case theory.[15] These non-finite Specs can only check null case and null case can only be carried by PRO. Thus, only PRO can appear in these positions.

The distribution of PRO, then, is relegated to case theory, specifically the case properties of non-finite "control" Infls and null case. The advantage of this in MP terms is that this accounts for the distribution of PRO in terms of

Spec-Head feature checking.[16] This in turn permits the interpretive facts noted in (21) and (23) to be explained in terms of the ambiguity of PRO. By making the distributive properties of PRO the province of case theory, the assumption that PROs are pronominal anaphors is no longer required. Rather, OC PRO is an anaphor and NOC PRO is a pronoun. At no time need PRO be *both* at once. The interpretational differences can now be seen to conform to whatever semantic properties differentiate anaphors from pronouns.

In sum, MP treats the distribution of PRO as a case theoretic phenomenon in contrast to GB's binding theoretic approach. This theoretical reapportionment, which is forced on both theory internal and empirical grounds within MP, has as a side benefit the simplification of the theory of control. In particular, how PRO is interpreted can be related to whether PRO is anaphoric or pronominal. In cases of OC it is the former and displays the paradigm in (21). In NOC cases it is pronominal and behaves like (23). The differences between OC and NOC then follow on general grounds and so need not be stipulated as part of an independent control module.[17]

Despite the virtues reviewed above, this account has a few inelegancies. The next section reviews these.

3   Some Problems

The picture that emerges from section 2 is the following. There is an important difference between OC and NOC PRO. OC PRO behaves like an anaphoric reflexive. NOC PRO has the properties of a pronoun. This suggests that PRO is not one expression but two. OC PRO is a reflexive while NOC PRO is a pronoun. Though reasonable, this conclusion forbids treating PRO simultaneously as an anaphor and a pronoun as required by the PRO theorem. Fortunately, the PRO theorem approach to the distribution of PRO seems theoretically (given MP) and empirically inadequate. An alternative is required. One option is to link the distribution of PRO to case theory. Chomsky and Lasnik's particular proposal is that non-finite T^0s are case checkers and that PROs carry the "null" case that such Infls check. PROs appear in the Spec IPs of non-finite T^0s because only these categories can check the case that PROs carry.

This story has some problems. The most glaring is that it essentially stipulates the distribution of PRO. Null case is special in two ways. First it is designed to fit only one expression – PRO. Lexical expressions don't bear null case nor do other phonetically null expressions such as WH-t or NP-t. Second, only non-finite T^0s can check/assign it. In effect, the case properties of PRO and non-finite T are constructed to exactly fit the observed facts. Had the data been otherwise, the theory would change accordingly. This comes close to restating the observations; PROs appear in the Spec IPs of non-finite clauses.

It is possible that this is the best that we can do theoretically. However, it is worth observing just how anemic an "explanation" this is. What is particularly fishy is the stipulation that only PROs bear null case. To date, only null case distinguishes its bearer entirely in phonetic terms.

Null case has a further problem.[18] A null case marked PRO fails to block contraction, in contrast to other case marked empty categories. Lightfoot (1976) observes that WH-traces block 'wanna' contraction but NP-ts do not. Jaeggli (1980) accounts for this in terms of case; case marked traces block the phonological phrasing of 'to' with 'want' to yield 'wanna'.

(27)   a.   Who do you want [WH-t to vanish]
             *Who do you wanna vanish
       b.   John's going [NP-t to leave]
             John's gonna leave

PROs pattern with NP-ts rather than WH-ts.

(28)   I want [PRO to leave]
       I wanna leave

If PROs are case marked expressions, as the theory of null case proposes, they should pattern like WH-ts and block contraction. Their behavior like NP-ts argues that they are more like non-case marked NP-traces than like case bearing WH-traces (see below).

A second problem with the story in section 2 is that it still requires a rather elaborate PRO module. This module functions to specify the antecedent, the "controller," of the OC PRO. The module will of necessity be rather elaborate if it addresses the core empirical issues. These include the following:

A.   In clauses of one nominal argument and a sentential argument the subject controls the OC PRO.

(29)   John$_i$ hopes/expects/wants [PRO$_i$ to leave]

When the matrix verb has two nominal arguments and a sentential PRO complement the structure is typically one of object control rather than subject control.

(30)   a.   John$_i$ persuaded Bill$_j$ [PRO$_{*i/j}$ to leave]

In fact, subject control, e.g. in 'promise' constructions, appears to be quite marked and emerges rather late in the acquisition process (see C. Chomsky 1969).[19] The Minimum Distance Principle (MDP) captures the observations in (17) and (19) (Rosenbaum 1970).[20] The MDP and the data it summarizes raise several questions: Why is OC the typical case in (19)? What sort of grammatical principle is the MDP; is it a primitive generalization or does it follow from deeper principles? If the latter, what does it follow from? From a MP perspective, the MDP bears a striking resemblance to the Shortest Move Requirement (SM).[21] Both prohibit structures like (31) in which there is a closer potential antecedent to 'ec', be it PRO or NP-t.

(31)   [... NP$_i$ ... NP$_j$ .. ec$_{*i/j}$ ..]

(31) points to a possible redundancy between the MDP and SM and raises the obvious question: can the MDP and SM be collapsed into a single condition?

B.   In contrast to complement control, PRO headed adjuncts seldom permit object control.[22] Why is object control into adjuncts not permitted and why is there a complement/adjunct asymmetry as regards the controllers of PRO in OC configurations?[23]

(32)   a.   John$_i$ saw Mary$_j$ without/before PRO$_{i/*j}$ leaving the room[24]

A third problem with the account in section 2 is that there appear to be cases of control where PRO is in a non-Spec IP position.[25]

(33)   John$_i$ washed/dressed/shaved (PRO$_i$/himself$_i$)

The examples in (33) relate a thematic subject 'John' to a thematic object. This object can be lexically realized or not. When it is not overt, the sentence is interpreted reflexively. These are the properties we would expect if the object were an OC PRO. Note that like the cases in (21) above, the OC PRO alternates with a locally bound reflexive. Given standard assumptions, the object position cannot be any empty category other than PRO given that its antecedent is thematically marked. However, cases like (33) are problematic as they suggest that PRO can appear in other than Spec IP position. If this is correct, it argues that the Chomsky and Lasnik theory is incomplete and that the relevant issue is not the null case marking/checking capacities of non-finite T^0.[26]

A fourth problem is that the account of control in section 2 exploits the properties of anaphors in accounting for the basic facts about OC. The theory of anaphora, however, is also in need of some minimalist rethinking. The standard GB version in Chomsky (1986) exploits locality notions, e.g. governing category, of dubious standing in MP. Other approaches introduce redundancies into the grammar by crucially exploiting locality conditions characteristic of movement, e.g. the chain condition in Reinhart and Reuland (1993). Such redundancies are partially allayed by requiring anaphors to move at LF. However, this raises other problems in an MP context for like all other forms of movement, this LF operation requires featural motivation. The problem is that it is unclear what features this movement would be checking. Anaphors appear to have case so movement to the antecedent would not be motivated as it is in existential constructions, for example. Another spur to movement could be the requirement to check phi-features. However, if these are interpretable (Chomsky 1995), then they need not be checked. Furthermore, if it is phi-feature checking that is at issue why is it that we do not find reflexives in finite subject positions? What would block the (LF-) movement in (34) if reflexives moved at LF to their antecedents to check phi-features?[27]

(34)   John thinks that *herself/*himself is handsome

In sum, the theory of anaphora raises problems for MP. It would therefore be nice if we could deal with the properties of OC without relying too heavily on any particular current account of anaphora. Chapter 5 addresses some of these issues in the context of a minimalist reanalysis of principles A and B of the binding theory.

Finally, the deepest question concerning PRO given minimalist inclinations is the very existence of a formative like PRO. PRO is a theory internal construct. In GB, PRO is structurally analogous to NP-traces and WH-traces. All have the same shape, viz. '[$_{NP}$ e]'. The main difference between traces and PRO is the source of their indices, the former derive from movement while the latter are assigned via the control module. In MP, however, this technology is all suspect. There is little reason to think that traces (qua distinctive grammatical constructs) exist at all.[28] Traces are not grammatical formatives but the residues of the copy and deletion operations necessary to yield PF/LF pairs. Traces as such have no common structure in MP as they do in GB. They are simply copies of lexical material and so have no specific shapes whatsoever. As such, they cannot be structurally analogous to PRO. This leaves the theoretical status of PRO up in the air. What kind of expression is it and why do grammars have them?

Section 1 provides answers to these questions. PRO exists because of θ-theory. If chains could bear more than a single θ-role and if θ-roles could be accreted in the course of a derivation, there would be little reason to distinguish PROs in OC configurations from NP-traces. These restrictions on theta assignment are hardly conceptually necessary. In a minimalist context this fact weakens the theoretical basis for distinguishing PROs from NP-ts. Put more bluntly, distinguishing trace from PRO requires *additional* assumptions about theta assignment and chains. The burden of proof, therefore, resides with those who favor such assumptions. In the next section, I argue that forgoing these stipulations permits a more empirically and theoretically adequate account of OC. The proposal in section 4 is that PRO, like NP-t, is the residue of movement. Strictly speaking, then, there is no grammatical formative like PRO (or trace). Rather, PRO is simply a residue of movement, simply the product of copy and deletion operations that relate two theta-positions.[29]

4   An Alternative

I have argued that the null hypothesis is that OC PRO is identical to NP-t, i.e. it is simply the residue of movement.[30] NOC PRO is 'pro', the null pronominal analogous to the null pronoun found in various Romance and East Asian languages.[31] This section is concerned with displaying the empirical virtues of these assumptions. The main focus is on OC PRO as handling the OC data requires the most radical departures from standard GB and MP technicalia. For what follows, I adopt the following assumptions.

(35)   a.   θ-roles are features on verbs
      b.   Greed is enlightened self interest
      c.   A D/NP "receives" a θ-role by checking a θ feature of a verbal/predicative phrase that it merges with
      d.   There is no upper bound on the number of θ roles a chain can have

(35a) treats θ-roles as morphological features.[32] This is required if OC involves movement to θ-positions and movement to θ-positions (like movement in general) conforms to the principle of Greed. (35b) interprets greed as requiring at least one of the relata to check a feature (Lasnik 1995a). Thus, if A moves to merge with B then at least one feature of either A or (the head of) B is checked. Treating θ-roles as features on the verb or predicate allows a D/NP to move to a θ-position and respect greed by checking this feature.[33] Analyzing θ-roles in this way permits us to "mechanize" θ-role assignment as in (35c): to receive a θ-role just is to check the relevant θ-feature of the predicate. One might think of this as "transferring" the verbal θ-feature to the nominal expression. In effect, checking conforms to Chomsky's vision of syntactic operations as the "rearrangements of properties of the lexical items of which they are ultimately constituted," i.e. the features of the elements in the array (c.f. Chomsky 1995: 226). (35d) is logically required to analyze OC in terms of movement given that control involves the relation of at least two θ-positions. It is also the null hypothesis, I believe. The requirement that chains be restricted to a single theta-role needs substantial empirical justification.[34]

The assumptions in (35) suffice to accommodate OC in embedded clauses in terms of movement given standard minimalist technology. Their empirical virtue is that they permit a radical simplification of the grammar of Control and a derivation of the basic properties of OC structures. Consider the details.

First consider the basic interpretive properties of OC structures. As noted in section 2, OCs require c-commanding local antecedents (c.f. (21a–c)). This is what one expects if OC PROs are formed by movement like NP-traces. For illustration consider (36).

(36)   a.   John hopes to leave
      b. $[_{IP}$ John $[_{VP}$ John [hopes $[_{IP}$ John to $[_{VP}$ John leave]]]]]

The derivation begins with 'John' merging with 'leave' thereby checking the verb's θ-role. 'John' then "raises" to (i.e. is copied and merges with) Spec of the embedded IP to check the D-feature of the IP.[35] This is *not* a case marking position, so the case of 'John' cannot be checked here. 'John' raises again to Spec VP of 'hope'. It checks the external θ-feature of the verb. By (35c), each time 'John' checks a θ-feature of a predicate it assumes that θ-role. Thus, 'John' (or the chain it heads) has two θ-roles, the leaver-role and the hoper-role. 'John' raises one last time to Spec IP of the matrix where it checks the D-feature of the IP and nominative case. This is the only place where 'John' checks case. On the assumption that it was inserted into the derivation with nominative case features, the derivation converges.

In more conventional notation, the copy 'John' in the embedded Spec IP corresponds to PRO and the copy in the matrix Spec IP is the antecedent. The requirement that OC have a local c-commanding antecedent follows from the fact that PRO is an intermediate link in an A-chain. Being such, it must have an antecedent. Furthermore, the antecedent must conform to general A-chain strictures and thus both c-command the traces in the A-chain, i.e. the PRO in Spec IP, and be local to it given conditions on movement like SM.

In short, the first three properties of OC PRO (illustrated in (21a,b,c)) follow from the fact that it corresponds to an expression which is the residue of movement. Because it is so formed, "OC PRO" must have an antecedent. Because the movement is A-movement, the antecedent must be local. Because the movement occurs in overt syntax, it must be to c-commanding positions.[36] This last property follows from the Extension condition. Here's how. Movement is simply Copy and Merge. For movement within single rooted subtrees, the standard case, obeying extension implies that the Copy must Merge with the whole available structure. For example, in 36Aa the only legitimate place to Merge A is to the root of DP. So merged, the copy of 'A' will c-command DP and everything it contains including the lower copy of 'A', as in 36Ab.

36A   a.   A "merge" $[_{DP} D^0 \ldots \ldots [\ldots \ldots A \ldots \ldots] \ldots]$
      b. $[_{DP} A [_{DP} D^0 \ldots \ldots [\ldots \ldots A \ldots \ldots] \ldots]]$

Thus, the basic properties of OC PRO are similar to those of simple raising constructions because they are formed in essentially the same way. The only difference being the kinds of features that get checked in the course of the derivation.

Treating OC PRO as the residue of movement also derives the prohibition against split antecedents. Two (non-conjoined) expressions cannot both antecede OC PRO because they cannot have both moved from the same position. In effect, the ban against split antecedents in this case is equivalent to the ban against one and the same trace having two distinct antecedents.

In MP, this prohibition follows from the theory of Bare Phrase Structure (BPS) (Chomsky 1995). Bare Phrase Structure makes no distinction between positions and their contents. For example, if an expression A merges with an expression B, then the position that A occupies with respect to B did not "exist" prior to the merger rather it came to exist as a result of the Merge operation. This contrasts with prior X'-theories of phrase structure in which the distinction between a position and the expression that fills it is exploited to define substitution operations and structure preserving processes.[37] Without this distinction it is literally impossible to claim that two expressions merge into the very same position. As such they cannot possibly both move *from* the same position. If OC is a function of movement, then it is impossible for an OC PRO to have split antecedents.

This fact is interesting for in a PRO based theory of OC this prohibition against split antecedents must be independently stipulated. The reason is that (37) is otherwise well formed.[38]

(37) $[DP_i \ldots DP_j \ldots [PRO_{i+j} \ldots]]$

Thus, the movement based approach to OC derives a property that PRO based theories must stipulate.

The required sloppy reading of OC PRO follows as well. Note that in raising constructions only a sloppy reading is available.

(38)   John seems to be happy and Bill does too

(38) must be understood to mean that it seems that Bill is happy. For the same reason, OC PRO must carry the sloppy reading as it too is functionally equivalent to an NP-t.[39]

The movement story also accounts for the required 'de se' interpretation of OC PRO. The movement underlying OC PRO ends up assigning two θ-roles to a single expression, e.g. in (36a), 'John' has two θ-roles. The semantic form of the predication in (36) is equivalent to (39), a predication that ascribes a reflexive property to the subject 'John'.

(39)   John λx [x hopes x leave]

Movement, then, semantically forms a compound monadic predicate by having one and the same expression saturate two argument positions. Salmon (1986) discusses these semantic issues at some length. Of importance here is his observation that relating the semantic value of an expression to two θ-positions via the formation of a reflexive predicate is semantically very different from relating two expressions in different θ-positions to each other via coreference. The former operation results in changing the semantic argument structure of the predicate while the latter leaves it intact. The former operation reflexivizes the predicate and thus forces a 'de se' reading while the latter does not. Treating OC as the reflex of movement, then, yields the correct interpretation for the structures; the one exemplified in (39).

Finally, the observed reading in (21g) (repeated here as (40)) follows as well.

(40)   Only Churchill remembers giving the BST speech

The reading in which someone other than Churchill could recall this event requires the paraphrase in (41).

(41)   Only Churchill remembers Churchill giving the BST speech

This cannot underlie the structure of (40). The PRO here is of the OC variety. This means that 'only Churchill' has raised from the embedded position and has the reflexive property noted in (42). This is semantically equivalent to the reading in which Churchill alone has the required memory.

(42)   Only Churchill λx [x remembers x giving the BST speech]

In sum, the six basic properties of OC reviewed in section 2 follow directly from assuming that OC PRO is identical to an NP-t, the residue of movement. In addition, these properties are derived without the problems reviewed in section 3. Once again, consider the details.

The distribution of OC PRO does not require the services of null case. This case, specially designed for PRO by Chomsky and Lasnik, is unnecessary if OC PRO is an NP-t. In fact, the existence of null case in Spec IP of control infinitives is *incompatible* with the movement analysis as it would prevent raising out of the embedded Spec IP. Thus, treating OC PRO as the residue of movement is incompatible with null case.

Note that abandoning null case in this context does not lead to any empirical difficulties. Recall that null case has been postulated to replace the assumption that PRO must be ungoverned. Its principal empirical effect is to block the derivation of (43) and license PRO only in Spec IP of non-finite clauses.

(43)   *We never expected [PRO$_i$ to appear to t$_i$ that . . .

(43) is ruled out on the same basis in the present theory as one that postulates null case. On the latter story, 'PRO' cannot move to Spec IP of the embedded clause because PRO is moving from one case marking position (inside PP) to another (Spec IP). This either violates greed or results in feature mismatch. The derivation fails to converge under either option. However, if Spec IP contains an *intermediate* NP-t, as it would be on the present proposal, then the exact same reasoning prohibits movement through this position. In effect, a PRO in (43) should be no better than an NP-t in (44).

(44)   *We$_i$ were expected [t$_i$ to appear to t$_i$ that . . .

Note, furthermore, that on the current account we expect to find OC PRO in positions from which movement is licit. This should roughly coincide with non-case marked positions, such as the Spec IP of non-finite clauses. Note that this is compatible with treating the inherent reflexive verbs like 'wash', 'dress', 'shave', etc. as simply (optionally) not case marking their objects. In effect, as allowing derivations like (45) to be licit.

(45)   a.   John washed
       b.   [$_{IP}$ John [past [$_{VP}$ John [wash John]]]]

Case is checked in Spec IP. 'John' receives two theta-roles as it checks both the internal and external θ-role of 'wash'.[40]

In effect, then, by assuming that PRO is an NP-t, we derive its distribution without having to assume null case. Note, two further benefits. First, this allows us to treat 'wanna' contraction over PRO and NP-t as one and the same phenomenon (see section 3 examples (27) and (28)).[41] Second, the null phonetic status of PRO is explained in whatever way we account for the null phonetic status of NP-t. One natural assumption is that case is required for phonetic "visibility." Both NP-t and PRO will therefore fail to meet the requirements for having phonetic content.[42]

The movement approach to OC PRO also accommodates the classical data used to distinguish raising from control. It was argued, for example, that idiom chunks and expletives could raise but not control.

(46)   a.   The shit seems [t to have hit the fan]
       b.   There seems [t to be a man in the garden]

(47)   a.   *The shit expects [PRO to hit the fan]
       b.   *There expects [PRO to be a man in the garden]

The distinction between these cases is preserved in the present account even if 'PRO' in (47) is just an NP-t. The basis for the distinction is that in (47) 'the shit' and 'there' bear the external theta-role of 'expect'. If this theta-role is not checked then, I assume, the derivation fails to converge as there is an unchecked feature at LF.[43] However, the only nominals that can check them, 'there' and 'the shit' are not expressions that can bear theta-roles due to their inherent idiomatic or expletive semantics. As such, we retain a difference between raising and control structures in cases such as these but attribute it not to an inability to control PRO but the inability to support a theta-role that must be discharged for grammaticality to ensue.

This section has demonstrated that OC structures can be treated in terms of movement and that there is considerable empirical payoff in doing so.[44] In particular, we can dispense with null case, and we can derive the six basic properties of OC exemplified in (9) above. The next section turns to perhaps the biggest advantage. It appears that treating OC PRO as the residue of movement comes very close to allowing us to eliminate the PRO module entirely.

5   The MDP Reduced to Shortest Move (SM)

The PRO module has two primary functions. First, it designates the controller in an OC structure. Second, it determines how a controlled PRO is to be interpreted in a given configuration, e.g. does it permit split antecedents, is it mandatorily 'de se' etc. The latter function of the PRO module is no longer required. The various interpretive options of OC and NOC PRO follow from whether the PRO in question is a null pronominal – 'pro' – or a residue of A-movement – an NP-t.[45] Still left to be explained is how the controller in OC cases is determined. Note that this is not an issue for NOC configurations as in these cases no antecedent is required. This is the topic of this section.

The chief descriptive principle regulating this part of the PRO module is the Minimal Distance Principle (MDP).[46] Its effect is to designate 'NP$_i$' the controller in the configurations in (48).

(48)   a.   NP$_i$ [V [PRO ...]]
       b.   NP [V NP$_i$ [PRO ...]]

Thus, the MDP picks the closest c-commanding DP as controller, i.e. α is the controller of PRO iff α c-commands PRO and for all β different from α that c-command PRO, β c-commands α. The MDP picks the subject to be the controller in (48a) and the object in (48b). If treated as a markedness condition, this makes verbs like 'persuade' the unmarked case and verbs like 'promise' highly marked. This descriptively coincides with the observed data and I assume its accuracy here (see C. Chomsky 1969).

The MDP makes perfect sense seen from the perspective of a movement approach to OC. We have already seen the derivation of a structure like (48a) in (36b). Consider the derivation of an object control sentence.

(49) a. John persuaded Harry to leave
      b. [$_{IP2}$ John [$_{I^0}$ past [$_{VP3}$ John v+persuaded [$_{VP2}$ Harry persuaded [$_{IP1}$ Harry [to [$_{VP1}$ Harry leave]]]]]]]]

The array consists of the following set of expressions: {John, Harry, persuaded, to, leave, past, v, other assorted functional categories}. The derivation starts by selecting 'leave' and 'Harry' and merging them. This allows 'Harry' to check the θ-feature of 'leave' and assume the internal argument role – (35a,c). 'To' then merges with the VP headed by 'leave' and 'Harry' moves to Spec IP1 to check the D-feature of embedded clause, i.e. the EPP.

Note that this move violates economy as 'John' could have been inserted here. However, if 'John' had been so inserted the derivation would not have been able to converge. I return to the details after limning the rest of the derivation.

'IP1' then merges with 'persuaded' checking the propositional θ-role of the verb. 'Harry' then raises and merges with VP to form Spec VP2. This too is a θ-position of 'persuade' and this move provides 'Harry' with a second θ-role. Once again economy is violated as 'John' could have been inserted. However, had it been the derivation would have failed to converge so its insertion is blocked (see below). The next step is to raise 'persuaded' to merge with 'v'. Then 'John' is taken from the array and merged with the 'v+persuaded' projection forming Spec VP3. This is a θ-position and 'John' checks the external θ-role. 'Past' tense features then merge with 'VP3'. 'John' raises and forms Spec IP2. Here the D-features and nominative case features of Tense are checked as are the case features of 'John'. At LF, 'Harry' raises and forms an outer Spec of VP (or alternatively merges with AgrO and forms Spec AgrO) where it checks its case features and those of 'v+persuade'. All features that must be checked are checked and the derivation converges.

Observe that Spec IP1, the position of "PRO," is occupied by an intermediate copy of 'Harry'. 'Harry', like all nominals in a derivation, has been inserted with case features. Assume that it has accusative case, otherwise the derivation does not converge. Each move in the derivation is licit with respect to Greed as some feature is checked at every step. The two violations of economy must still be accounted for, however. Let's turn to them now.

'Harry' is inserted into the derivation with some case features.[47] If these features are accusative then there is no way to check the features on 'John'. There are two possibilities. If 'John' has accusative features then either its features or those on 'Harry' cannot be checked as there is only one accusative head around; viz. 'v+persuaded'. If the features on 'Harry' are nominative then SM will prevent movement of 'Harry' across 'John' if 'Harry' is inserted into Spec IP1 and raised again. The full LF phrase marker given this derivation is (50).

(50)   [$_{IP2}$ Harry [$_{I^0}$ past [John [$_{VP3}$ John v+persuaded [$_{VP2}$ John persuaded [$_{IP1}$ John [to [$_{VP1}$ Harry leave]]]]]]]]

To check nominative case requires moving 'Harry' to 'T$^{0'}$. This traverses several copies of 'John' all of which are closer. This is a violation of SM and so is illicit (see below).

Consider the second option. 'John' is inserted with nominative case, 'Harry' with accusative. 'John' is merged into Spec IP1. It then raises through the two theta positions of 'persuade' and 'v' up to Spec IP2 where it checks its nominative case and that of finite 'T$^{0'}$, as well as the D-feature of IP2. We still need to check the accusative features on 'Harry'. This could be done by moving to the outer Spec of VP3. The relevant LF is (51).

(51)   [$_{IP2}$ John [$_{I^0}$ past [Harry [$_{VP3}$ John v+persuaded [$_{VP2}$ John persuaded [$_{IP1}$ John [to [$_{VP1}$ Harry leave]]]]]]]]

(51) must be illicit if the derivation in (49b) is well formed as required by the present analysis. The derivation of (51) violates SM on the assumption that 'John' in Spec IP1, Spec VP2 or Spec VP3 prevents the movement of 'Harry' in Spec VP1 to the outer Spec (or Spec AgrO) of VP3 to check accusative case at LF. This, in turn, requires that copies formed by movement be relevant for SM. 'Harry' cannot check its case because it is further from the relevant case checking position than are *copies* of 'John'. If we make the assumption that such copies are visible to the computational system (and so can block movement across them via SM) then the derivation in (51) does not converge. This, in turn, permits the violation of economy in the derivation of (49b).

Interestingly, the assumption that copies are relevant for the SM/MLC is required independently once the assumption that only trivial chains can be θ-marked – (35d) above – is dropped. Given the assumption that there is no upper bound to the number of theta-roles an expression can have ((35d) – a conceptually necessary assumption if OC is to be reduced to movement –) (52) provides independent motivation for making the SM/MLC sensitive to copies. Chomsky (1995: 345) asks why (52b) doesn't exclude (52c).

(52)   a.   I expected someone to be in the room
       b.   [$_{IP1}$ I expected [$_{IP2}$ I to be [someone in the room]]]
       c.   [$_{IP1}$ I expected [$_{IP2}$ someone to be [someone in the room]]]

The derivation of (52b) proceeds as follows. The small clause 'someone in the room' is constructed via successive mergers. The result is then merged with 'be' and then with 'to'. 'I' is merged in the Spec IP2 position discharging the D-feature on the embedded Infl. The result is merged with 'expected'.

Chomsky argues that this structure is illicit because 'I' cannot receive a θ-role given either the assumption that only trivial chains can be θ-marked or the assumption that θ-features do not count for greed so that movement via the Spec VP of 'expect' is illicit. Either way, 'I' has no θ-role. If convergence requires nominals to have θ-roles, then (52b) does not converge. This then licenses the derivation in (52c) in which economy is violated. In other words, instead of merging 'I' to Spec IP2, 'someone' can be raised, violating economy. This is permitted as the derivation which honors economy, viz. (52b), does not converge. This is how (52a) is licitly derived.[48]

The assumptions in (35) preclude adopting this analysis. Given (35b,d) there is nothing that prohibits moving 'I' to the Spec VP of 'expect' to get a θ-role. Thus, the reason that (52b) fails to converge cannot be due to the requirement that nominals have θ-roles. However, the derivation can be excluded in the same way that (51) above is. 'Someone' needs to check its case features. The only available case position is the outer Spec of 'expected' (or the AgrO above it). Movement to this outer Spec is blocked by 'I' in Spec IP2 if copies count for the SM/MLC.[49] In short, the same reasoning required for (51) extends to cover this case as well.

(52) is of particular interest for it indicates that treating copies as the computational equals of originals from the array is virtually unavoidable if OC is reduced to movement in the context of MP. (52b) must be prohibited from converging. θ-theory is unavailable once one gives up the last vestiges of D-structure as (35b,d) do. In particular, there is nothing amiss with the derivation in (52b) if 'someone' can check case. Thus, it must be that it cannot. This is accomplished if the 'I' in Spec IP2 triggers SM.

The above has been in the service of a single conclusion; that object control can be derived via movement given a general MP setting amended by (35). There is a further conclusion. Subject control in 'persuade' clauses is ungrammatical. To derive a structure of subject control involves violating SM. Consider the derivation of a subject control structure like (53a).

(53) a. John$_i$ persuaded Harry [PRO$_i$ to leave]
      b. [$_{IP2}$ John [$_{I^0}$ past [$_{VP3}$ John v+persuaded [$_{VP2}$ Harry persuaded [$_{IP1}$ John [to [$_{VP1}$ John leave]]]]]]]

The relevant structure is provided in (53b). If 'John' is the controller, it must have been merged with 'leave' and raised to Spec IP1, the locus of "PRO." 'Harry' has the object-of-persuade theta role, as indicated by its merger in Spec VP2. Now, the external θ-feature of 'v+persuaded' must be checked. In (53b) 'John' is raised to Spec VP3. Note that it crosses 'Harry' in Spec VP2. This violates SM and is prohibited. Thus, subject control in structures like (53) cannot be derived as they violate the SM. As noted earlier, this is consistent with the traditional observation that subject control verbs like 'promise' are highly marked.

To conclude. I have argued that a derivational approach to obligatory control can account for the prevalence of object control with 'persuade' verbs. This is what is expected given MP technology supplemented with the assumptions in (35). In effect, OC structures conform to the traditional MDP just in case their derivational histories respect the Shortest Move condition. The control module and the MDP are superfluous in cases like these.

6   Control into Adjuncts: The Basic Account

Our account, to this point, has concentrated on control into complements. Adjuncts also manifest properties of obligatory control. Consider structures like (54) embodied in sentences like (55).

(54)   NP$_i$ V NP$_j$ [$_{adjunct}$ PRO$_{i/*j}$ ...]

(55)   John$_i$ heard Mary$_j$ [without/while/before/after [PRO$_{i/*j}$ entering the room]]

These constructions exhibit the hallmarks of OC structures. PRO headed adjuncts require local, c-commanding antecedents.[50]

(56)   a.   *John$_i$ said [that Mary left after PRO$_i$ dressing himself]
     b.   *John's$_i$ picture appeared after PRO$_i$ shaving himself
     c.   *It seemed that Bill left before PRO$_{arb}$ noticing

(56a) is unacceptable under the indicated indexation as the antecedent 'John' is too remote. (56b) involves a non-c-commanding antecedent. The arbitrary reading of PRO in (56c) is unavailable, as it would be if PRO here did not require an antecedent. Put positively, the absence of a reading for (56c) analogous to "It seemed that Bill left before anyone noticed" follows from the requirement that this PRO needs a grammatical antecedent.

The PROs in these adjuncts do not tolerate split antecedents:

(57)   a.   *John$_i$ said that Mary$_j$ left after PRO$_{i+j}$ washing themselves
     b.   *John$_i$ told Mary$_j$ a story after PRO$_{i+j}$ washing themselves

PRO headed adjuncts only have sloppy readings under ellipsis.

(58)   John left before PRO singing and Bill did too

Thus, (58) only has the reading paraphrased in (59a). It cannot be understood as (59b).

(59)   a.   .. and Bill left before Bill sang
     b.   .. and Bill left before John sang

In "Churchill" sentences – (60), they cannot take 'Churchill' as antecedent. In other words, (61) is not an adequate paraphrase of (60).

(60)   Only Churchill left after PRO giving the speech

(61)   Only Churchill left after Churchill gave the speech

   In sum, where applicable, adjunct control structures pattern like structures of obligatory control.[51]
   They have a further distinctive property noted in (54) and (55); they do not permit object control.[52] This last property is typically accounted for by assuming that objects do not c-command adjuncts and so cannot bind the PRO. In MP terms, this requires assuming that objects fail to c-command adjuncts *at LF*, the locus of binding requirements in a minimalist theory. This assumption, however, is doubtful. Objects can license bound pronouns within adjuncts as in (62).

(62)   John read every book$_i$ without reviewing it$_i$

If 'every book' can bind 'it' then 'every book' c-commands 'it' at LF. If so, it c-commands PRO as well.
   There is a larger problem with this proposal, however. It does not account for the OC properties of PRO headed adjuncts. The OC properties of these constructions suggest that the PRO found here is actually the residue of movement. In what follows, I show how to analyze these constructions as formed by MOVE and how this derives the lack of object control exemplified by (55).
   Analyzing adjunct control as movement requires a further assumption. We need to assume that movement out of an adjunct is possible. This in turn requires reanalyzing standard CED effects. We return to this in chapter 3. For the present, let's simply assume that movement out of an adjunct is indeed possible in some cases. Moreover, we must assume that this movement is a species of sidewards movement discussed extensively in Nunes (1995).

(63)   Sideways movement exists

Sidewards movement occurs when an element in one subtree is merged to a position in another "unconnected" subtree. In short, such movement is interarboreal.[53] The characteristic property of such movement is that movement is not to a c-commanding position.[54] We return in chapter 3 to a more detailed analysis of sidewards movement. For the present let's simply assume that it exists and see how it can be put to use to account for the properties of adjunct control.
   Consider the derivation of (55). The numeration for (55) consists of the set of items {John, heard, Mary, without, entering, the, room, assorted functional categories}. We build the adjunct phrase by merging 'the' to 'room' then merging 'the room' with 'entering' and merging 'John' with 'entering the room'. The two theta-roles of 'enter' are checked by the merger of the two D/NPs. The 'ing' heads its own Infl projection. This merges with the previously formed VP small clause. The strong feature of this Infl is checked by raising

'John'. Observe that this violates economy. We return to this after completing the proper derivation. At this point we have a structure like (64) after the adjunct has merged with the IP.[55]

(64) [$_{adjunct}$ without [$_{IP}$ John [$_{I^0}$ ing [$_{VP}$ John [entering the room]]]]]

Next we build the main clause. 'Mary' merges with 'read'. The internal theta role is thereby discharged.

(65) [$_{VP}$ saw Mary], [$_{adjunct}$ without [$_{IP}$ John [$_{I^0}$ ing [$_{VP}$ John [entering the room]]]]]

Note that in (65) we have two unconnected subtrees in the derivation. This is where sidewards movement becomes relevant.[56]

Let's continue with the derivation. The external θ-feature of 'saw' must be checked. If we move 'John' then the derivation proceeds as follows: 'John' raises and discharges the external θ-role by merging with the VP of 'saw'. This is an instance of sideways movement as the target of movement is not a c-commanding position. Indeed it is not even in the same subtree.

(66) [$_{VP}$ John [saw Mary]], [$_{adjunct}$ without [$_{IP}$ John [$_{I^0}$ ing [$_{VP}$ John [entering the room]]]]]

The next step is to merge the adjunct and the VP.

(67) [$_{VP/VP}$ [$_{VP}$ John [saw Mary]] [$_{adjunct}$ without [$_{IP}$ John [$_{I^0}$ ing [$_{VP}$ John [entering the room]]]]]]

The derivation then terminates with 'John' raising to Spec IP to check its own case, those of Infl, and the latter's D-features. At LF, 'Mary' raises to check accusative case in either the outer Spec of VP or in AgroP. The derivation converges with the overt structure in (68).

(68) [$_{IP}$ John [$_{I^0}$ past [$_{VP/VP}$ [$_{VP}$ John [saw Mary]] [$_{adjunct}$ without [$_{IP}$ John [$_{I^0}$ ing [$_{VP}$ John [entering the room]]]]]]]]

This derivation requires comment at three points.

First, the movement of 'John' to Spec of 'ing' within the adjunct violates economy. 'Mary' could have been inserted. However, had we done this 'John' could never have checked its case features. 'Mary' or a copy of 'Mary' would have blocked movement out of the adjunct to a case position in the matrix. In short, once again the SM/MLC would prevent a convergent derivation. Thus, economy is violable at this point.

Second, 'John' moves to check the external theta-feature of 'saw'. Doesn't this violate the MLC/SM? In other words, isn't 'Mary' closer to this position and shouldn't 'Mary' block this movement? The MLC/SM is not involved in this move. The reason is that 'Mary' in the complement position of 'saw' and

'John' in the Spec IP of the adjunct do not c-command one another nor does the target of movement c-command them both.[57] Thus, they are not in a "closeness" relation relevant for the MLC/SM. The combination of movement from an adjunct and movement to a non-commanding position makes it possible for 'Mary' and 'John' to be equidistant from the Spec VP of 'saw'. Hence there is no violation of the MLC in moving 'John' to Spec VP. Note, furthermore, that if 'Mary' moves to Spec VP in place of 'John' then the derivation cannot converge for the case features on 'John' would not be checked.[58] Thus, the only convergent derivation is the one reviewed in (64)–(68).[59]

Third, this is the most economical derivation that converges. In particular, it is not possible to have object control for it would require unnecessary violations of economy. To see this, consider the derivation at the point where the adjunct has been formed. The structure is provided in (64) repeated here.

(64)   [$_{adjunct}$ without [$_{IP}$ John [$_{I^0}$ ing [$_{VP}$ John [entering the room]]]]]

Still remaining in the array are 'saw' and 'Mary'. We place 'saw' into the derivation. To get object control would require moving 'John' and merging it with 'saw' to receive the internal θ-role. However, this movement is blocked *at this point of the derivation* as merging 'Mary' (which is in the array) is cheaper. Recall that if MOVE=COPY+MERGE then Merging 'Mary' involves fewer operations than copying and merging 'John'. As such, the derivation is forbidden from moving 'John' at this point of the derivation. This is what accounts for the absence of object control in these sorts of adjuncts. Object control is not derivable as it would involve a violation of economy, an instance of premature movement.[60] This is the desired result for it deduces, correctly, that OC PROs inside adjuncts like (55) are controlled by subjects.[61]

In sum, this section has provided evidence that adjunct control is a form of OC. We have shown in section 4 that the properties of OC follow given a movement analysis. This section has shown that a movement analysis can be extended to cases of adjunct control if we allow sidewards movement into the grammar as argued by Nunes (1995).

7   Some Further Empirical Issues

Section 5 and section 6 make the assumption that copies are relevant for the evaluation of grammatical computations. For example, they enter into calculations of Shortest Move/Minimal Link considerations. This section considers a further application of this reasoning to accommodate Object Preposing (OP) constructions in Italian (Burzio 1986: ch. 1). In addition, we revisit certain claims concerning quantifier scope ambiguities in raising versus control structures. The discussion is based on Burzio (1986: ch. 3). Lastly, we examine a problem for the assumption that one can freely move into θ-positions. This is critical to the analysis above and there are some empirical obstacles in the way of fully adopting it.

7.1   *Object Preposing (OP)*[62]

(69b) exemplifies an OP construction in Italian.

(69) a.   Si leggerà volentieri [alcuni articoli]
          Si will read willingly a few articles
     b.   [Alcuni articoli] si leggerano volentieri
          a few articles   SI will read (pl) willingly

(69b) has a passive-like interpretation and is roughly synonymous with its non-OP counterpart (69a). Burzio (p. 46) notes that the preposed object behaves just like a subject: it triggers verb agreement, can undergo raising and be re-placed by a 'pro'. In addition, it is clearly related by movement to the thematic object position as it meets the selectional requirements of the verb (idioms can be preposed as well) and there is a gap in post verbal position (p. 47).

Burzio (p. 48) further argues that 'si' *moves* to its surface position and is marked with the subject θ-role. In addition, 'si' must check (nominative) case (p. 50). Thus, for example, it is illicit in infinitivals where there is no case to check.[63]

Burzio's analysis of these constructions relies on treating the preposed object and the 'si' as part of a single complex chain. He uses this to get (nominative) case marking on the 'si'. He also uses this to account for another property of interest in OP constructions; it is possible in raising contexts but not control configurations. The relevant contrast is (70) (Burzio 1986: 52; (78)).

(70) a.   [quei prigionieri]$_i$ risultavano [t$_i$ esser*si* già liberati t$_i$]
          Those prisoners turned out SI-to be already freed
     b.   [quei prigionieri]$_i$ vorrebbero [PRO$_i$ essersi già liberati t$_i$]
          Those prisoners would want PRO SI-to be already freed

Burzio accounts for this contrast by claiming that in the control example in (70b), 'si' fails to form a chain with the preposed object 'quei prigionieri'. This relies on the GB assumption that PROs head their own chains and contrast with raising in not being formed by MOVE.

It is possible to reanalyze these data in terms compatible with the present MOVE based analysis of (obligatory) control. Before doing this, however, we must translate Burzio's GB-based proposal into a minimalist idiom. Burzio notes his analysis is somewhat odd in a GB context. In particular, it requires having a chain with two θ-roles, the one carried by 'si' and the one carried by the preposed object. It is non-standard from a GB perspective in a second way: the chain contains two distinct phonetic expressions, 'si' and the preposed object, and both get to check case against the same head, i.e. the nominative T^0. To see what implications OP constructions have for the movement theory of control, we must first see what a minimalist account of OP constructions might look like.

Burzio argues that OP constructions are formed by movement. As such, in a MP context, it must be driven by feature checking requirements. The preposed object determines clausal agreement. It is thus natural to assume that it checks features of finite I^0. This drives the relevant movement of the object to Spec IP.

'Si' also enters into a checking relation with I^0. Recall that 'si' must associate with a case position. In addition, OP constructions only allow third person DPs to prepose (p. 49; (72)). This restriction can plausibly be tied to the case checking requirements on 'si'. If 'si' must check case by movement to I^0 then the φ-features that it carries might impose requirements on the checker. The 'si' found here is of the impersonal variety, as (69a) indicates, thus the imposition of a third person restriction makes sense. Only an inflection with third person features can check the case of 'si'. This can account for the person restriction on the preposed object on the assumption that OP constructions involve I^0s that can multiply check case.

In effect, OP constructions involve a type of multiple specifier structure in which several expressions ('si' and the preposed object) check the same feature (viz. case) against a single head (viz. I^0).[64] Multiple Specifiers are the technical counterpart in MP to Burzio's proposal that OP chains can assign case to both the preposed object and the 'si' in a single chain.

To sum up so far, the object preposes to Spec IP to check various features (including case and φ-features) and the 'si' moves to I^0 to check case. The fact that one and the same I^0 checks the features of two DPs, one of them ('si') being third person, allows us to explain the restriction to third person preposed objects.

The second point that needs clarification in developing a minimalist alternative relates to the domains of case checking and θ-role assignment. MP typically assigns θ-roles within lexical projections and checks case and other morphological features within functional projections. In effect, MP adopts the predicate internal subject hypothesis and refrains from assigning θ-roles in Spec IP positions. In OP constructions, for example, 'si' in (69) receives the subject θ-role within the projection of 'leggerano' before moving to I^0 to check case.

With these assumptions in hand, consider the contrast in (70). The structures of these sentences is given in (71) on the assumption that control is actually the result of movement through various θ-positions.

(71) a. [quei prigionieri]$_i$ risultavano [t$_i$ esser*si*$_j$ già t$_j$ liberati t$_i$]
      b. [quei prigionieri]$_i$ [t'$_i$ vorrebbero [t$_i$ esser*si*$_j$ già t$_j$ liberati t$_i$]]

These two structures differ in one important respect. The control structure (71b) has a trace (i.e. a copy) in the Spec VP of the matrix verb. There is no analogous trace in (71a). The reason for this is that 'vorrebbero', being a "control" predicate has an external θ-role to assign. The raising predicate 'risultavano' has no external θ-role to assign. On the way to the matrix case position, 'quei prigionieri' moves through the external θ-position of 'vorrebbero' (in overt syntax) to check this θ-feature.

At LF, 'si' still needs to check case. To do so, assume that it must move to matrix I^0 position, just as it overtly does in (69). This movement is licit in (71a). There are no intervening expressions that 'si' crosses that are "closer" to the matrix I^0. Thus, there are no minimality violations and the shortest move/ minimal link condition is adhered to.[65] The relevant LF phrase marker for (71a) is (72).

(72)   [quei prigionieri]$_i$ si$_j$+I^0 risultavano [t$_i$ esser-t$_j$ già t$_j$ liberati t$_i$]

The unacceptability of (70b) can now be explained as a shortest move/ minimal link violation. The copy of 'quei prigionieri' in the matrix Spec VP blocks 'si' from raising to check case. Note that this is a typical minimality violation induced by the presence of a DP in the trajectory of a DP moving across it.[66] The relevant illicit LF is (73).

(73)   [quei prigionieri]$_i$ si$_j$+I^0 [t$_i'$ vorrebbero [t$_i$ esser-t$_j$ già t$_j$ liberati t$_i$]]

The movement of 'si' across 't$_i''$' violates minimality.

To sum up. The contrast in the possibility of object preposing in raising and control structures can be accounted for without abandoning the claim that (obligatory) control is formed by MOVE. The contrast reduces to the fact that control structures induce a minimality violation due to the presence of a copy in the Spec VP of the matrix control predicate. This is absent in raising structures and so the LF raising required to check the case of 'si' is not blocked.

7.2   Quantifier Scope

Burzio (1986: 201–4) reports another asymmetry between raising and control structures. English simplex clauses with multiple quantifiers display scope ambiguities.

(74)   a/some politician will address every rally

(74) is ambiguous with either 'a/some politician' or 'every rally' taking wide scope. This ambiguity is preserved in raising constructions.

(75)   A/some politician$_i$ is likely [t$_i$ to address every rally]

Burzio reports that the scope ambiguity disappears in control structures. In (76) 'a/some politician' scopes over 'every rally'.

(76)   A/some politician tried [PRO to address every rally]

Why the assymetry if indeed both constructions are in fact formed by movement, as argued above?

This question actually has two answers. The first is that the facts are somewhat more complicated than Burzio reports. Thus, many speakers find little difference between (75) and (76), allowing both to be ambiguous.[67] Control predicates differ in that some allow the matrix subject to scope under a quantified D/NP in the embedded clause and some do not. For me, it is relatively easy to get scope ambiguities with 'want', 'expect', 'try' and 'persuade'. I find it very difficult to get the ambiguity with 'hope' or 'demand'. However, it appears that there is considerable idiolectal variation in this regard.

Note that if this is correct, then there is no asymmetry to explain and things are just as expected if both raising and control are formed by movement.

The second answer takes Burzio's description at face value. Let's briefly consider what to say if we accept that Burzio is correct and that control and raising predicates contrast as he reports. This too can be accounted for if we adopt the account of relative quantifier scope outlined in Hornstein (1995, 1998).

The idea there is that relative quantifier scope piggy backs on A-chain structure. A raising construction such as (75) has an LF with multiple copies of the raised expression, two being of particular interest; the one in the Spec VP of 'addressed' which is the θ-position and the one in the matrix Spec IP, which is the case position. In addition, 'every rally' has a copy in the outer Spec of VP where accusative case is checked.

(77)   A/some politician is likely [a/some politician to every rally [a/some politician address every rally]]

Assume that all but one copy must delete prior to the LF phrase marker being fed to the CI-interface. If the lowest copy of 'a/some politician' is retained and the higher copy of 'every rally' is retained then we have a phrase marker in which the universal DP scopes over the existential.

The same structure, however, is not necessarily available for the control structure (76). Let's annotate the LF phrase marker more fully, making explicit where case and θ-roles are assigned.[68] I use "−" to indicate a checked case and "+" to indicate an assigned θ-role.

(78) $[_{IP}$ A politician $[−Nom, +θ_{try}, +θ_{address}]$ I^0 $[_{VP}$ A politician $[+Nom, +θ_{try},$ $+θ_{address}]$ try $[_{IP}$ A politician $[+Nom, +θ_{address}]$ I^0 to $[_{VP}$ [every rally $[−Acc,$ $+θ_{address}]]$ $[_{VP}$ A politician $[+Nom, +θ_{address}]$ address every rally $[−Acc,$ $+θ_{address}]]]]]$

Observe that in this phrase marker, only the top copies of 'a politician' bear both the θ-role of 'try' and 'address'. If we assume that all θ-roles must be expressed in the interpretation provided by the CI-interface, then this prevents the deletion of the upper copies. However, if one of these copies must be retained, then we account for why 'a politician' must have scope over 'every rally'.[69,70]

7.3   A Problematic Example

The account of OC structures above relies on moving into θ-positions. We considered Chomsky's (1995) argument against allowing movement into θ-positions and showed that the data he mentions could be accommodated without prohibiting such movement. There is another problem, however, that leads to the same conclusion. Consider (79a) with the structure in (79b).[71]

(79)   a.   *John expects to seem that he is smart
       b.   [$_{IP1}$ John [$_{VP}$ John expects [$_{IP2}$ John to seem [$_{CP}$ that he . . .]]]]

The derivation indicated in section 7.2 is that 'John' is merged into the Spec of IP1. It then raises to the Spec of VP checking the external θ-role of 'expect' and then raises to Spec IP1 to check case and D-features. This derivation is ruled out if one cannot move to a theta position or if only trivial chains can get θ-roles. However, these assumptions are rejected here and so another way must be found to prevent the derivation in (79b). Consider three possible ways of doing this.

The first option is to deny that 'John' can be inserted into the Spec of IP2 as it fails to check some relevant feature. One possibility is that the I^0 of a control predicate is different than the one in a raising construction. This is argued for in Martin (1996: ch. 2) following earlier work by Stowell (1982) on the tense of infinitives. The proposal is that these infinitives have a +Tense feature. Thus raising infinitives are distinguished from control infinitives in that the latter have +Tns Infls while the former have −Tns Infls. Say that this is correct. We now make a further assumption concerning +Tns infinitives: assume that the +Tns infinitive Infl (in contrast to raising Infls which are −Tns) has a feature that can only be checked by a D/NP which has a theta-feature, i.e. is theta-marked. For concreteness assume that the D-feature associated with +Tns infinitives can only be checked by a +θ-marked DP. Recall that the current story treats θ-roles as features that an expression receives by checking the θ-features of a predicate under merger. In effect the θ-features of the verb are transferred to the DP that merges with it. If they are indeed features then we would expect them to enter into typical checking relations. The proposal is that this is what happens in control IPs, viz. only θ-marked DPs can check the Infl of +Tns OC infinitives. Note that this will prevent the derivation in (79b) for 'John' merged into Spec IP2 is not yet θ-marked. It only receives a θ-feature by moving to Spec VP. Thus, it cannot check the postulated θ-sensitive feature of the +Tns infinitive Infl. This effectively blocks the illicit derivation in (79b).

Note that this same assumption will suffice to block control by expletive arguments like 'it' in sentences like (80).

(80)   *It was hoped to be believed that Fran left

(80) cannot be interpreted as parallel to (81).

(81)   It was hoped that it was believed that Fran left

The question is why not? The relevant structure is (82).

(82)   [$_{IP2}$ It was hoped [$_{IP1}$ it to be believed [that . . .

This is illicit if we assume that 'it' is not endowed with a θ-role (or endowed with the "wrong kind" of pseudo argument θ-role in the sense of Chomsky (1986)) and cannot check the postulated feature of the embedded +Tns infinitive that 'hope' selects.

Observe that if PRO were a base generated formative, it is not clear how (82) would be ruled out except by stipulating that PRO cannot be bound by a non-θ-marked antecedent in these sorts of constructions or that PRO must be θ-marked to be licit. The latter stipulation is a notational variant of the proposal made here which requires the subject of a control complement to be θ-marked.

In short, the postulation of a feature on control infinitives that must be checked by θ-marked DPs suffices to handle (79a). Furthermore, this proposal finds independent support as it explains why OC PROs cannot be controlled by expletives.

A second option for dealing with (79a) is to recognize that when predicates like 'seem' take finite complements then they require 'it' subjects. If, as Chomsky 1986 suggests, 'it' carries a weak kind of θ-role, then one can treat this requirement as a selection fact about predicates with finite complements; they select thematically marked subjects like 'it'. If so then (79a) is out because it violates a selection restriction. Note that the intimate relation between 'it' and finite complements has long been observed. The proposal here is to exploit the fact to block the derivation in (79a). A similar sort of account would block the derivation of (83) that Chomsky (1995) treats as a selection restriction violation.

(83)   *I expect [$_{IP1}$ John to seem [that t left]]

This raising should be licensed by the requirement to check the D-feature in IP1. The raising is blocked if the finite complement requires that 'seem' have an 'it' subject.

Consider a third possibility. Chomsky (1998) raises the possibility that MERGE like MOVE is subject to Greed. In effect, this would require all grammatical operations to be driven by feature checking. Chomsky (1998) also suggests that the EPP not be treated as involving feature checking. These assumptions together suffice to prevent direct Merger (at least of a lexical DP) into the Spec IP of a non-finite clause. As such, the derivation of (79a) above is blocked.

There is one last approach that hinges on denying that the EPP (or its equivalent) holds for non-finite clauses. Observe that (79) is derived by merging 'John' into the embedded Spec TP position. Say that non-finite clauses do not have Spec TPs. Then this sort of merger could be blocked. However, if this merger is illicit, then the unwanted derivation is unattainable.

Castillo, Drury and Grohmann (CDG)(1999) have recently proposed that raising clauses do not have subjects. They observe that the requirement that all clauses have subjects is largely supported on theory internal grounds and that there are ways to reanalyze most (if not all) of the remaining empirical support.[72] The proposal here is to assume, as CDG do, that there is no EPP effect in control infinitives either.

Technically, we need the following assumptions. First, that non-finite T^0 does not license a Spec (at least in the standard case). This means to say that there is no feature that such T^0s have that needs checking. Second, that merger, like movement, is greedy. This follows Chomsky (1998) in extending greed to Merge. Observe that the extension of greed to Merge operations is required given the assumptions we have been exploring here. The reason is that it is impossible to restrict it to movement operations once one makes two further assumptions: (a) that Move is the composite of Copy and Merge and (b) that copies are indistinguishable from "originals" in their grammatical powers. Once one adopts these two assumptions it is impossible to say that greed only applies to movement for movement *per se* is not a grammatical operation and copies cannot be singled out for special treatment. In effect, the extension of greed to Merge is required.[73]

These two assumptions together prevent the derivation in (79). In addition, they account for why it is that there is no control by expletives, as in (80) above. The reason is if we put aside the EPP, then movement in control structures is from one theta-position to another. There is no intervening movement via a non-theta-position. But if this is so, then there is no way that an expletive can "control" as expletives cannot be theta-marked.

For current purposes all four of these approaches suffice to eliminate the problem posed by (79). I personally favor the last of these.[74] However, all of the approaches are compatible with the basic assumptions required for a movement theory of OC.

8   Non-Obligatory Control; The Elsewhere Case

The upshot of the last three sections is that a Control Module is superfluous if OC PRO is treated as a residue of movement, essentially equivalent to NP-t. We can account for the distribution of OC PRO in terms of case theory; it appears where case is not checked. Typically this coincides with the Spec IP position of non-finite Infls.[75] However, it can also occur in verbs like 'dress' and 'shave' that have the option of not needing to check accusative case. OC PRO's lackluster phonetic properties follow from the assumption that PROs are simply NP-ts; hence their inability to block 'wanna' contraction as well as their lack of phonetic content. In addition, we have deduced the interpretive properties of OC PROs. They require non-split local antecedents because they are formed by movement. They are interpreted 'de se' because chains that involve PROs form compound (reflexive) predicates, i.e. predicates in which an argument has two theta-roles. Last of all, we have provided a theory of controllers; why object control holds in 'persuade' type verbs, why subject control is required in OC PRO headed adjuncts. In short, reducing control to movement allows for the elimination of any special control module and for the further simplification of grammatical theory along MP lines.

One last point. By reducing OC to movement, the empty category in (23) above (repeated here) is expected to be an NOC PRO. The reason is that, in the relevant examples, movement from Spec IP is prohibited as the relevant launch sites are within islands.

(23) a.   It was believed that PRO shaving was important
      b.   John$_i$ thinks that it is believed that PRO$_i$ shaving himself is important
      c.   Clinton's$_i$ campaign believes that PRO$_i$ keeping his sex life under control is necessary for electoral success
      d.   John thinks that PRO getting his resume in order is crucial and Bill does too
      e.   The unfortunate believes that PRO getting a medal would be boring
      f.   Only Churchill remembers that PRO giving the BST speech was momentous

In the cited examples, PRO is in the subject position of a subject sentence. Given that subject sentences are islands, movement from the Spec IP of these structures is prohibited. As such, OC is also barred. Only NOC is permitted, as attested.

I have said very little about NOC PRO. I have silently assumed that it is analogous (if not simply identical) to 'pro', the null pronominal found in various Romance and East Asian languages. This 'pro' can be interpreted as a pronoun, either definite (so similar to 'he', 'they', 'she' etc.) or indefinite (like English 'one'). The latter underlies the so-called arbitrary reading. This requires assuming that 'pro' can be licensed in English in NOC configurations. Chomsky (1993) has 'pro' licensed in the Spec of certain Infls. If the above is correct, it indicates that 'ing' and 'to' can so license 'pro' and that 'pro' can check whatever features of these Infls need checking. Importantly, however, the distribution of 'pro' is not free. One does not find the free alternation of OC and NOC structures. Rather, NOC typically obtains when movement is prohibited, e.g. from WH islands as in (84). OC and NOC are effectively in complementary distribution. This suggests that NOC is the "elsewhere" case.

(84) a.   John told Sam how PRO to hold oneself erect at a royal ball
      b.   *John told Sam PRO to hold oneself erect at a royal ball

One way of implementing this observation would be to treat 'pro' on a par with 'do' in English. 'Do' support is regularly treated as a costly last resort operation.[76] When all other grammatical options fail to yield a convergent derivation, 'do' can insert to "support" an otherwise deadly morphological residue. Just how to treat this "last resort" nature of 'do'-support in MP is somewhat unclear.[77] Strictly speaking, 'do' cannot be part of the array for if it were sentences with and without 'do' would not be comparable and so the intuition that 'do' sentences are less economical (more costly and hence to be avoided if possible) than those without it cannot be redeemed. Rather 'do' is a formative of the computational system of English that can be inserted in any derivation, though at a cost and, hence, only when all other relevant grammatical options have failed. A similar treatment of 'pro' in NOC structures would yield the correct empirical results. Consider some details.

In NOC configurations, movement is impossible as the sentences in (85) indicate.

(85)   a.   It is believed that Bill's/pro shaving is important
       a'.   *Bill's is believed that shaving is important
       b.   It is impossible for Bill/pro to win at Roulette
       b'.   *Bill is impossible to win at Roulette

Consider in more detail (85a) with the 'pro' subject in the embedded position. To license this structure, the Spec IP must have its features checked. There is no way to do this by moving an expression through this position to check the relevant features of Infl and then moving it again to check its own (e.g. case) features, as movement from this position is prohibited. Thus, we find no OC "PRO"s in these slots. However, the features of the embedded Infl must still be checked if the derivation is to converge. Assume that 'pro' can be inserted to meet this requirement. In short, assume that 'pro' needs no case but can check the relevant features of Infl.[78] Note that English is not a 'pro' drop language so the features of 'pro' must be quite anemic. 'Pro' then has two important properties: (i) it is able to check the requisite features of infinitival Infls and (ii) using 'pro' to check such features is derivationally costly. The second assumption, viz. that the grammatical use of 'pro' in these cases is uneconomical, suffices to account for why it is that 'pro' and PRO are in complementary distribution. Thus, for example, (22) cannot have an NOC inter-pretation for all features can be checked without inserting it, as the derivation in (22b) indicates.

(86)   a.   John hopes to win
       b.   [$_{IP}$ John [$_{VP}$ John hopes [$_{IP}$ John to [$_{VP}$ John win]]]]

When this sort of derivation is impossible, however, 'pro' can be inserted and the derivation saved, as in (85a) above. This account mimics the standard one for 'do' point by point. In particular, in MP terms, NOC 'pro' cannot be part of the array but is a formative used as a last option to save an otherwise doomed derivation.[79]

To sum up then. OC PRO is the residue of movement and has all the char-acteristics of an NP-t. The only real distinction between raising and control structures is that the former involves raising a D/NP to a non-theta-position while the former raises expressions to theta-positions. Both raising and control chains (generally) terminate in case positions. NOC PRO, in contrast, is simply 'pro' and it is licensed *at a cost* in the Spec IP of non-finite CP complements.

9   Q-float, Raising and Control

The analysis presented here treats OC and raising as a natural class. They both involve movement and the formation of an extended chain. They both contrast with NOC configurations such as (87), for example, in which the relation between 'John' and 'pro' is an inter-chain, not *intra*-chain relation.

(87)   John$_i$ thinks that [[pro$_i$ shaving] is a duty]

In this section, I would like to use Q-float to "count" chains. The idea is the following. For concreteness, let's assume Sportiche's (1988) theory of Q-float.[80] On this account, floated Qs result from NP movement. For example, (88) results from leaving the Q behind under movement of 'the men' to Spec TP.

(88)   The men have [$_{VP}$ [all [the men]] eaten supper]

Assume that this is correct. Next, observe that examples like (89) are quite odd.

(89)   a.   ??The men each have each eaten supper
     b.   ??The men all have all eaten supper
     c.   ??The men both have both eaten supper
     d.   ??The men both have all eaten supper
     e.   ??The men all have each eaten supper

We can account for its oddity by noting that (90) is also quite unacceptable.[81]

(90)   a.   ??Both the men both have eaten supper
     b.   ??Both the men all have eaten supper
     c.   ??Each of the men all have eaten supper

The problem in (90) is clear: there are too many quantifiers per nominal. If floated Qs are the residue of nominal movement, then this same account extends to account for (89). In effect, the oddity of (89) follows from that of (90) if we assume that we cannot have too many quantifers per nominal *(A-)chain*. The attested oddity, then, can be used as a chain detector. Where it appears, there is but a single chain, where it is absent there is more than one chain.

   Note that the reasoning extends to cases of raising. The examples in (91) share the status of those in (89).

(91)   a.   ??The men all seemed to have all eaten supper
     b.   ??The men seemed each to have each eaten supper
     c.   ??The men seemed both to have both eaten supper

   A second Q-float diagnostic that similarly discriminates chain structure involves multiple *different* Q-floated sentences. (92) and (93) seem to be of comparable unacceptability.

(92)   a.   ??The men all have each/both eaten supper
     b.   ??The men both have all/each eaten supper
     c.   ??The men each have all/both eaten supper

(93)   a.   ??The men all seemed to have each/both eaten supper
     b.   ??The men both seemed to have all/each eaten supper
     c.   ??The men each seemed to have both/all eaten supper

Both these types of cases are unacceptable because cases like (94) are.

(94)   a.   ??Both men all/each have eaten supper
     b.   ??All the men each/both have eaten supper
     c.   ??Each of the men all/both have eaten supper

Consider now how these two diagnostics work in the case of OC and NOC configurations. The OC examples in (95) are on a par with the raising cases in (91) and (93).[82]

(95)   a.   ??The men both hope to have both eaten supper (by 6)
     b.   ??The men each hope to have each eaten supper (by 6)
     c.   ??The men all hope to have all eaten supper (by 6)
     d.   ??The men both hope to have all/each eaten supper (by 6)
     e.   ??The men all hope to have each/both eaten supper (by 6)
     f.   ??The men each hope to have all/both eaten supper (by 6)

These contrast with the NOC cases in which the corresponding multiple Q-floated configurations seem quite acceptable.

(96)   a.   The men both think that both/each having eaten supper at 6 was a good idea
     b.   The men all thought that all/each dancing with Mary was fun
     c.   The men each thought that all/each dancing with Mary was fun

This is what we expect if indeed the OC structures are formed via A-movement (and hence form a single A-chain) while the NOC structures are not.[83]
    One last point. Adjunct control configurations pattern together with OC. This provides confirmation for the analysis of adjunct control in terms of sidewards movement.

(97)   a.   ??The men both sang while both eating supper
     b.   ??The men both sang before all eating supper
     c.   ??The men each sang after all eating supper

10   Conclusion

This chapter has argued in favor of eliminating the control module from the grammar. In place of subtheories specially designed to account for the distribution and interpretation of PRO the present proposal has relied on movement to account for OC and 'pro' to handle NOC. The price paid for thus eliminating the PRO module has been to remove the last residues of D-structure from the grammar and to dispense with the assumption that expressions (or chains they head) are restricted to a single theta role. Both assumptions are required to permit movement from one θ-position to another; the very minimum required if OC is to be analyzed as movement. Technically this has also required treating θ-roles as features on predicates and θ-role assignment as a species of feature checking that licenses greedy movement. It is for the reader to judge whether this price is too high for the benefits garnered. In my view, the theoretical adjustments required to gain the elimination of the PRO module are methodologically preferable to the theoretical stipulations they have replaced. As such, even if the gains were paltry, the burden of proof would be on those who insist on maintaining the restrictions on theta-roles, chains and merger that have been dispensed with.

The most controversial assumption made in the analysis above is that theta-roles are features in sense that they can license greedy movement. This is what leads to the elimination of the bi-uniqueness restriction on chains and theta-roles. Therefore, it is worth pointing out once more that this assumption follows very directly given three more general currently widely held assumptions: (a) that Move is Copy and Merge, (b) that Copies are grammatically indistinguishable from "originals," i.e. that traces have no special status within the grammar and (c) that Merge as well as Move is subject to greed (see Chomsky 1998). These three independently desirable assumptions have as their consequence that theta-roles are sufficient to license an operation as greedy. And this is all that is required to make the present analysis viable.

This said, the present analysis raises several additional questions and suggests various extensions. Let's assume that the story outlined above is roughly correct. It enables us to eliminate one central class of construal rules, those involved with OC, from the grammar. This suggests looking at the other major source of construal processes; the Binding Theory to see to what extent this module of the grammar is required. We do this in chapter 5.

Another issue raised by the present analysis relates to the elimination of 'PRO' as a grammatical formative. As noted, it is undesirable theoretically on grounds of parsimony. We have shown how it can be dispensed with. There are other purely theory internal objects such as the 0-operator involved in parasitic gap structures, relatives, purpose clauses, and 'tough'-constructions. Do these really require 0-operators or can they be reanalyzed. Nunes (1995) goes a long way in suggesting how to reanalyze some of these constructions so as to eliminate the need for 0-operators as primitives. The next chapter reviews this work and considers its relation to adjunct control structures more generally.

Notes

1 This chapter is a revised version of Hornstein (1999).
2 There is one more standard set of data from Burzio (1986) associated with the control/raising distinction. Burzio notes that some quantificational dependencies are sensitive to the distinction. See section 7 below for discussion.

Burzio further describes a second set of data. He notes that one can margin-ally allow 'each' to be bound by a plural inside a 'to' phrase under passive and raising:

(i)   a.   ?One interpreter each$_i$ was assigned to the visitors$_i$
      b.   ?One interpreter each$_i$ is likely to be assigned to the visitors$_i$

This contrasts with control cases which are deemed much worse:

(ii)   *One interpreter each$_i$ was trying to be assigned to the visitors$_i$

Unfortunately, for many speakers, the first set of raising data are very marginal. Moreover, if one considers control predicates other than 'try' the second set of cases improve.

(iii)   ?One interpreter each$_i$ hoped/asked to be assigned to the visitors$_i$.

As such, it is hard to assess the impact of the purported contrast.

    There is a third set of data concerning object preposing in Italian and French discussed in section 7 below.

3   This conception goes back to the earliest models of generative grammar. The thematic properties of D-structure are roughly identical to those enjoyed by Kernel sentences in a *Syntactic Structures* style theory. Kernel sentences were input to transformational processes and were the locus of (what we now call) theta-roles. *Aspects* substitutes the base for kernel sentences. The base is a pre-transformational phrase marker generated by phrase structure rules. Like kernel sentences, it is the input to the transformational component and the locus of thematic information. This role for the base has been retained in some form in all subsequent theories.

4   Several technical details are glossed over here for convenience.

5   This is not quite accurate. Recently control has become a hot area of research. The proposal below shares with O'Neill (1995) the intuition that control should be reduced to movement. Though the details of the two approaches differ, they are conceptually very similar. There are two other approaches to control set within MP assumptions. Martin (1996) develops a theory exploiting the notion of null case proposed in Chomsky and Lasnik (1993) to account for the distribution of PRO. Manzini and Roussou (forthcoming) develop a theory of control in terms of feature movement of heads at LF. The wealth of approaches is to be welcomed given the awkward position that the control module has in MP. In what follows, I lay out a view of control that differs from those noted above. For reasons of space, I keep comparisons to a minimum and relegate them to the notes.

6   David Lightfoot has pointed out to me that it is not clear how cases like (13a) are to be handled given standard GB assumptions. If one takes case marking to be a diagnostic under government, then the unacceptability of (13a) with 'Mary' as subject indicates lack of government. However, this should then make (13a) with 'PRO' in embedded subject position acceptable. The only way to resolve this prob-lem is to assume that the embedded subject position is governed, hence 'PRO' is not a viable embedded subject, and that case marking is blocked by something like adjacency, hence 'Mary' is not a viable embedded subject. This move, however, is quite problematic once one moves to a minimalist account. First, there is little reason to think that adjacency holds for accusative case marking once one moves

to a theory of case like that in Chomsky (1995), as Chomsky (1995: 330 ff) observes. Solving the problem likely requires abandoning the idea that either 'PRO' or 'Mary' are actually in Spec IP in these configurations.

7   This is based on definitions in Chomsky (1981). See also Aoun (1986).

8   A similar argument can be based on Chinese data. See Huang (1983) for discussion.

9   This sort of reasoning is in fact used in Kayne (1991).

10   (9a–e) are presented in Lebeaux (1984–5). (9f) is discussed in Higginbotham (1992). (9g) is first discussed in Fodor (1975). In what follows I take the paradigm in (21) as properties of OC. This view of OC differs from that in Williams (1980) in that I leave out some of his diagnostics for OC, e.g. I reject his assumption (which follows the standard practice dating to Rosenbaum (1967)) that OC configurations are in complementary distribution with structures in which an overt lexical subject appears and his assumption OC and non-OC structures are in complementary distribution in having overt antecedents for PRO. This latter assumption leads Williams to deny that one has OC in cases like (i) given the well-formedness of cases like (ii).

(i)   John's desire [PRO to win]
(ii)   The desire [PRO to win]

For discussion of these latter cases see chapter 3.

    To put things in a slightly misleading manner, the main difference between the approach taken here and that of Williams is that I do not identify "structures" of OC so much as PROs that are OC. Hence I allow for the possibility that one and the same "structure" sometimes has an OC PRO and sometimes a non-OC PRO.

11   It is even possible to "control" an NOC PRO across a sentence boundary. This was first noted by Bach (1979).

(i)   John$_i$ even shaved for the interview. PRO$_i$ making himself presentable is very important to the success of the project

12   This does not mean that reflexives can *always* replace OC PRO or pronouns NOC PRO. Rather, where this is possible then OC PRO shows up as a reflexive and NOC PRO as a pronoun.

13   In fact, the entire paradigm noted in (21) and (23) is duplicated when local and non-local reflexives are considered. See chapter 5 for discussion.

14   Adopting the assumptions in Chomsky (1995), the offending sentences would be out because the case of the embedded I^0 is not checked or because case checking has resulted in feature clash within the PP. The movement does not violate greed for the D-feature of the embedded Infl is checked by the movement. However, its case feature cannot be checked by the raised PRO as it has been checked prior to raising within the PP or because the case on PRO and the case on PP do not match and the derivation terminates. At any rate, the unacceptability of the construction reduces to whatever blocks the derivation in (14).

15   The idea of tracing the distribution of PRO to case theory is due to Bouchard (1984). The Chomsky–Lasnik approach is a variation on Bouchard's theme.

16   This is similar to how Chomsky (1993) treats the distribution of small 'pro'. Its distribution is related to the feature structure of certain types of Infls.

17   The interpretive advantages of replacing the PRO theorem with null case are also noted in Bosković (1995).

18   See Boeckx (2000) for a more elaborate discussion of the point made briefly here.

19   There are several ways that this markedness fact can be incorporated into the theory. One way is to treat the object of 'promise' as in fact the object of a pre-position, perhaps null. In nominal forms, the "object" of 'promise' in fact surfaces with a 'to' preposition rather than the 'of' preposition characteristic of objects.

(i)   John's promise to Mary to leave

If this is correct, then the object of 'promise' in (ii) is not analyzed as a possible antecedent as it does not c-command the PRO.

(ii)   John promise [P Mary] [PRO to leave]

The presence of a null preposition might cause problems of acquisition and hence account for C. (Chomsky's observations.)

I am sure that there are other possible ways of handling the exceptional status of 'promise'. My point here is that however one treats these cases they are plausibly treated as outliers and should not be taken as revealing the basic properties of control configurations. This position might in fact be incorrect. Recently Culicover and Jackendoff (forthcoming) have argued that 'promise' should be treated as the central case of control and that its correct analysis suggests that control is actually a fact about the conceptual system, not a reflex of the grammar. It is possible that for some cases of control they are in fact correct. However, for the nonce, I put aside this possibility and examine what a more grammatical approach to control given minimalist strictures might look like.

20   Observe that what the controller in a given sentence is must be considered a structural fact not a lexical fact. To see this consider a verb like 'ask'. It optionally takes an object. When it does it requires object control – (i). When there is no object present it requires subject control – (ii).

(i)   John asked Mary$_i$ PRO$_i$ to leave the party
(ii)   John$_i$ asked PRO$_i$ to leave the party

These facts are accurately described by the Minimal Distance Principle. One cannot describe these data by claiming that 'ask' is either a subject or an object control verb.

21   Also known as the Minimal Link Condition. Linking some types of control to Shortest Move is also characteristic of the other minimalist approaches to control in Martin (1996) and Manzini and Roussou (1999).

22   There are cases of such control in rationale clauses such as (i):

(i)   John arrested Harry for PRO driving his car too fast

We return for a discussion of these constructions in chapter 3.

23   The reason that is implicitly assumed is that objects cannot bind into adjuncts, in contrast to subjects (see Chomsky 1995: 272 ff). The empirical basis for this contrast is not very clear. Note that objects can license bound pronouns. As these are typically thought to be licensed under c-command, it appears that objects can bind into adjuncts.

(i)   John greeted every girl$_i$ without her$_i$ knowing it

For discussion see section 6.

24   Cases like (32) are not always classified as configurations of OC, as I do here. The reason is that these structures permit overt lexical subjects.

(i)   John kissed Mary without Frank/PRO leaving the room

Nonetheless, with respect to the properties listed above, these configurations pattern just like those that do not have lexical alternates.

(ii)   John kissed Mary before *Frank/PRO leaving the room

25   What is meant by control here is that the subject appears to bear both the theta-role of the subject and that of the object. Lasnik (1995a) discusses these cases and attributes his observations that these appear to be control-like to Alan Munn. Lasnik, like Munn, suggests that these cases be treated in terms of movement. The account below develops this suggestion for all cases of OC. Note, incidentally, that this is another instance in which there is no complementary distribution between a PRO and an overt lexical item. Moreover, it is possible to put a full reflexive in place of the PRO in these cases.

26   The most elaborated version of the Chomsky–Lasnik approach is Martin (1996). He argues that null case must be tied to properties of certain T^0s. These data are a problem for this view.

27   Chomsky (1986: 176) blocks this case in terms of the ECP. Movement of the reflexive at LF violates this condition. The details of this proposal are not replicable in an MP framework as it appears to rely on lack of proper government to block the derivation. See Hornstein (1995) for discussion of the place of the ECP in MP.

28   See Nunes (1995) for an elaborate critique of traces as grammatical primitives. Chomsky (1998) makes a similar point.

29   It is interesting to observe that earlier theories of control that distinguished OC and NOC assume that OC PRO is governed (see, e.g. Manzini 1983, Hornstein and Lightfoot 1987). In many versions of the ECP, government by a head is required for all empty categories resulting from movement (see, e.g. Aoun, Hornstein, Lightfoot, and Weinberg 1987, Rizzi 1990). The fact that OC PROs are the head governed ones once again suggests that they, like traces in general, are the residues of movement.

30   The term 'NP-t' is here used descriptively. All traces are merely copies. The point here is that OC PRO is no different from NP-t in that both are copies formed via movement.

31   NOC 'pro' is discussed more fully in section 8.

32   This has already been proposed in Bosković (1994), Lasnik (1995b), and Boskovic and Takahashi (1998).

33   Chomsky (1995) suggests that it is odd to think of theta-roles as features. This is correct if one thinks of them as properties of D/NPs. There is no "paradigm" that groups nominals by their thematic status. However, one does group verbs (and other predicates) by their addicities. In other words, verbs *are* categorized by their thematic status. This makes it quite natural to treat theta roles as features of predicates.

34   A similar point is made in Brody (1993). He too distinguishes between the bi-uniqueness restriction on arguments and theta-roles and the rest of the theta-criterion. He observes that whereas the latter parts of the theta-criterion are plausibly seen simply as parts of the Principle of Full Interpretation, this is not so for the bi-uniqueness condition. Brody argues, as I do here, against retaining this restriction.

35   This assumes that the Extended Projection Principle is to be handled in terms of checking a D-feature. This is not at all obvious. See Martin (1999) and Chomsky (1998) for discussion.

36   This only holds for standard cases of movement, those that take place within a single rooted subtree. In these cases, the Extension Condition guarantees that the copy must merge in a c-commanding position. In cases of sidewards movement, movement between subtrees, c-command is not guaranteed and in fact we find cases of apparent OC without c-command. For further discussion see section 6.

37   Chomsky (1998) reconstructs the distinction between structure preserving "substitution" operations and adjunction given a theory like BPS. This is required given that BPS eliminates literal substitution as a possible operation.

38   The same reasoning applies to theories that treat traces as formatives and base generate chains. The problem is to find a way to prohibit split antecedents for a trace, say two DPs both sharing a theta-role by together binding a trace. Once again this follows trivially on a movement theory with a Bare Phrase Structure component.

39   This does not say how sloppy readings are derived, whether interpretively (Sag 1976, Williams 1977) or via some deletion operations at PF under some sort of parallelism requirement (Chomsky 1995). For current purposes which of these proves to be correct is irrelevant. All that is required is that whichever approach proves correct it treat all A-movement in a uniform fashion.

40   There remains the question as to why this operation is not generally valid. See chapter 5 for discussion.

41   We similarly provide a rationale for why it is that it is governed PRO that Manzini (1983) and others took to be the OC PRO. The ECP is an empirically useful diagnostic of movement, whatever its theoretical shortcomings in minimalist terms. The reason that OC PRO is governed, is that it is the residue of movement, i.e. it meets the same descriptive requirements as other traces.

42   This is essentially the suggestion proposed in Jaeggli 1980. It is not relevant here whether it is correct. All that is required is that PRO's phonetic status will be accounted for in the same way as NP-t's. For another approach see Nunes (1995).

43   If one is reluctant to require that theta-features be checked, we can recast the theta-criterion to require that every theta-role be "expressed" by being attached to a DP. This would then make the above a theta-criterion violation. Note, the analysis proposed above requires dropping the assumption that a DP can bear but a single theta-role. It does not require dropping the assumption that all theta-roles must be assigned.

44   Bosković (1994) provides independent evidence for the claim that movement via multiple theta-positions is possible. If he is correct, then simplicity favors treating obligatory control in the same terms. Put negatively, a hybrid theory that relates multiple theta-positions in structures like those Boskovic considers via movement but treats control as involving a PRO-like element is less favored than one that unifies both in terms of movement. I mention this for Martin (1996) seems to be the most sophisticated example of such a theory. It is unclear how this theory could accommodate Boskovic's cases. The main reason is that Boskovic's cases do not appear to involve IPs of the sort where a null case theory could gain a foothold. Without null case, however, the prospects for a PRO-based account are dim.

45   There remains the issue of when 'pro' headed propositions are permitted. We return to this in section 6 below.

46   This is first formulated in Rosenbaum (1970).

47   The standard assumption, adopted here, is that nominal expressions cannot be doubly case marked, at least in the unmarked case.

48 There are other ways of blocking Chomsky's derivation that do not require that copies be treated as relevant for SM. This involves dropping the assumption that the EPP (or some functional equivalent) holds in non-finite clauses. If there is Spec TP in such constructions, then the envisioned derivation in (52b) cannot get off the ground as merging into the embedded Spec TP is not an option. Other assumptions are required to flesh out this argument. See below for further discussion.

49 Note that strictly speaking the 'I' in the embedded Spec IP is not a copy but the original element selected from the array. The higher 'I's are the copies if movement is copy+deletion as Chomsky assumes. The point in the text above is that the grammar does not (and should not) distinguish copies from originals in any relevant sense. This is contrary to Chomsky's (1995) position where the foot of a chain is different from the head in not being visible to the computational system. Chomsky's proposal amounts to encoding in MP terms a distinction between expressions and their traces. In effect, the proposal implicitly postulates the existence of traces as grammatical formatives. As usual, the postulation of abstract entities must be empirically justified. The null position is that NP-ts as distinctive grammatical objects do not exist. This is what the copy theory presupposes and I assume here. For further critical discussion of this assumption see Nunes (1995).

   The treatment of all copies as grammatically equal raises the question of whether chains are "real" objects, i.e. have distinctive properties of their own. When introduced in Chomsky (1981) chains were notational shorthands used for summarizing the properties of local movement. Rizzi (1986) was the first to argue that chains had an independent grammatical existence. In the context of MP it is not at all clear that chains should be treated as independent entities. For example, their existence appears to contradict "inclusiveness" (Chomsky 1995: 228) which bars the addition of "new objects" in the course of the computation from the numeration to LF. Chains are not lexical objects. As such, inclusiveness should bar their presence at LF. This is not to deny that movement exists. The existence of "displacement" operations in the grammar is undeniable. However, this does not imply that chains exist with well-formedness conditions of their own. For further discussion of these issues see Hornstein (1998).

50 I illustrate using 'after'. However, the diagnostics work just as well with the other adjuncts, 'before', 'without' and 'while'.

51 The requirement that OC PROs receive an obligatory 'de se' reading is hard to test as such readings require embedding under propositional attitude predicates which we do not have here.

52 As noted in section 2, this is not entirely correct. I return to a fuller discussion of other adjuncts in chapter 3.

53 This term is due to Bobaljik and Brown (1997).

54 Nunes (1995) assumes that c-command is not part of the definition of MOVE but part of the chain formation requirements. For current purposes I accept the divorce between MOVE and c-command. We return to whether c-command must be stipulated to hold of chains in chapter 3.

55 I stay agnostic on the exact status of the adjunct, i.e. whether it is a complementizer or head of a PP.

56 We return to a fuller discussion in chapter 3. However, observe that if MOVE is really just Copy+Merge, then there is no obvious reason why this movement should be illicit. There may be objections to this kind of operation if MOVE is defined in terms of Attract, as attraction makes little intuitive sense across subtrees. We return to these issues in chapter 4. For now, let's see what sideways movement can do for us here.

57   There are a variety of ways to define relative closeness. One can define it (i) only for expressions that c-command one another or (ii) only for expressions both c-commanded by the target or (iii) for expressions that c-command one another and are both c-commanded by the target. What the relevant relation is is an empirical issue. (i) appears to be an accepted necessary condition for defining closeness. Theories that see ATTRACT as a basic component of movement would naturally adopt something like (iii). For present purposes (i) suffices. In fact, sidewards movement does not fit well with definitions of closeness stated in terms of the target. I discuss this in chapter 4.

58   This raises an interesting problem. What blocks 'Mary' from having nominative case and 'John' from bearing accusative and thereby deriving (i), in which 'John' checks its case at LF?

(i)   *Mary saw before John entering the room
(ii)   [$_{IP}$ Mary [$_{I^0}$ past [$_{VP/VP}$ [$_{VP}$ Mary [saw Mary] [$_{adjunct}$ before [$_{IP}$ John [$_{I^0}$ ing [$_{VP}$ John [entering the room]]]]]]]]]

As (ii) indicates, 'Mary' would have two theta-roles and 'John' would check its accusative case at LF.

This derivation is plausibly blocked by the CED. Note that at LF, the adjunct and the VP form a constituent. In the derivation in the text, the movement from the adjunct takes place prior to merging it to VP. See chapter 3 for a detailed discussion of CED effects.

59   Observe that this argument requires that we adopt a non-Larsonian approach to adjuncts, i.e. they are not like syntactic arguments. In fact, the difference between where we merge adjuncts and complements is central explaining why we have object control (typically) in the latter case while we have subject control in the former. For further arguments against adopting a Larsonian structure see Hornstein (1995 ch. 8).

60   This reasoning should sound familar. It is identical to the reasoning Chomsky (1995) uses to account for the unacceptability of sentences like (i):

(i)   *There seems a man to be here

61   The facts are more involved and the argument actually more subtle than shown here. We return to this in chapter 3.

62   The data below follow Burzio (1986: 46–53). He observes that the same phenomenon exists in French.

63   Burzio (1986: 50; example 73a–c) provides evidence that this 'si' cannot appear in PRO headed clauses of either the OC or NOC variety. This is interesting for it argues against the view that this is a case marked position, at least in the usual sense. 'Si' cannot check its case in these configurations though it can in standard case positions.

One further point of interest. His example (73c) is a case of OC control into adjuncts. The 'si' cannot move at LF to check its case in the matrix. This conforms to the view expounded in note 58 above that once the adjunct is adjoined, it functions like an island. See chapter 3 for further discussion of CED effects.

64   See Chomsky (1995) for discussion of multiple Spec constructions.

65   Note, we are assuming that the 'si' and the trace/copy of 'quei prigionieri' in the embedded Spec IP are equidistant from the matrix I^0 as they are essentially multiple Specs of the embedded I^0. See Chomsky (1995: 356; (189)–(190)) for the relevant definitions.

One more technical point. I assume that moving the preposed object over the 'si' subject inside the VP shell is not a problem. This is standardly so because the object moves via the outer Spec of VP to check accusative case. This is not so in the OP construction as the preposed object does not have accusative case. However, as (71a,b) indicates, the preposed object agrees with 'liberati' with respect to number. This suggests a predicate internal movement of the object prior to moving to the Spec IP of the embedded clause. I assume that this suffices to permit the object to cross the subject by placing them in the same domain.

66   The account here is entirely analogous to the one in Chomsky (1995: 186) in which a trace in the subject theta-role position of Spec VP blocks movement of the object to Spec IP.

67   See Kennedy (1997) for example.

68   We make the standard assumption that derivations proceed bottom up. See Hornstein (1998) for further discussion of this issue.

69   A QR based theory can similarly account for the contrast of scoping possibilities in raising versus control configurations. Following May (1977, 1985) we can allow QR to lower and adjoin the quantifier to the embedded Spec IP in raising constructions. This would allow the lowered quantifier to have the same scope as it would enjoy in a simple clause. This lowering leaves an unbound trace in the matrix. However, the trace has no thematic properties and this lowering plausibly has no ill effects. Lowering in control structures, however, would leave a trace with a theta-role unbound and this plausibly leads to a full interpretation violation.

There is yet another option. It is well known that infinitives are more porous than finite clauses. This might allow QR to move adjoin 'every rally' to the matrix IP and thereby allow it to scope over 'a politician'.

70   A problem remains, however. We can account for why all control structures should allow ambiguity and why all should prevent it. What we need, however, is to find a way of explaining how to allow some control verbs to permit a scope ambiguity while preventing others from doing so. One way of doing this technically is to adopt the account of quantifier scope ambiguities in Hornstein (1998). There I proposed that derivations could proceed bottom up (in overt syntax) or top down (at LF) and that these alternative derivations would lead to different scope realizations. If one assumed that control verbs differed in whether the theta roles of the control predicate (the matrix) were weak or strong then one could track the possibility of ambiguity in this way. For example, say that 'hope' does not allow a scope ambiguity in (i):

(i)   Someone hopes to see every movie

One could track this fact by treating the external theta-role of 'hope' as strong. Recall, theta-roles are simply features here so they should come in weak and strong varieties. If it is strong, this forces a bottom up derivation which in turn forces the reading in which 'someone' scopes over 'every movie'. In cases where the control clauses are ambiguous this is consistent with treating the matrix theta-feature as weak and so checkable at LF. In this case, lowering is possible at LF and so a top down derivation is available. For details on derivational directionality see Hornstein (1998).

More clearly needs to be said. However, it is interesting to observe that the data can be accommodated using this approach. It is unclear whether this is generally so as it is unclear on most accounts why control structures should differ in their permissiveness with respect to relative quantifier scope.

71 This case was brought to my attention by Juan Carlos Castillo (see also Martin (1996: 26, example 21)).

72 The main type of support comes from ECM constructions such as (i)

(i) John believes Bill to be here

However, if one has accusative case checked overtly in English then this sort of example ceases to be evidence for the EPP. This has recently been argued to be true on independent grounds by Koizumi (1995) and Lasnik (1995c).

Castillo, Drury and Grohmann (1999) review much of the other evidence in favor of the EPP and reanalyze it. In support of their efforts, it is worth observing that the EPP has proven to be remarkably refractory to insightful theoretical analysis.

73 Note one further consequence of this extension. If greed is extended to Merge then merger into theta-positions must be greedy. In other words, we are adopting the assumption made here that theta-role checking is sufficient to license operations that must be greedy.

74 The elimination of EPP requirements within raising and control constructions has a further interesting consequence for the analysis of 'wanna' contraction. The current best analysis of these effects relies on the assumption that it is case marked traces that are the culprits blocking contraction (see Jaeggli 1980). This suggests that case is what makes an expression a phonetic "intervener." Though this clearly works, it has never been clear why case has this power. A better analysis would be that *any* nominal trace blocks contraction (see Lightfoot 1976). Note that this option is blocked under the requirement that all clauses, including non-finite raising and control clauses, have subjects. In effect, it is the EPP that prevents adopting the latter story and complicating it with restrictions to case marked nominals. If, however, the EPP is dropped for non-finite clauses, then the simplest account of 'wanna' contraction is viable and all reference to case marked traces can be dropped. Note that case checking independently forces subjects to move to Spec TP in finite clauses, the environment in which 'wanna' contraction is blocked.

75 Non-finite +Tns Infls if Martin (1996) is correct. The distinction he motivates is compatible with the theory outlined so long as one does not conclude, as he does, that case is assigned in the Spec of such infinitival heads. Note that I have here returned to assuming that the EPP holds for non-finite clauses. If it doesn't, then, strictly speaking, there is no analogue of PRO at all in control structures, i.e. there are not even residues of movement in the Spec TPs of non-finite clauses. Observe that if this is correct it undercuts the Chomsky–Martin view of null case quite directly.

76 See, for example, Chomsky (1995: ch. 2) and Lasnik (1995c).

77 To my knowledge, Arnold (1995) is the first place that the problem of how to implement "elsewhere" reasoning of the 'do' support variety into a minimalist framework is addressed. What follows is largely influenced by this work. See Arnold (1995) for discussion.

78 That 'pro' need not be case marked is proposed in Authier (1992). If we drop the requirement that non-finite sentences have subjects then 'pro' might be within the VP and check whatever features need checking there, presumably theta-features. Rizzi (1986) has noted that 'pro' occurs within VPs in Romance. It is plausible that licensing this instance of 'pro' is different from the licensing of 'pro' in the Spec of finite TP. Rizzi treats the two cases rather differently. If so, this suggests that the 'pro' drop parameter is largely concerned with the generation of null pronominals in the subject position of finite clauses.

79 See chapter 5 where a mechanism for "inserting" pronouns into the derivation is provided.

80 I adopt Sportiche's analysis for it has the right properties. However, all I require in what follows is that the number of acceptable floated Qs correlates with the number of separate chains. This follows on Sportiche's theory. However, Barry Schein and Tim Stowell have convinced me that it likely follows just as well given other assumptions.

81 The cases in (90) are worse than those in (89) to my ear. I assume that this is not significant however.

82 It is perfectly acceptable to Q-float within a control structure.

    (i)   a.   The men all hope to have eaten supper by 6
          b.   The men hope to have all eaten supper by 6

83 One final note of interest. It seems that it is not equally acceptable to float quantifiers everywhere. In particular, consider the cases in (i).

    (i)   a.   The men are unlikely to have all/both/each eaten supper by 6
          a'. The men are unlikely all/both/each to have eaten supper by 6
          b.   The men hoped to have all/both/each eaten supper by 6
          b'. The men hoped all/both/each to have eaten supper by 6
          c.   The men tried to all/both/each eat supper by 6
          c'. The men tried all/both/each to eat supper by 6

(ia',b',c') seem worse than (ia,b,c). It is my experience that this contrast is quite sharp for some speakers but not for all (see Castillo, Drury and Grohmann 1999 for example). For others, the a, b, c cases are slightly "more natural" but not strongly so. Note that the existence of a contrast suggests the absence of movement to Spec TP in raising and control clauses. Of course, it remains to be explained why the contrast is so weak for some speakers. I have nothing to say on this score.

3

Adjunct Control and Parasitic Gaps

Introduction

Chapter 2 analyzes adjunct control (AC) constructions like (1) as instances of sidewards movement.

(1)   John saw Mary [before PRO leaving the party]

The proposal is closely modeled on the analysis of parasitic gaps (PG) proposed in Nunes (1995) which uses sidewards movement to derive many of the salient properties of PG constructions. In this chapter, I contrast PGs and AC structures. Though they share many properties in common, they are not entirely identical. Contrasting their differences sheds light on the mechanics of their shared theoretical common core. It also affords us the opportunity to consider certain larger theoretical themes concerning the role of derivations in UG and the status (and interpretation) of Binding Principle C within a minimalist system.

   The chapter proceeds as follows. Section 1 starts with a quick review of the chapter 2 analysis of ACs. Section 2 offers a revised version of Nunes' (1995) proposal and shows how a sidewards movement analysis can be used to derive virtually all of the salient properties of PGs. I then focus on a key difference between the two construction types. This leads into a discussion of Principle C in section 3. Section 4 addresses an obvious problem for these analyses: if PGs and ACs are derived by sidewards movement then adjuncts are not strict islands. How then are CED effects (e.g. the fact that WH movement is illicit from adjuncts) to be analyzed? Section 5 extends the analysis in section 4 to a variety of other cases including noun-complement constructions and constructions in which object control is possible. Section 6 considers yet another problem for the analysis and proposes a constraint on derivations to accommodate these. Section 7 outlines extensions of the analysis to other 0-operator constructions such as relative clauses, 'tough'-constructions and purpose clauses.

1   A Review of Adjunct Control

Let's quickly review the analysis of adjunct control structures in the context of the derivation of (1). The relevant array includes the items in (2) plus assorted functional elements (not listed).

(2)   {John, saw, Mary, before, leaving, the, party}

The "adjunct" is constructed first.[1] 'The' merges with 'party' forming a DP, then 'the party' merges with 'leaving' which thereby checks its internal θ-role and transfers it to 'the party'. Next 'John' merges with this VP thereby checking the external θ-role. 'John' then raises to Spec IP and then the IP merges with 'before' to form the adjunct. The relevant structure is provided in (3). The notation below indicates that 'John' bears an (as yet) unchecked nominative case (+Nom) and bears a θ-role (+θ).

(3)   after [$_{IP}$ John [I [$_{vP}$ John v [$_{VP}$ leaving the party]]]]
            +θ/+Nom +θ/+Nom

   The matrix is constructed next. 'Saw' merges with 'Mary' to produce the VP 'saw Mary'. Next, 'John' moves sideways (or "inter-arboreally") out of the "adjunct" to Spec vP and gets its second θ-role. The "adjunct" then merges with 'vP' to form an adjunct structure. 'John' then moves to Spec IP and the derivation converges. The structure prior to Spell Out is shown in (4). Observe that the matrix copies of 'John' are each marked with two θ-roles. In addition, the copy in matrix Spec IP is marked '–Nom' meaning that its nominative case feature has been checked.

(4)   [$_{IP}$ John [I [$_{vP/vP}$[$_{vP}$ John [$_{VP}$ saw Mary]] [after [$_{IP}$ John [I [$_{vP}$ John v
         +θ/+θ/–Nom +θ/+θ/+Nom   +θ/+Nom +θ/+Nom
      [$_{VP}$ leaving the party]]]]]]]]]

   There are several details of this derivation worth highlighting. First, we account for the fact that ACs like those in (1) are subject control structures in terms of local economy. Economy requires 'Mary' to merge with the matrix 'saw' before 'John' moves to Spec vP. That 'John' must move is required by convergence as it needs to check its case features. However, that it move after 'Mary' merges follows from considerations of derivational economy. It follows because MERGE is cheaper than MOVE since MOVE, being a complex of two operations COPY and MERGE, contains MERGE as a subpart. Hence simply merging an element from the array is cheaper than first copying an element and then merging this copy (i.e. MOVE) as it involves fewer operations at the relevant point in the derivation. Economy, therefore, prohibits first moving 'John' to the embedded VP position and then merging 'Mary' to Spec vP (see Chomsky 1995, 1998). Were this latter derivation licit, object control into ACs like (1) would be acceptable.[2]

   Second, movement out of an adjunct is permitted. In fact, 'John' in the derivation above *must* move out of the "adjunct" if it is to check its case features given that there is no relevant case checking configuration within the "adjunct." This reverses the GB assumption embodied in the CED that prohibits all movement out of adjuncts. This in turn places a demand on the current analyses; to explain why movements like those displayed in (5) are illicit. In other words, an explanation is required that specifies when the CED is violable. We return to this below.

(5)   *Which book did you read Moby Dick before reviewing

Third, applications of MOVE in the derivation illustrated in (3)–(4) all strictly adhere to the principle of GREED understood as "enlightened self interest." Every application of MOVE yields a structure in which a feature is checked; either a feature of the moved expression or a feature of the target. For example, moving 'John' to Spec vP allows the external theta-role of the matrix 'v' to get checked. Further movement to the matrix Spec IP results in the checking of the case and agreement features of 'I' as well as the case features of 'John'. To strictly adhere to this version of GREED requires treating θ-roles as features that enter into calculations of GREED on all fours with morphological features like case. Without it, movement to θ-positions would necessarily be illicit given the minimalist assumption that MOVE must be greedy to be an instance of MOVE at all (see Chomsky (1995: 269, (32))).

Fourth, every operation in the derivation, including adjunction, obeys the Extension Condition, i.e. every operation, including adjunction, that affects a subtree does so by having the input structure properly contained as a constituent within the output structure. This is contrary to Chomsky (1993) in which adjunction is specifically excluded from the purview of Extension. However, as Nunes (1995) and Uriagereka (1998) note, one of the principal virtues of allowing sidewards movement is that adjunction need no longer be viewed as an exception to the Extension Condition.

This is well illustrated by overt V-raising, an instance of head movement. Consider V^0-to-T^0 raising for illustration. It occurs in a structure like (6a) and yields (6b).

(6)   a. $[_{TP} T^0 [_{VP} \ldots V \ldots]]$
    b. $[_{TP} T^0+V_i [_{VP} \ldots t_i \ldots]]$

As Chomsky (1995) observes, this adjunction operation violates extension and it is (largely) to accommodate head movement that adjunction operations are removed from the purview of the Extension Condition. However, once sidewards movement is permitted, it is possible to derive (6b) as follows: Form the VP. Then take 'T⁰′' from the array. Move 'V' sidewards and adjoin to 'T⁰′'. Then Merge 'T⁰+V' with VP. This derivation is displayed in (7).[3]

(7)   a. $[_{VP} \ldots V \ldots]$
    b. $T^0, [_{VP} \ldots V \ldots]$
    c. $T^0+V_i, [_{VP} \ldots t_i \ldots]$
    d. $[_{TP} T^0+V_i [_{VP} \ldots t_i \ldots]]$

The most interesting feature of the derivation in (7) is that it allows head movement to conform to Extension. The crucial step is (7c) where sidewards movement obtains. By allowing sidewards movement of V to 'T⁰′', MOVE can apply in accord with Extension. In other words, by generalizing MOVE so that it is not restricted to single rooted subtrees, Extension can govern all cases of MERGE including adjunction (of the head movement variety).

Generalizing MOVE to allow sidewards movement also makes conceptual sense given the internal logic of the minimalist program. MOVE is basically a sub-case of MERGE. The main difference between the two operations being what gets merged; copies in the former case and "originals" from the array in the latter. If MERGE is to obey extension then it must be allowed to apply in non-single rooted subtrees. The derivation of (8) illustrates this point.

(8)   The man saw Mary

(8) is derived via the merger of two subtrees constructed in parallel. First, 'saw' merges with 'Mary'. Then 'man' and 'the' merge. The next step merges the two subtrees to form 'the man saw Mary'. Observe two things. First, a trivial point. Extension holds for MERGE only if we interpret it as saying that the *affected* subtree is extended (as in (7) above). That the other phrases remain unchanged is irrelevant for the purposes of Extension. Second, note that one cannot first merge 'man' with 'saw Mary' only then merging 'the' with 'man' as this *would* violate Extension. MERGE must be able to operate on phrase markers constructed in parallel that share no root. In other words, if Extension is to govern the applications of MERGE then it must be interpreted as meaning that subtrees can be constructed in parallel and that the condition regulates how these subtrees "grow."

Now for the punchline: if MOVE is really just COPY plus MERGE then it is hard to see why it should be confined to operating exclusively in single rooted structures though MERGE is not. In fact, it is not even clear how one would state the restriction against interarboreal movement once the copy theory of movement is adopted. The restriction cannot be placed on the MERGE operation for, as noted above, MERGE can take place when there are multiple subtrees. Nor is it obvious how to restrict COPY so as to prevent it from applying when there are multiple subtrees. Put more baldly, there is no apparent conceptual reason why COPY should be confined to apply only within single rooted structures. But if neither MERGE nor COPY are naturally restricted to single rooted structures then it is unclear why MOVE, the composite of the two, should be so restricted. The simplest assumption is that it isn't and this suffices theoretically to permit sidewards movement.[4]

If this is correct, then whether sidewards movement exists is an empirical question. There are no natural conceptual grounds for excluding it as a viable possibility.

2   The Properties of Parasitic Gaps[5]

Now consider PGs. They similarly involve relating a theta marked expression to an empty category inside an adjunct. This suggests that PGs too are formed by sidewards movement in overt syntax as argued for persuasively in Nunes (1995). With one important difference that we highlight below, the same assumptions deployed in section 1 suffice to derive all the salient properties of PGs. Before demonstrating this, consider a sample derivation of a PG construction.

(9)   Which book$_i$ did you read t$_i$ before Fred reviewed t$_i$

(9) has the array in (10), functional categories excluded for convenience.

(10)   {which, book, you, read, before, Fred, reviewed}

Begin the derivation with the adjunct. 'Which' merges with 'book'. Then 'which book' merges with 'reviewed', the latter thereby checking its internal θ-role. 'Fred' then merges with this constituent checking the external θ-role of 'v'. 'Fred' then raises to Spec IP to check the features of 'I^{0}' (viz. case, agreement and (possibly) D features). Assume, that 'which book' then moves to some outer spec of IP or CP via WH movement.[6] The structure of the adjunct looks something like (11).

(11)   before [which book [Fred I [Fred [reviewed which book]]]]

Next 'read' is taken from the array. We then sidewards move 'which book' and combine it with 'read'. Observe that this violates economy (viz. the preference for MERGE over MOVE) as we have merged 'read' with a copy of 'which book' rather than merge it with 'you' from the array. As merging 'you' is locally more economical than moving 'which book' it should block the indicated derivation. We return below to why this apparent violation of Economy is permitted.

The next step is to merge 'you' into the Spec vP position of 'read which book'. Then the adjunct merges with vP. After this 'you' raises to Spec IP and 'which book' moves to Spec CP of the matrix to complete the derivation.

Several points of this derivation are worth noting.

First, every step obeys Extension. Even merging the adjunct to vP meets the condition.

Second, every application of MOVE satisfies GREED (but see note 6).

Third, this analysis allows an expression that bears a θ-role to move into a θ-position. 'Which book' merges into a θ-position in the adjunct and moves to the internal θ-position of 'read' in the matrix.

Fourth, movement is permitted from an A' to an A position. Note that 'which book' moves from an A'-position in the adjunct to an A-position in the matrix. This kind of movement is generally considered illicit.

Nunes (1995) does not derive PG structures in this fashion. However, there are some benefits to doing things in the way indicated here which I return to. However, if the execution in Nunes (1995) is correct then perhaps it might be possible to retain the prohibition against A' to A movement. The real question is whether retaining this stricture is worthwhile within MP. Why should A' to A movement be generally prohibited? After all, we have cases of A to A' movement, A to A movement and A' to A' movement. Why should A' to A movement be the sole case of "improper movement"? In GB, this improper movement reduces to some version of Principle C (see May 1983). We return to whether or not Principle C is relevant in all instances of A′ to A movement.

Fifth, the derivation crucially relies on a violation of Economy. Why is Economy bypassed in this instance? To fix the problem more clearly, observe that the derivation of AC structures in section 1 crucially assumes that Economy regulates movement out of adjuncts. This is what explains the fact that ACs only permit subject control. The relevant question is what distinguishes PGs from ACs with respect to Economy? We return to this question presently.

Assume for the time being that the steps of this derivation can all be justified. It permits a derivation of the salient properties of PGs. Consider some of these.

Chomsky (1986a) observes that PGs cannot be generated within islands within the adjunct.

(12)　a.　*Which book did you read t before Fred met someone who reviewed pg
　　　b.　*Which book did you read t before Fred asked Bill whether you reviewed pg
　　　c.　*Which book did you read t before Fred denied the claim that you reviewed pg
　　　d.　Which book did you read t before Fred said that you reviewed pg

(12a) locates the parasitic gap (pg) within a relative clause, (12b) within a WH island and (12c) within a noun-complement clause. These examples are less acceptable than (12d) which shows that a pg can be embedded arbitrarily deep inside a non-island. The degree of unacceptability induced by the various examples tracks that exemplified in standard island violations. Chomsky (1986a) reasonably concludes from this that parasitic gaps are the residues of movement.

The derivation of PGs in (9)–(11) above explains the paradigm in (12) by moving 'which book' to the head of the adjunct. This movement is subject to the standard locality conditions on A′-movement and accounts for why pgs cannot appear within islands inside the adjunct.

Why is the movement to the head of the adjunct required? Note that elements that move here then move out of the adjunct. One possible reason for the movement is that the shortest move condition (SMC) would prevent 'which book' from leaving the adjunct unless it raised there. The subject 'Fred' would be closer to any position that 'which book' could reach if we measure proximity in terms of c-command. 'Fred' c-commands 'which book' unless the latter raises. So 'which book' cannot move out of the adjunct unless it first moves to the top of the adjunct. In short, there is a plausible minimalist reason driving the movement of 'which book' to adjunct initial position that accounts for the subjacency data noted by Chomsky (1986a).[7,8]

This sort of sidewards derivation has a further additional benefit: It accounts for why it is that 0-operators are phonetically null. Note that the derivation involves movement out of a CP-like position inside the adjunct. All traces within "intermediate" CPs must delete. Thus, if PGs are formed via sidewards movement through an embedded CP we expect the copy therein to similarly delete. This suffices to account for its null phonetic quality. We discuss below some mechanics for deletion.

A second salient property of PGs is that they cannot involve adjunct WHs.

(13)   a.   *Why did you read Moby Dick t [after Bill reviewed it pg]
      b.   *How did you word the letter t [after Bill phrased the note pg]

(13) cannot be paraphrased as "For what reason did you read Moby Dick after Bill reviewed it for that reason" nor can (13b) be understood as "In what manner did you word the letter after Bill phrased the note in that way".

GB accounts for this difference between adjuncts and arguments in terms of what can license the 0-operator that moves to adjunct initial position. It is assumed that adjuncts cannot "identify" this 0-operator and so the movements are illicit.

It is actually quite unclear why adjuncts are so impotent. One proposal is that 0-operators are actually PRO or 'pro' so that adjuncts, which are not nominals but PPs, cannot bind them.[9] However, it is not clear that this is empirically correct. For example, though PP subjects are not very common in English, when they occur, they seem able to control into adjuncts.

(14)   In the bathroom is a great place to hide without PRO really being a good place to live

Furthermore, it is unclear that 0-operators are congenial objects in the kind of minimalist theory adopted here. Chapter 2 argued that PRO does not exist as a primitive formative of UG. The properties of obligatory control PRO are equivalent to those of an intermediate NP-t with the latter just being a copy with certain unchecked features.

Nor are 0-operators small-'pro's. Non-obligatory control occurs when small 'pro' occurs. Small-'pro' is an elsewhere expression; something that is inserted into a position when movement from that position is impossible. If 0-operators were 'pro's then we would find them just in case movement from the indicated position was impossible. However, given that the present theory countenances movement from adjuncts in the analysis of ACs, it is unclear why movement should not be permitted in this case as well. If so, a 0-operator could not be a small-'pro' either.

Even with these considerations to one side, it remains unclear whether 'pro' could accomplish what we want it to. Recall that PGs are licensed at SS in GB. In MP terms, they are licensed prior to Spell Out. GB gets this result by stipulating that the 0-operator, i.e. 'pro', must be licensed at SS. Stipulations are always suspect, even more so given minimalist mores. Moreover, this stipulation does not travel well. It finds no home in minimalist accounts as SS does not exist as a grammatical level in MP. As such, it is unclear how this fact about PGs can be integrated in MP without deforming its basic architecture, i.e. without adverting to a level akin to SS and without adding a novel kind of process like predication.

Nunes (1995) notes that the overt licensing of PGs follows if they are formed by sidewards movement. However, this conclusion only holds if there are no 'pro's or 0-operators that could move within the adjunct and get bound at some later point in the derivation, e.g. LF, the primary grammatical level in MP. In effect, what Nunes (1995) tells us is that the simplest theory, the one with the fewest unmotivated empty categories, the sparsest kinds of rules and the most general view of movement provides a principled account for why PGs are licensed "at SS."

Interestingly, if this is correct then the fact that adjuncts cannot license PGs also follows.[10] We have assumed that movement is greedy. In other words, every application of MOVE must result in some feature of the copy or the target getting checked. We have also assumed that θ-roles count for GREED. Sidewards movement of arguments is greedy as the movement is to a θ-position. In (9), movement out of the adjunct is licensed by checking the internal θ-role of 'read'. Adjuncts differ from arguments in not bearing θ-roles. Thus, one cannot move an adjunct out of an adjunct as this movement must violate greed because adjunct positions are not feature checking positions, i.e. neither case nor θ-roles are checked in adjunct positions.[11] Indeed minimalist analyses generally prohibit all forms of adjunct movement precisely because such movement violates greed (see Chomsky 1995 ch. 4). The upshot is that we can directly explain why adjuncts cannot license PGs if PGs are formed by sidewards movement.[12]

This account can be extended to explain why PPs fail to license PGs.

(15)   *About which book did you talk before Frank read

The unacceptability of (15) follows if we assume that PPs are not θ-role bearers. Prepositions can still be thought of as thematically linked to verbs in that they combine with verbs to assign θ-roles to their objects. However, PPs don't themselves bear θ-roles or case so PPs cannot move greedily and hence cannot move sidewards to form PG constructions.[13]

There are two other properties of PGs that Nunes accounts for and are adopted here (though in somewhat revised form). PGs are only acceptable where overt movement to an A'-position obtains.

(16)   a.   *you read every book$_i$ before Fred reviewed pg$_i$
       b.   Which book did you read t$_i$ before Fred reviewed pg$_i$

The contrast in (16) indicates that 'every book' cannot move from the adjunct the way 'which book' does.

Nunes (1995) traces this ultimately to the workings of the Linear Correspondence Axiom (LCA). The way he puts it is that a chain cannot be linearized unless all but one copy is deleted. Without deletion of all but a single copy, a chain cannot be coherently assigned a linear order. For example, if two members of a chain bracket a third expression, then the LCA will require that the chain both precede and follow that expression, which is incoherent. Nunes' conclusion is that if linearization is necessary for convergence, deletion of copies must apply.

I adopt the main features of this account but with a twist. I assume that it is not chains that are linearized but expressions in the array. In other words, in order for a derivation to converge the ARRAY of items selected from the lexicon must be interpretable at both interfaces. Linearization of items in the array is a precondition for interpretation at the AP interface. Thus, for a derivation to converge, every item in the array must be assigned a unique linear position in the phrase marker. This forces all copies but one to delete for unless all but one does so, the array cannot be consistently linearized for the reasons that Nunes identifies. On the assumption that successful linearization is required for Full Interpretation, the deletion requirement amounts to saying that derivations must result in fully interpretable structures to be convergent. Or put another way, linearization is a bare output condition. Consider the derivation of (16b) in this light.

Prior to deletion it has the structure in (17).

(17)   Which book [you Tns [[you [read which book]] [before [which book [Fred Tns [Fred reviewed which book]]]]]]

The copies are the residues of movement in overt syntax. For example, there are two copies of 'you' as it has moved from Spec vP, its θ-position, to the Spec IP in overt syntax. 'Which book' has moved several times; from the complement of 'reviewed' to an A'-position in the adjunct, to the complement of 'read' to the Spec CP of the matrix. The copies track this "movement." Note that 'which' and 'book' are both elements in the array so they must be linearized. However, if we retain all the copies then these have no determinate linear position. The LCA would place them before all other elements if the copy in Spec CP is considered, to the right of 'read' if the copy in the complement of 'read' is considered, etc. Moreover, unless all copies but one are deleted the LCA appears to impose the absurd requirement that 'which book' must both precede and follow itself! In short, if the LCA is a convergence condition that requires that elements of the array be linearized then deletion of copies is required.[14]

How does the deletion rule operate? Nunes (1995) assumes that it can only take place within chains.[15] This has the effect of requiring copies to be in c-command relations if deletion is to be operative. Observe that if this is correct, then the reason that (16a) is ill formed can be traced to the fact that the two copies of 'every book', the one that is complement of 'read' and the one which is complement of 'reviewed', are not in a c-command relation and so neither can delete. But if so, the array cannot be linearized as the two lexical items 'every' and 'book' cannot be assigned unique linear positions by the LCA.

A similar problem does not beset (16b). Here the 'which book' in Spec CP commands both other copies though the two copies in VP complement position do not c-command one another. This allows deletion to operate to reduce the number of copies to one. There is still the question, however, of which copy survives. Why is the copy in Spec CP pronounced rather than a copy in one of the complement positions? The answer relates to movement and greed. Generally, when an expression moves its feature composition changes. For example, when 'which book' moves from the adjunct to the matrix, it adds a θ-role that it didn't have before by checking the θ-features of 'read'. Similarly, when 'you' moves to Spec IP in (17) it checks its case feature and the one on 'T⁰'. In effect, movement quite generally changes the feature composition of a moved expression.[16] If we assume that 'which book' in the matrix Spec CP has a different feature composition from the other copies, and if at least one of the features by which it differs and which is checked in the +WH Spec CP is uninterpretable at PF, then the only copy that can survive is the one in Spec CP as the others bear at least one feature (the one the +WH 'C⁰' checks) that would cause the derivation to crash.

This is conceptually congenial. Hornstein (1995) argues that covert A′-movement fits poorly with minimalist assumptions. In other words, MP should prohibit covert A′-movement operations and restrict A′-movement to overt syntax. Assume that this is correct. One way of enforcing this requirement is to assign expressions that move to A′-positions features that are uninterpretable at PF. In other words, any expression in an A′-position must have checked a PF uninterpretable feature in moving to that A′-position.

Observe that if this is correct it allows deletion (of copies in overt syntax) to apply deterministically. There is no "choice" as to which expression survives as all copies but one will generally derail the derivation. If this is correct then it is unnecessary to make deletion sensitive to c-command relations, at least in these cases. Recall that c-command is exploited in differentiating between the acceptable (16b) and the unacceptable (16a). The latter derivation fails if deletion requires a c-command relation between the copies. The problem with (16a) is that the copy of 'every book' in the matrix fails to c-command the copies in the adjunct. However, if deletion must be deterministic, i.e. expressions delete only if retaining them would crash the derivation, then there is another reason why (16a) fails. The copies are essentially equivalent with respect to PF restrictions and so there is no reason for deleting one rather than another. In short, there is no *forced* choice in these cases. If deletion must be deterministic, then deletion cannot apply in this case and the derivation crashes as it violates the LCA.

Let me be a bit more specific. The derivation of (16a) has the structure in (18).

(18) [you Tns [[you [read every book]] [before [every book [Fred Tns [Fred reviewed every book]]]]]]

(18) parallels (17) in moving 'every book' via an embedded A′-position in the adjunct.[17] There are three copies.

Consider two scenarios. First, assume that movement via the A′-position in the adjunct results in some kind of feature checking. If so, then the copy in the A′-position in the adjunct and the one in the matrix have the same feature composition with the exception that the matrix has a θ-role that the other two copies lack. If θ-features are not PF active, as seems reasonable, then there is no reason for choosing the copy in the matrix over the one in the Spec CP to survive deletion and get pronounced.

Consider a second option. Movement to the adjunct A′-position checks no feature at all. If so, the three copies have all the same checked PF features. Consequently, there is no reason to delete any of the copies. Once again the derivation crashes due to an inability to linearize.

In sum, if we are sufficiently careful in specifying how GREED works in these cases and if we treat deletion as restricted to expressions that bear features that crash a derivation, then it is unnecessary to restrict deletion to c-command configurations.[18]

To this point, the analysis has accounted for most of the salient properties of PGs: (i) they are licensed in overt syntax by an expression in an A′-position, (ii) the pg cannot be inside an island inside the adjunct and (iii) the pg cannot be an adjunct trace or a PP-t. Two final properties remain: (iv) the real gap cannot c-command the parasitic gap – (19a) and (v) PGs are not licensed under A-movement – (19b).[19]

(19)   a.   *Which book t was read t by Bill before Frank reviewed pg
       b.   *Moby Dick was read t by Bill before Frank reviewed pg

Chomsky 1982 accounted for these cases of ill formed PGs by tracing them to Principle C violations. In (19a), the matrix variable (the trace in Spec IP), c-commands the variable in the adjunct (i.e. the pg). This is plausibly a Principle C violation. Similarly for (19b). Here the matrix r-expression "Moby Dick" c-commands the pg it is coindexed with. This too is plausibly a Principle C violation.[20] However, how Principle C should be stated and how it operates in cases like (19) needs careful consideration.

3   Principle C

This section has several ambitions. First, it aims to clarify the status of Principle C. Principle C is odd in that it holds over an unbounded domain, in contrast to principles A and B. Its status calls for yet more clarification in the present context given the aim of eliminating both principles A and B from UG.[21] If there are no binding principles governing the distribution of anaphors and pronouns why should R-expressions be the object of special grammatical concern? Consequently, one aim of the following is to rethink Principle C from a minimalist point of view.[22]

Two empirical considerations will help drive the exercise. First, we want a reason for why the sentences in (19) are not equally unacceptable. (19a) seems rather more acceptable than (19b). Second, we still need an account for why it is that only subjects can "control PROs" in adjuncts while they are prohibited from licensing PGs. The technical issue concerns how to understand the role of economy in the derivation of PGs. The derivation of PGs by sidewards movement requires a violation of economy, in contrast to ACs where it is (crucially) respected. What licenses this violation of economy in PGs? The proposal is that principle C is what permits MOVE to supersede MERGE in the derivation of PGs.

Let's start with the second concern first. To refresh memories, recall that in the derivation of (9), repeated here, we copy 'which book' from the adjunct and merge it with 'read' rather than simply merge 'you' in this position from the array. This violates economy.

(9)   Which book [you Tns [[you read which book] [before [which book [Fred Tns [Fred reviewed which book]]]]]]

(9) contrasts with the derivation of an AC in (4) in which 'Mary' is merged with 'saw' before 'John' moves to the matrix Spec vP. The steps in (4) respect economy and this explains why ACs only allow subject control. The relevant structure is repeated here.

(4)   [$_{IP}$ John [I [$_{vP/vP}$ [$_{vP}$ John [$_{vP}$ saw Mary]] [after [$_{IP}$ John [I [$_{vP}$ John v
      +θ/+θ/−Nom +θ/+θ/+Nom   +θ/+Nom +θ/+Nom
      [$_{vP}$ leaving the party]]]]]]]]

Why the difference? Note, first, that within MP, the derivation in (4) re-quires no further justification. The derivation converges and is economically optimal. The real question is why (9) allows a violation of economy. We have an answer if we assume that violating Principle C crashes a derivation. Were this so, then MOVE could licitly apply in place of MERGE as violating economy would permit compliance with a convergence condition, viz. Principle C, which would otherwise be flaunted. This line of reasoning is well illustrated by con-sidering the derivations of (19a) and (9). Consider first the structure of (19a).

(19)   a.   *Which book *t* was read t by Bill before Frank reviewed pg

The 'pg' and the 't' in Spec IP of the matrix are case marked A'-bound expres-sions, i.e. variables. As such, they are subject to Principle C.[23] Observe that 't' c-commands 'pg', violating Principle C.[24]

Now turn to (9). (20) is its LF structure with copies that are interpreted as variables indicated.[25]

(20)   Which book [you Tns [[*which book* [you read which book]] [before [which book [Fred Tns [Fred [*which book* reviewed which book]]]]]]]

(20) conforms to Principle C as the variables are not in a c-command con-figuration. Note, however, that if the derivation had adhered to economy then 'you' and 'which book' in the matrix would exchange places. The resulting configuration would violate Principle C in just the way that (19a) does. In sum, *if* Principle C is a convergence requirement then MOVE can apply in place of MERGE because thus violating economy would prevent a derivation from crashing. This would license the derivation of (9) and explain the deviance of (19a) where the "real" gap is in subject position.[26]

Contrast the derivation in (4). It obeys economy. This is expected if Principle C does not apply to NP-traces, as standardly assumed. The analysis here takes "PROs" in ACs to be equivalent to "NP-ts". The Spec IP position is *not* a case position.[27] As such, traces in such positions are not variables in the sense relevant to Principle C. Consequently, moving to Spec vP of the matrix and then to Spec IP will not lead to a Principle C violation as the copy in Spec IP of the adjunct is not a variable. As convergence is possible without violating economy, economy considerations forbid its violation. This suffices to derive the fact that only subject control is permitted in these ACs.

The above, if correct, makes two important points. First, it indicates that the present account requires a distinction between different kinds of residues of movement. We must distinguish "traces" that get interpreted as variables, i.e copies in case marked positions that are A'-bound, from NP-traces that are not so interpreted. Second, it argues that Principle C is required and that it has the status of a convergence condition. If it were not a convergence requirement that phrase markers conform to Principle C, economy could not be finessed in PGs. This second point sharpens the question of just what Principle C is and how it fits into minimalism. We turn to this now.

Consider once again the examples in (19) repeated here.

(19)   a.   *Which book t was read t by Bill before Frank reviewed pg
       b.   *Moby Dick was read t by Bill before Frank reviewed pg

(19a) has been accounted for in terms of Principle C. What of (19b)? Principle C can be used here as well if 'Moby Dick' and 'pg' fall under Principle C. There is no problem categorizing 'Moby Dick' as an r-expression. What of 'pg'? It falls under Principle C if it is a variable. What's a variable? Case marked traces that are operator bound, i.e. bound by contentful A'-expressions, are clearly variables.[28] Using this definition, 'pg' is not a variable as it is not A'-bound by an operator. However, it is case marked. So one option is to assume, as Chomsky (1982) does, that variables are case-marked traces and that operator binding is not relevant to identifying them. If this is assumed, then (19b) violates Principle C. (21) is the relevant LF structure. The case checked copies are indicated.

(21)   *Moby Dick* was [[read Moby Dick by Bill] [before [Moby Dick [Frank Tns [*Moby Dick* [Frank reviewed Moby Dick]]]]]]

If we assume these copies are r-expressions, then Principle C suffices to rule out (19b).

There is an objection to treating both the examples in (19) in the same way that may also shed light on Principle C. The sentences are not equally un-acceptable. This suggests that they should answer to different conditions. Put another way, if both are just Principle C violations, then why is (19a) better than (19b)? We can make room for the differences in unacceptability if the two derivations derail in different ways. With this in mind let's return to asking how to think about Principle C.

Here's the proposal.[29] Assume there exists an algorithm for assigning expressions in an LF phrase marker a "scope order". This is an LF analogue of what occurs at PF with the LCA. Essentially, this "Scope Correspondence Axiom" (SCA) functions like the LCA in saying that if α c-commands β then α scopes over β. Moreover, just as the LCA can be thought of as preparatory for phonological interpretation, i.e. AP processes are order sensitive, one can think of the SCA as readying expressions for the operations of the CI systems. Furthermore, just as the LCA forces the deletion of copies to allow linearization of the array so too the SCA will force at most one copy of an expression to survive at the CI interface to allow expressions to have fixed and coherent scopes.[30]

To help fix ideas, consider how this operates. It seems reasonable to think of scope as being irreflexive and transitive; viz. an expression E cannot scope over itself and if α scopes over β and β scopes over γ then α scopes over γ. If we assume that the SCA must "scopify" the array, i.e. assign all elements of the array (and, derivatively, the expressions they combine to form) a scope, much as the LCA must assign all expressions in the array a linear position, then consider what happens if more than one copy survives to the CI interface.

One possibility is that the expressions are in a c-command configuration, as in (21) above. In this case, 'Moby Dick' cannot be assigned a coherent scope as the two copies that survive are in a c-command configuration. The SCA then asserts that 'Moby Dick' scopes over itself, an impossibility. If the SCA, like the LCA, is a convergence requirement, this suffices to crash the derivation in (21).

Another possibility is provided by (22).

(22) a. *You read every book before Frank reviewed pg
      b. [you Tns [[*every book* [you [read every book]]] [before [every book
          [Fred Tns [*every book* [Fred reviewed every book]]]]]]]

(22b) is the relevant LF structure. It assumes that 'every book' moves from the adjunct via an A'-position to the object position of the matrix clause. Following Nunes (1995) I propose that this sentence violates the LCA. It also violates the SCA. The two underscored copies are the ones that have checked case at LF by movement to either Spec AgrO or an outer Spec of v. Assume that after deletion of copies (indicated by bracketing) the structure fed to CI is (23).[31]

(23) [you Tns [[*every book* [(you) [read (every book)]]]] [before [(every book)
      [Fred Tns [*every book* [(Fred) reviewed (every book)]]]]]]]]

The scope assigned to 'every book' by the SCA violates transitivity. Thus, 'Fred' c-commands 'every book' and 'every book' c-commands 'read'. This means that 'Fred' should scope over 'read'. If we assume, as we do for the LCA, that if α scopes over β then α c-commands β, then this structure violates the SCA. In short, copies cause problems at LF analogous to the ones they induce at PF once we assume a (more or less) linear mapping between (asymmetric) c-command and some property like linear order or scope.

The violation of the SCA discussed in (23) can be used to account for an interesting restriction that PGs impose on the functional interpretation of WHs. Hornstein (1995, ch. 8, section 5) observes notes that PGs prevent the functional interpretation of WHs. Consider the contrast in (24).

(24)   a.   What did everyone review
        b.   What did everyone review before I read

(24a) is ambiguous. It can have a pair-list reading (i.e. different reviewer per item) or an individual reading (i.e. same book for all reviewers). (24b) only has an individual reading. It fails to have a pair-list reading. Hornstein (1995, ch. 7) argues that pair-list readings rely on reconstructing the WH in Spec CP back to its base position. In short, at LF, the pair-list reading relies on (24b) having the structure in (25) after deletion.

(25)   [(what) [everyone [[*what* [(everyone) review (what)]] [before [(what) I [*what* [(I) read (what)]]]]]]]

In short, we have retained the lower WH copies so that they can be interpreted functionally.[32] However, this is an illicit LF structure given the SCA. Observe, (25) has the same structure as the ungrammatical (23). In short, we account for why the pair-list reading disappears with PGs.

It is interesting to note that the individual reading is *not* prohibited in (24b). This indicates that we can have two variables in this construction, one in the matrix and one in the adjunct and that this does not violate the SCA. Why not?

MP assumes that variables are essentially case checked copies that are operator bound. This simply translates the GB account using MP technology. The relevant LF structure of (24b) with this reading is (26).

(26)   [what [everyone [[*what* [(everyone) review (what)]] [before [(what) I [*what* [(I) read (what)]]]]]]]

Why doesn't (26) run afoul of the SCA? The reason is that variables are scopeless expressions. Unlike contentful lexical items, variables have their scope determined by the operators that bind them. For example, in (26), the 'what' in Spec CP is the scope bearer. The copies that it binds are variables with no scope of their own. In effect, variables at LF act with respect to the SCA the way that traces at PF act with respect to the LCA. Chomsky (1995) proposes that traces are invisible for purposes of the LCA. They have no phonetic content and hence need not be prepped for AP operations by being linearized. Similarly, variables are not assigned a scope as they are scopeless expressions whose scopal powers reside in the operator that binds them. This licenses the individual level reading for (26) by rendering the copies of 'what' in case positions that are bound by the copy in Spec CP invisible to the SCA. In sum, variables are to the SCA what traces are for the LCA. Their inherent interpretive properties allow them to fall outside the purview of the respective "linearization" conditions.

With this in mind, consider again the structure of (19a), repeated here.

(19) a. *Which book was read by you before Fred reviewed pg

It has the LF structure (27).

(27) Which book [*which book* Tns [[read (which book) by you] [before [(which book) [Fred Tns [Fred [*which book* reviewed (which book)]]]]]]]

Earlier, we suggested that this structure was unacceptable because of Principle C. However, if Principle C reduces to the SCA and variables are not subject to the SCA, then why is (27) ungrammatical? I would like to propose that the problem is that the case checked copy inside the adjunct is not immediately operator bound. Recall that variables are case checked copies that are operator bound. If we require that they be *immediately* operator bound then '*which book*' inside the adjunct is not interpretable as a variable.[33] However, if it cannot be interpreted as a variable, the SCA rules the structure out. Furthermore, if we assume that SCA violations result in stronger unacceptability than does this condition on variables, then we can account for the difference between (19a,b). In effect, the relative acceptability of (19a) resides in the fact that we can "compensate" for the violation of the condition on variables in (19a) and interpret the copy inside the adjunct as a variable despite this being a grammatical violation in this structure. Because this is not strictly kosher, the sentence is unacceptable. However, interpreting a case checked copy as a variable in such structures is less unacceptable than subjecting the structure to the SCA, with which it necessarily fails to comply if the relevant copy is not interpreted as a variable. (19b) cannot similarly finesse the strong effects of the SCA as it contains no copies interpretable as variables as there is no A'-operator present. This possibly accounts for the difference in acceptability between the examples in (19).

This account, if correct, has an interesting consequence. It relies on (19b) not having an operator-variable structure at LF. This is turn relies on quantified NPs not being subject to QR at LF. To see this contrast (28) and (19b).

(19) b. *Moby Dick was read by Bill before Frank reviewed

(28) *Every book was read by Bill before Frank reviewed

There is no appreciable difference in acceptability between these two examples. However, if QR applied at LF to quantified expressions, then the structure of (28) would be virtually identical to that of (19a). QR would raise 'every book' adjoining it to IP (or move it into some Spec position) leaving a copy in Spec IP which would be interpreted as the variable bound by the A'-operator. The LF structure would look like (29), with variables indicated.

(29)   [every book [*every book* was [[read (every book) by Bill] [before [(every book) [Frank Tns [*every book* [Frank reviewed (every book)]]]]]]]]]

The problem that arises is why (28) is not on a par with (19a) given their structural similarity at LF. Observe, if QR does not exist, then there is nothing more to explain and we expect (29) to pattern with (19b), as seems to be the case. This lends support to the view that minimalism fits poorly with QR and no rule like it operates in UG to modify the c-command positions of quantified expressions at LF.[34]

This section has proposed ways of accounting for the fact that PGs can only be licensed by "real gaps" in non-subject positions. If correct, the main difference between ACs and PGs is due to the different grammatical requirements placed on variables and NP-traces. The former are subject to Principle C while the latter are not. We have considered how this difference suffices to distinguish the licensers if controlled "PROs" inside adjuncts are actually "NP-ts" (i.e. copies in non-case positions) while pgs are variables (i.e. copies in case positions). This supports the view that "PRO" does not check case, not even null case (pace Chomsky and Lasnik 1993 and Martin 1996).

In addition, this section reconsidered just how to interpret Principle C. We have resolved the data involving variables into a condition analogous to the LCA that assigns scope to expressions in the array and to a definition of variable as a case checked immediately A'-bound operator.[35] Both conditions essentially elaborate the mapping between LF and CI in ways quite analogous to what has been proposed for the PF to AP mapping.

A virtue of this approach to Principle C is that it explains why Principle C has no domain limitations, in contrast to principles A and B. The SCA (like linearization at PF) applies to *all* items in the array and assigns each a unique scope (or position). Scope and linear order are thus defined over the whole constructed expression in virtue of applying to each member of the array. If Principle C effects are simply the reflex of a process like the SCA then it accounts for the global character of its effects.

There remains one last property of PGs to discuss. We turn to this now.

4   Adjunct Islands

To this point, the analysis has not addressed perhaps the most salient feature of PG constructions; parasitic gaps must be licensed by real gaps. Sentences like (30) are strongly unacceptable.[36]

(30)   *Which book did you read Moby Dick before Frank reviewed t

In GB, real gaps license pgs by "identifying" the 0-operators that form them. The present account dispenses with 0-operators and the SS licensing conditions characteristic of GB analyses of PGs so the question arises what it means to say that real gaps are needed to have acceptable PG constructions. It means the following: *expressions can move out of adjuncts only by sidewards movement*. In other words, only sidewards movement can evade the strictures of the CED. Why so? To put this question another way: what prevents the derivation of (30) in which 'which book' moves from the adjunct CP to the matrix CP? It cannot be a general prohibition against movement out of adjuncts, like the GB CED condition for example, given that the analysis above crucially exploits such movement to generate PGs and ACs. What then distinguishes these movements from those in (30)? The answer relies on the interaction of the island conditions and the cycle, in particular the Extension Condition. Let me elaborate.

GB reduces island effects to the Subjacency Condition (see Chomsky (1986a) for example). In effect, extraction out of the adjunct in (30) is prevented as it involves movement across two barriers, the one that the non-θ marked adjunct induces and the one that the matrix IP inherits from the adjunct. Other island effects that are handled in essentially the same fashion are subject islands, relative clause islands and noun complement islands. WH islands fall under subjacency if one adds the prohibition against multiply filled Spec CPs.

This approach to islands combines with the theory of sidewards movement to account for the distinction between acceptable PGs and unacceptable extraction out of adjuncts. Sidewards movement crosses at most one barrier, the one that encumbers the adjunct. The matrix IP is irrelevant for sidewards movement as the moved expression does not cross it. However, the IP is relevant for movement out of the adjunct to the matrix CP *if the adjunct is adjoined prior to this movement taking place* as now the IP is crossed.

Note that the VP in sidewards movement cases is not relevant on the assumption made in Chomsky (1986a: 14) that domination is a precondition for barrierhood. In sidewards movement, the VP does not dominate the "adjunct" from which movement occurs *at the point* at which movement takes place. Consider the derivation of (9) repeated here.

(9)   Which book [IP you Tns [VP/VP [VP you read which book] [Adj before [which book [Fred Tns [Fred reviewed which book]]]]]]

The relevant step of the derivation is the one where 'which book' moves from the adjunct to the object of 'read'. At this point the two subtrees have not yet been merged. What (9) displays is the end product. However, note that even in the fully formed tree, VP does not dominate the adjunct so it cannot be a barrier to movement. Nor can the IP or VP/VP as neither of these are crossed in the movement. In sum, if subjacency is computed in terms of Barriers as in GB sidewards movement need not worry about the barriers that encumber the landing site. By *not* moving to a c-commanding position sidewards movement will (at most) only encounter the barrier offered by the adjunct.

Contrast this with the derivation of (30) where 'which book' moves upwards to a c-commanding position. The final product is shown in (31).

(31)   Which book [IP you Tns [VP/VP [VP you read Moby Dick] [Adj before [which book [Fred Tns [Fred reviewed which book]]]]]]

(31) is identical to the derivation of (9) inside the adjunct. Then the two derivations diverge. In (31) 'read' merges with 'Moby Dick' then the whole VP merges with 'you'.

There are now two possible continuations of the derivation, both of which are illicit. The first option is to merge the adjunct. This is no problem. Merging the adjunct at this point adheres to the Extension Condition. Then, 'Tns' merges with the VP and 'you' raises to Spec TP. All these steps are kosher. However, the next step crosses two barriers. 'Which book' moves from the adjunct to the matrix Spec CP. The two relevant barriers are the adjunct which is not θ-marked and the IP which dominates the adjunct and inherits barrierhood from the adjunct. This move is illicit as it violates subjacency.

The other option is to move from the adjunct prior to merging the adjunct. This derivation goes as follows. We have the VP and the adjunct. Merge 'Tns' with the VP. Move 'you' to Spec TP. Move 'which book' from the adjunct to Spec CP. Then merge the adjunct to VP. The movements are all fine and conform to Subjacency. However, the final adjunction violates the cycle, more specifically, the Extension Condition, and this suffices to block the derivation. Thus, if Extension holds of all MERGE operations including adjunction (clearly the methodologically best assumption) then this second derivation is blocked as well.[37]

The upshot is very positive. The Extension Condition combines nicely with sidewards movement to explain why PG constructions require real gaps. These are the tracks of sidewards movement. As moving in this way is the only way to licitly leave an adjunct it follows descriptively that PGs require real gaps to "license" them. The assumptions that are crucial here include the following: (i) sidewards movement is licit, (ii) all (overt) MERGE operations (crucially including adjunction) obey the Extension Condition, (iii) the relevant adjuncts are merged below CP and above VP. (i) is required here on independent grounds; (ii) is methodologically the best assumption and so minimalistically prized; and (iii) is a standard assumption in the GB literature.[38]

These three assumptions work in concert to derive two consequences: adjuncts are typically islands for A'-movement and they are porous for A-movement operations. We have up to this point considered one class of adjuncts; those headed prepositions like 'after'/'before' that plausibly hang in the mid-portion of the clause. Below in section 6 and section 8 we consider adjuncts that appear to hang lower down in the phrase marker. Before leaving the topic of adjunct islands, however, I would like to briefly consider the case of an adjunct that hangs relatively high up, say, for discussion, it adjoins to CP. Assuming the analysis above, it should be possible to A'-move from such an adjunct. The reason is that it should be possible to move out of the adjunct greedily to Spec CP before the adjunct is adjoined (all the while cleaving to the Extension Condition) and thereby frozen. The structure of interest is (32).

(32)   [$_{CP}$ [$_{CP}$ WH [$_{IP}$ . . . .] [$_{Adjunct}$ . . WH . .]]

Etxepare (1998) has recently argued that this sort of movement is in fact attested. He considers apparent violations of adjunct islands in Spanish. He observes the following contrast:

(33) a. que libro dijiste [que si Ricardo leia alguna vez] abandonaria la
         Linguistica]
         'Which book did you say that if Ricardo ever read he would aban-
         don linguistics'
     b. *que libro quieres [que [si algun lee]] abandone la Linguistica
         'Which book do you desire that if anyone reads, he would abandon
         linguistics'

Etxepare argues that the 'si'-adjunct in (33a) is adjoined to a focus projection.
These are available in reporting verbs like 'say' but not desire verbs (see
Etxepare (1998) for the relevant evidence). He further assumes that Spec FP is
an escape hatch for WH elements. If so, then given the analysis above, it
should be possible to first move a WH from the adjunct to Spec FP, then adjoin
the adjunct to Spec FP and then move the WH to Spec CP. This derives the
apparent island violation in (33a). As 'quieres' does not have a similar FP
projection, this is not an option in (33b) so island effects are expected to
surface, as they do.

   It is worth observing that the English glosses point in the same direction as
Etxepare's Spanish data. The gloss in (33a) is quite acceptable and far better
than the one in (33b). Note, furthermore, that if the position of the 'if'-clause
is an indication of its being adjoined to FP then we also expect that when the
'if'-clause is to the right (rather than the left as in (33)) then the island status
should reassert itself. This seems to be correct. Contrast the gloss in (33a)
with (34).

(34) *Which book did you say that Ricardo would abandon linguistics if he
      ever read

   The analysis above adopts the GB approach to islands in terms of subjacency
defined in terms of barriers. This is done more for convenience than from
conviction. The technical apparatus that sits behind the Barriers approach to
locality fits poorly with minimalist commitments. As such, a reanalysis in
other terms is welcome.[39] However, whatever accounts for island conditions,
whether it be something like the Subjacency condition or something else, will
serve present purposes equally well so long as it permits sidewards movement
but prohibits upwards movement from an adjunct. What the above account
trades on is the fact that sidewards movement evades locality restrictions that
upwards movement falls prey to. It requires that adjuncts are not inherently
islands but are porous under the right circumstances. The analysis of ACs and
PGs exploits this loophole. What is further required is that upwards movement
be prevented from doing so as well. The combination of sidewards movement
plus the standard barriers-based approach to subjacency fills this twin bill well.
It is likely that other combinations fare just as well. What is crucial is that they
license the conclusion that only sidewards movement can escape an adjunct.[40]

5   Noun Complement Constructions

Section 4 argues that extraction from an adjunct is possible just in case the moved expression escapes the adjunct by moving sidewards. For PGs and ACs, if we adopt the standard assumption that adjuncts merge to VP (forming a VP/VP constituent), this entails that the landing site be a θ-position. A curious property of noun-complement (NC) constructions provides further support for this conclusion. It is well known that NCs manifest control but are incompatible with raising. The contrast in (35) illustrates this.

(35)   a.   John's$_i$ desire [PRO$_i$ to score a goal]
      b.   *John's$_i$ appearance [t$_i$ to score a goal]

The phrases in (35) are the nominal analogues of (36).

(36)   a.   John$_i$ desired [PRO$_i$ to score a goal]
      b.   John$_i$ appeared [t$_i$ to score a goal]

The problem is why control is acceptable in the nominal analogues of obligatory control verbs while raising in the analogue of raising verbs is not. (37) is a dramatic example of this. 'Promise' has both a control and a raising reading, illustrated in (38). Only the control nominal, (37a), is acceptable.

(37)   a.   John's promise [PRO to score a goal]
      b.   *The weather's promise [t to turn cold]

(38)   a.   John promised PRO to score a goal
      b.   The weather promised to turn cold

GB accounts for this contrast by supposing that movement is not permitted inside nominals.[41] One way of preventing such movement is to deny that complements within nominals are truly syntactic complements. If all noun internal arguments are actually adjuncts in some sense, then the lack of movement from adjuncts follows from the CED.[42]

This analysis cannot be adopted, if control in ACs is the result of movement from the adjunct, as argued for here. However, the contrasts in (35) and (37) can be accommodated on the basis of the assumptions above coupled with a proposal in Stowell (1981) that sentential complements in NCs are actually in adjunct positions.[43] Stowell proposed this for finite complements only. I assume here that it holds quite generally. If so the structure of NCs with sentential complements is as in (39). Note that the complement is an adjunct to the N^0 it is related to.

(39)   [$_{DP}$ . . D^0 [$_{NP/NP}$ [$_{NP}$ . . N^0 . .] [$_{clause}$ . . .]]]

Assume further that genitive case gets checked in Spec DP, as standardly assumed (Abney 1987).

With this in mind consider the derivation of (35a). The PRO is the residue of sidewards movement. 'John' bears genitive case. (40) illustrates the derivation: (i) the adjunct is formed. Note that 'John' has a θ-role and is case marked, presumably with genitive case. (ii) We take 'desire' from the array and MOVE 'John' to the θ-position of 'desire'. This copy of 'John' has two θ-roles and still bears an unchecked case. Note that this movement is analogous to the ones discussed in section 1 for ACs. (iii) The adjunct and 'desire John' merge. This forms a NP/NP adjunct structure, following Stowell's suggestion about the adjunct status of sentential complements in NCs. (iv) The NP/NP merges with 'D⁰'. (v) 'John' moves to Spec DP to check its genitive case. Note that at all points the derivation obeys Extension and Greed.

(40) i.   [John to [John score a goal]]
           +C+θ   +C+θ

    ii. [desire John] [John to [John score a goal]]
           +C+θ+θ +C+θ   +C+θ

    iii. [$_{NP/NP}$ [desire John] [John to [John score a goal]]]
               +C+θ+θ +C+θ   +C+θ

    iv. [D⁰ [$_{NP/NP}$ [desire John] [John to [John score a goal]]]]
                  +C+θ+θ +C+θ   +C+θ

    v.   [$_{DP}$ John [D⁰ [$_{NP/NP}$ [desire John] [John to [John score a goal]]]]]
           −C+θ+θ   +C+θ+θ +C+θ   +C+θ

Contrast this with the derivation of a raising structure. The relevant part is illustrated in (41). Step (i) is the same. However, there is no analogue of step (ii) as, by assumption, raising predicates do not contain a θ-position for 'John' to move into. This is the same assumption made for raising verbs and it carries over to their nominal counterparts. Step (iii) merges the adjunct and 'appearance', just as was true for 'desire'. The problem is that 'John' is now stuck. Note that Spec DP c-commands the adjunct. Therefore the restriction against raising out of adjuncts comes into play. The subjacency condition invoked in section 4 serves here to block raising to Spec DP as well.[44] Thus, this derivation cannot converge.

(41) i.   [John to [John score a goal]]
           +C+θ   +C+θ

    ii. [$_{NP/NP}$ [desire] [John to [John score a goal]]]
                  +C+θ   +C+θ

    iii. [D⁰ [$_{NP/NP}$ [desire] [John to [John score a goal]]]]
                     +C+θ   +C+θ

    iv. [$_{DP}$ John [D⁰ [$_{NP/NP}$ [desire] [John to [John score a goal]]]]]
           −C+θ   +C+θ   +C+θ

There is an alternative derivation but it too is ungrammatical. Move 'John' from the adjunct and merge it into Spec DP. Then adjoin the adjunct to NP. This derivation violates Extension and so is illicit.

(42) i.   [John to [John score a goal]]
            +C+θ   +C+θ

      ii.   [desire] [John to [John score a goal]]
                     +C+θ   +C+θ

      iii. [D⁰ [desire]] [John to [John score a goal]]
                          +C+θ   +C+θ

      iv.   [$_{DP}$ John [D⁰ [desire]] [John to [John score a goal]]
            −C+θ   +C+θ   +C+θ

      v.   [$_{DP}$ John [D⁰ [$_{NP/NP}$ [desire] [John to [John score a goal]]]]]
            −C+θ   +C+θ   +C+θ

The analysis relies on some secondary assumptions worth highlighting.

First, it assumes that sentences are adjuncts to NP, not DP. This makes sense given Stowell's original observations that the sentential complement actually functions to specify the content of the head noun. If this is correct, then treating the adjunct as modifying the NP seems appropriate.[45]

Second, I assume that nouns have the same thematic structure as their verbal analogues as far as their nominal arguments are concerned. This is what licenses the movement out of the adjunct and allows it to merge with the noun. If this were not correct, then this move would violate greed and so be illicit. It is not clear to me whether this is incompatible with the idea that all complements inside NPs are actually adjunct-like syntactically (see Grimshaw (1990) and Zubizarreta (1987)) as it is also generally assumed that these adjuncts assign θ-roles inside the noun similar to those assigned by verbs in clauses. This plausibly suffices for current purposes.

Note that it is critical to the present analysis that raising within the DP is permitted (pace Williams 1982). The analysis supposes that the genitives in Spec DP arise from movement. The standard alternative relies on some general relation R that relates genitive nominals to the rest of the noun if directly generated in genitive position. A typical interpretation of such directly merged expressions is that they bear some sort of "possession" relation to what follows. So, for example, (43) has an interpretation in which John possesses the photograph.

(43) John's photo

If there is no movement within D/NPs however, the semantic content of R must have a wider range of contextually determined interpretations. For example, 'John' in (43) can also be interpreted as the subject of the photo or the creator of the photo. Similarly what constitutes possession is not terribly clear. Presumably owning a photo is not the same thing as having a desire yet if there is no movement then the relation R covers both if neither (43) nor (35a) are formed via movement.

A problem with the proposal banning all movement within nominals is that it fails to explain why a structure like (44) is illicit.

(44) John's$_i$ appearance [PRO$_i$ to score a goal]

In (44) 'John' is merged in Spec DP. This operation places it in some relation R with the nominal. Its position should allow it to bind 'PRO'. If this were possible, the distinction between raising and control in nominals would be unobservable. Thus, (i) must be ill formed. The problem is to specify the grounds of its ungrammaticality.

There are two options.

One is to specify the range of possible relations that genitives can enter into contextually and show that the one that is relied on here is not one of them. This is no easy task given the wide range of possible roles the genitive can assume in the standard analyses.

The second option is to explain why PRO cannot be generated here. This is not easy to do. The most general assumption is that 'appearance' has all the lexical properties of its verbal counterpart, except perhaps the capacity to govern into the clause. The latter difference prevents raising as it would induce an ECP violation given standard GB assumptions (see Hornstein and Lightfoot 1987). However, if this position is ungoverned why can't PRO be generated there? One answer is that 'appearance' is a "raising" predicate and cannot tolerate PRO. But what does this mean, except to restate that PRO cannot appear here? Another possibility is to say that the distribution of PRO depends on the properties of I^0. The ones in raising nominals are the wrong kind (see Martin (1996) for an elaboration of this proposal). It is unclear, however, in what way they are wrong. If this too is rejected, there is no obvious way of excluding (44).

Let me put this point another way. The problem is actually twofold. In "Noun Complement" constructions the non-finite clause is either treated as a complement or as an adjunct. If the former, then if selection is identical across N and V (the unmarked assumption) then unless something "special" is said about the grammatical powers of Nouns, one would expect raising to be possible. GB accounts have tried to come up with non *ad hoc* restrictions on raising in these cases, e.g. Ns are not proper governors (Kayne 1981, Hornstein and Lightfoot 1987). However, these are not natural within MP (nor, truth be told, very natural within GB). The second approach is to assume, with Stowell (1981) that the clauses within nouns are actually adjuncts not complements. But then it is unclear how to prevent PRO adjuncts from being generated and so deriving (44). One can, of course, always stipulate that they are to be excluded.[46] However, such stipulations fail to explain the relevant properties. None of this is a problem for the analysis in the text.

In sum, the assumptions exploited in section 4 plus Stowell's assumption that nominal sentential complements are actually adjuncts fit together (with some ancillary modifications) to derive the fact that control in nominals is acceptable while raising is not.

The present analysis of control in nominals has one further virtue. Chapter 2 outlined a list of properties characteristic of obligatory control (OC) structures. OCs require local, c-commanding non-split antecedents, require sloppy readings under ellipsis and require a 'de se' interpretation. Nominals display all these features save one.

(45)   a.   *Bill$_i$ opposed John's desire/plan [PRO$_i$ to leave]
  b.   *John's$_i$ campaign's desire/plan [PRO$_i$ to leave]
  c.   *Bill$_i$ opposed John's$_j$ desire/plan [PRO$_{i+j}$ to leave each other]
  d.   John's desire/plan [PRO to leave] is stronger than Bill's
  e.   The unfortunate's desire [PRO to get a medal] is strong

(45a,b,c) indicate that the antecedent must be local, commanding and non-split. (45d) only has the reading in which Bill's desire is that Bill leave, not John, i.e. (45d) cannot be paraphrased as "John's desire to leave is stronger than Bill's desire that John leave." (45e) has the de se interpretation exclusively. The only contrast with OC in sentences is that in nominals the PRO need not have a controller.

(46)   a.   *It was desired to shave (oneself)
  b.   The desire to shave (oneself)

This gap in the OC paradigm with nominals is quite puzzling for standard accounts of control. The latter generally key control to selection. Verbs are classified as verbs of "obligatory control" or "raising verbs." The nominal paradigm indicates that the nominal counterparts of OC verbs do not obligatorily require a controller though, if there is one available, the structures must be interpreted in an OC fashion. It is unclear how this generalization could be treated in standard approaches to control.[47]

The present analysis leads us to expect what we see. OC in nominals is a function of sidewards movement. We expect OC just in case such movement is grammatically sanctioned. If, however, there is nothing to move, then there is no reason to expect OC structures. In other words, OC is not predicate centered but movement based.[48]

This conclusion is buttressed once adjuncts become the focus of attention. Adjuncts are not selected. Thus, if OC were predicate dependent, i.e. a function of a specific verb for example, we should not witness OC in adjuncts. This indicates that whether OCs occur is not predicate dependent.

Control in nominals illustrates the same thing. Here too there is an adjunction structure. Here too, the gap is an OC PRO just in case it was formed by sidewards movement. The gap in the paradigm – (46b) – is expected as there is no nominal around that could have moved.

One final observation. Chapter 2 observes that non-obligatory control (NOC) is only possible when OC is not. In present terms, the NOC PRO is only available when movement could not have created the PRO gap. In the case of nominals we expect an NOC reading just in case there is no controller (witness the arbitrary reading in (46b)) and an OC reading otherwise (see (45)). As expected, the NOC PRO in (46b) functions just like a pronoun and shows the opposite paradigm to OC PRO.

(47)   a.   John$_i$ told Mary$_j$ to nix any plan/desire [PRO$_{i+j}$ to wash each other]
  b.   John$_i$ heard that Mary had condemned any plan/desire [PRO$_i$ to wash himself]

c. John's$_i$ committees supported the plan/desire [PRO$_i$ to nominate each other for vice president]
d. John approved of the plan/attempt [PRO to leave early] and Bill did too
e. The unfortunate vetoed the plan/attempt [PRO to get himself a medal]

(47a) indicates that NOC PRO can have split antecedents, (47b) that the controller can be remote and (47c) that the controller need not c-command the PRO. (47d) can have a strict reading, i.e. it can be paraphrased as "John approved the plan that John leave early and Bill approved the plan that John leave early." Finally, (47e) can have a non 'de se' reading, e.g. in the circumstance that the unfortunate, not knowing that he was the hero in question, nixed a plan in which the hero he believed himself not to be would receive a medal. (47) conforms to our expectations in light of (46b)'s demonstration that such PROs do not require antecedents.

This section argued that the facts concerning control inside nominals is fully consistent with the analysis of ACs in section 1. The alternation between NOC and OC inside D/NPs, depending on whether a controller is present, was also seen to fit snugly with the analysis presented here. It is not clear that as much can be said for the standard GB approach to control.

6   Other Cases of Adjunct Control

The account in section 1 and section 4 restricts adjunct control to subjects on the basis of two assumptions: controlled PRO is the residue of movement and adjuncts headed by 'before/after/without' are adjoined between vP and T'. Hornstein (1995: ch. 8) provides evidence that these sorts of adjuncts are higher than the θ-position of subjects. The argument in section 4 that accounts for CED effects requires that these adjuncts hang no higher than T'. In particular, if adjoined to TP then the latter cannot act as a barrier to movement and WH extraction from adjuncts should be permitted.[49] This section examines some cases with adjuncts that hang lower than the 'after/before/without' class do.

Let's analytically consider what we expect to occur if the adjunct adjoins below vP, say to v' or to VP.[50] For concreteness assume that it is adjoined to VP (though nothing hangs on this assumption so far as I can see).

(48)   . . Z . . [$_{vP}$ v [$_{VP/vP}$ [$_{VP}$ V . . W . .] [$_{Adjunct}$ . . XP . .]]]

Consider what happens if we move XP sidewards to W, i.e. copy XP and merge it with V. This move is greedy as a θ-role of V gets checked by the movement. Note that at most one barrier is crossed, that of the adjunct. However, this move may violate economy, e.g. if the matrix verb is transitive and there is another nominal in the array then merging that nominal would be less costly than copying and merging XP. The question arises, therefore, whether such a move is legitimate. It would be if the movement of XP is required for convergence and its movement cannot be delayed. In the case of adjunct control, which we are considering here, the movement from the adjunct is indeed required as the case of XP needs checking. Moreover, the movement cannot be delayed if the adjunct must be merged with VP, as assumed in (48). Once merged, the adjunct becomes frozen. In particular, movement targeting Z is illicit. Consider why.

To be greedy, XP must be moving into a θ-position, say the Spec of vP. However, once adjoined to VP the XP will have to cross at least two barriers; the one provided by the adjunct and vP. If crossing two barriers is illicit, then convergence requires violating economy. This permits movement of XP to W and forbids movement of XP to Z.

This account presupposes two things. First, that A-movement across one barrier, but not two, is allowed. Second that barriers are computed derivationally. To see this consider the structure that obtains after XP has moved:

(49) $[_{vP}$ XP $[_{v'}$ v $[_{VP/VP}$ $[_{VP}$ V . . W . .] $[_{Adjunct}$ . . XP . .]]]]

Note that after movement, the maximal projection (on the left edge) in (48) "becomes" an intermediate projection given a bare phrase structure approach to bar levels. In (49), therefore, there is only one barrier between XP in Spec vP and its copy inside the adjunct. Thus, if barriers are computed representationally the derivation indicated in (49) should be licit. If, however, it is computed derivationally, then the maximal vP projection in (48) blocks access to Z which is too far away. In sum, if something like the barriers story is correct in determining islands, then depending on how we compute locality determines whether object control is ever possible.[51] On the representational interpretation it never should be. On the derivational interpretation it should be.

As it turns out, there do appear to be cases where object control into adjuncts is permitted and subject control is prohibited.[52] This could be accounted for in the way sketched above if the 'for' clause in (50) hung low, i.e. adjoined to V' or VP.

(50) John$_i$ arrested Bill$_j$ [for PRO$_{*i/j}$ driving his car too fast]

There is evidence to support this placement of the 'for' adjunct. First, it seems that these sorts of adjuncts are very sensitive to the presence of external arguments. Thus, it is acceptable in transitive constructions and passives but not unaccusatives and middles.[53]

(51) a.   John sank the boat for running the blockade
      b.   The boat was sunk for running the blockade
      c.   *The boat arrived early for running the blockade
      d.   *The boat sank for running the blockade

The data in (51) make sense if 'for' clauses need to modify a 'v' and these are only present in clauses with external arguments (see Chomsky 1995: ch. 4).

It further makes sense to think that an adjunct modifies 'v' if adjoined to v' or VP.[54]

There is a second bit of evidence for a low adjunction site for these clauses: they must be in the scope of negation. These contrast with "because" clauses, in this regard. (52a) is paraphrasable as (52b) in the reading where the 'because' phrase hangs low and is in the scope of negation. However, there is a reading of (52b) that (52a) doesn't share in which the 'because' phrase is outside the scope of negation.

(52) a. John didn't berate Bill for driving fast
      b. Mary didn't berate Bill because he drove fast

Note further that the adjuncts in (52b) are preposable while the 'for' clause in (52a) is not.

(53) a. *for driving fast, John didn't berate Bill
      b. Because he drove fast, Mary didn't berate Bill

Adverbs that hang low are often awkward when preposed:

(54) a. *with panache, John kissed Mary
      b. ??in a hurry, the president signed the bill
      c. ??with charisma, John talked to the assembly

   Different adjuncts have different modificational powers. Their various effects are plausibly related to the different positions that they occupy. These differences, in tandem with the approach to sidewards movement outlined above, lead us to expect different restrictions on adjunct control. In effect, the height of the adjunct will determine where elements within it can move and lead to rather different convergence options. For this reason we expect to find that adjuncts differ as to whether they support subject or object control. The adjuncts analyzed in this section, together with those discussed in section 1 exemplify these possibilities.

7   Constructing Phrase Markers Economically: A Long and Involved Technical Digression Concerning COPY

The previous sections have argued that there is considerable empirical payoff in allowing sidewards movement out of adjuncts. The story has assumed that MOVE is not a primitive operation but is a composite of COPY and MERGE. This is a standard view of MOVE.[55] However, integrating this conception of MOVE into a general minimalist framework requires rethinking various economy and locality issues to prevent significant overgeneration. In short, the component operations that underlie MOVE – COPY and MERGE – must be constrained or chaos threatens. This section discusses how this might be done in ways consistent with general minimalist guidelines. The discussion is largely technical and presupposes knowledge of the details of current minimalist approaches to MOVE and MERGE.

The overgeneration arises in the following circumstance: one makes a copy of some expression E and then does nothing with it for a while. Under this scenario MOVE need never conform to any island or economy restrictions. To illustrate the problem as concerns islands, consider the CED violation in (55).

(55)   *Which book did you read Moby Dick before Frank reviewed

It can be derived as follows. Form the adjunct. Make a copy of 'which book' but do not merge it anywhere. Then build the matrix VP 'you read Moby Dick'. Then adjoin the adjunct to this VP. Then build IP and move 'you' to its spec. Continue merging functional categories and build the CP. Finally, merge the copy of 'which book' made earlier (and left unmerged until this point) into the Spec CP. This derivation obeys extension and greed at every point. What has gone wrong? Clearly, keeping the unmerged copy around is what gums up the works. We need to limit the option of making copies that "just hang around."

The problem is not unique to sidewards movement. Consider the derivation of (56).

(56)   *There seems a man to be here

Take 'a' and 'man' from the numeration. Make a copy. Then merge one of the copies with 'here'. Then continue as usual to build the VP adding 'be' and 'to'. Merge the second copy of 'a man' into Spec IP. Then merge 'seems' and 'there' to complete the derivation.[56]

The problem in both cases stems from analyzing MOVE in terms of COPY and MERGE. The derivations allow the COPY operation where MOVE is barred. This suggests restricting COPY so that it applies only where required. One way of doing this is to strictly prohibit (or assign a high cost to) making copies that are not quickly used, i.e. it is part of the definition of the COPY operation that they be used rapidly (or keeping copies is just very expensive).[57] In a derivational context, 'used' means integrated into a large substructure, i.e. copies must merge with something. They cannot be created and remain idle isolates. For concreteness, consider (57).[58]

(57)   A copy C made at step N of a derivation must be grammatically integrated at step N+1.

(58)   An expression E is grammatically integrated iff$_{def}$ E is a proper subset of a phrase marker.[59]

(58) defines "integrated" so that E is merged with some other expression E', e.g. a copy from the adjunct in a PG construction merges with the verb of the matrix. With this definition (57) prevents copies from hanging around. It requires that E be integrated into a larger phrase marker right after it is made.[60]

(57) allows MERGE and MOVE to be locally evaluated with respect to cost once MOVE is analyzed as COPY and MERGE. What I mean is this. Economy treats MERGE as cheaper than MOVE. Why? Because MOVE involves MERGE as a sub-operation. However, in the absence of (57) a derivation need not involve MERGE right away. However, if MERGE is delayed then how is it that at *a given point of the derivation* one evaluates whether it is better to merge or to copy at that point? Asked another way: as both MERGE and COPY are single operations why should MERGE be better than COPY if all one does is count operations? We can provide an answer if COPY must be quickly followed by MERGE for it is then possible to specify economy by noting that the local extension of the phrase marker is obtained via an extra operation (i.e copy) in one case but not the other.[61]

Note incidentally, if one can have partial parallel phrase markers in a derivation, as a bare phrase structure theory allows, then cost must be relative to extending a given phrase marker, not simply having partial unconnected subtrees. In other words, there is nothing wrong with parallel structures per se. So, having a copy in parallel is not in and of itself problematic. Rather what is costly are copies that have been made but not merged.[62]

To return to the problem at hand, (57) prohibits the derivational history that generates (55) (and (56)) as it prohibits making a copy of 'which book' (and 'a man') which remains unmerged until the CP is constructed.[63]

(57) prevents other cases of overgeneration. For example, the operations noted in the derivation of (55) can also allow the extraction of adjuncts from weak islands.

(59)   *Why did John wonder who left early (why)

(59) is unacceptable with 'why' interpreted as modifying the embedded clause. Chomsky (1995) reduces this to a shortest move violation. However, it is not clear how to state this condition if COPY can freely apply and leave copies indefinitely in "computational space." Consider the following derivation. For concreteness assume that 'why' adjoins to VP. Then build the VP. Take 'why' from the numeration and make a copy. Hold this copy until the matrix CP is built. Then insert 'why'. Under this scenario it is not clear in what sense 'who' is closer to the matrix than the copy of 'why' is. In fact, there is one sense in which *at this point* it is more economical to merge the copy into the Spec CP than it is to make a copy of 'who' and then merge it. If, however, we prevent copying 'why' until moving to the matrix is a real option, i.e. adopt (57), then it is clear in what sense 'who' is closer to the matrix Spec CP than 'why' is.[64] This locality can be built into the copying operation to define shortest MOVE. However, as the derivation of (59) indicates, doing this presupposes a condition similar to (57).

These cases should suffice to illustrate the utility of a principle like (57). The issue I would like to end with concerns the status of (57): is it primitive or just a generalization derivable from more general considerations? The latter is the more desirable prospect. Consider how it might be true.[65]

(57) says that COPY must be followed immediately by MERGE. This captures the intuition that copies cannot be made and retained indefinitely. Why should this be true? Consider what a convergent derivation does. It integrates the lexical items in the numeration while checking all features that must be checked. Assume that at any given point in the derivation operations that further this end are preferred to those that do not. In other words, operations that result in feature checking trump those that do not, up to convergence, i.e. COPY can apply in place of MERGE if convergence requires it.

Now, consider mergers which are substitutions. These are into θ-positions or into positions in which a feature is checked (given GREED). If θ-roles are features too, as has been argued for here, then all instances of (substitution) MERGE result in feature checking. It is reasonable to assume that operations that reduce the inventory of features that must be checked are locally preferred to those that do not, all things being equal. Thus, these cases of MERGE will be preferred to applications of COPY at the same point of the derivation. When will COPY be needed? Just in case further feature checking cannot proceed without it. This will restrict COPY in the desired ways. In (55) for example, 'which book' cannot be copied and held in computational limbo until the matrix is reached for the copy is not locally required to check anything. By the time it is needed, e.g. by the time we get to the matrix CP, the adjunct has been attached and it is no longer available for copying due to its island status.[66]

What of adjunction MERGE? There are several possibilities depending on whether or not adjunction involves feature checking. If this operation does not check a feature it should be about equal cost with COPY and we should expect to find adjunction and copying in local free variation. If it does involve feature checking then adjunction MERGE should be cheaper than COPY and we should find the latter always preceding the former. I have not been able to find convincing evidence to bear on these options so I leave the matter unresolved here.[67]

To recap: once MOVE is reduced to the pair of operations COPY and MERGE locality and economy conditions become threatened with vacuity. The problem can be solved by adopting a principle like (57) which prohibits making copies freely and letting them hang around indefinitely. This principle can itself be interpreted as the result of valuing operations to the degree that they (locally) lead to convergence. This makes COPY less preferred than MERGE as the latter results in feature checking where the former does not. As such, the latter will be delayed unless required for convergence. This has the desired effect of prohibiting making copies "early" that remain unused but allow locality and economy conditions to be skirted.[68]

8   Other 0-Operator Constructions

Sections 2 through 6 have outlined an approach to PGs that does not require the use of a 0-operator.[69] In the best of all possible worlds, 0-operators should

not exist. These are grammar internal constructs with little theoretical motivation. The prime reason for postulating them is the existence of dependencies
that seem immune to explanation in terms of A-movement; at least as this
operation is standardly construed within GB. In addition to PGs, some typical
0-operator constructions include, relative clauses, purpose clauses and easy-
to-please constructions. All these constructions leave a gap in a case marked
position that functions like a variable and can be arbitrarily remote from its
antecedent.

(60)   a.   The man [0$_i$ [John said that Fred saw t$_i$]]
       b.   John bought Moby Dick [0 [for Fred to say that Mary read t$_i$]]
       c.   John is easy [0 [PRO to confirm that Mary admires t$_i$]]

    In addition, the antecedent has a thematic connection to the gap site. For
example, 'the man' in (60a) is said by John to have been seen by Fred, 'Moby
Dick' in (60b) is said by Fred to have been read by Mary and 'John' in (60c) is
admired by Mary.

    The distinctive signature of these constructions, in short, is that they de-
scriptively blend A and A' properties. The amalgam is attributed to the special
characteristics of 0-operators: (i) they move like WH elements via A'-positions
and (ii) they head complex predicates. The antecedent that identifies them is
construed as subject of the complex predicate that the 0-operator heads. As
predication has thematic powers, the thematic properties that the antecedents
of 0-operators exhibit are due to the predication operation the GB postulates to
"identify" these 0-operators.

    Much of this machinery extends to the GB analysis of PGs. Here too the
dependency is unbounded, the gap is in a case position and functions like a
variable. Similarly PGs demonstrate thematic sensitivities in the observed
dependency between parasitic gaps and real gaps. This leads to the methodological hope that the elimination of 0-operators in the analysis of PGs might
permit their removal from these other constructions as well. This section limns
the silhouette of such an approach.

8.1   Relative Clauses

Consider first relative clauses (RCs). The most natural approach derives RCs
via promotion as first suggested by Vergnaud (1974) and recently advocated
in Kayne (1994). Let's see how to implement this sort of analysis given the
assumptions adopted above. I illustrate a typical derivation using (61) as a
sample relative clause sentence.

(61)   John met every man who Bill likes t

    The relevant array consists of {John, met, every, man, wh-, likes, Bill} and
various functional expressions. The promotion analysis relies on the assumption
that the 'who' is a residue of movement.[70] The derivation proceeds as follows.

First merge 'wh-' and 'man'. Then merge 'wh-man' with 'likes'. Next merge this complex with 'Bill'. Raise 'Bill' to Spec TP and move 'wh-man' to CP. The derivation at this point has the form (62).

(62)   [$_{CP}$ wh-man [$_{TP}$ T^0 Bill [$_{vP}$ Bill [v [$_{VP}$ likes wh-man]]]]]

All promotion analyses are similar up to this point. Hereafter, however, there are several possible alternative derivations. Let's consider these in turn.

Option 1: The next step is to take 'every' from the array and "promote," i.e. MOVE, 'man' sidewards to merge with it. Note that we must assume that 'John' cannot merge into this position, or at least, merging at this point would not lead to convergence. This seems like a safe bet in this case.[71] Note as well that we must assume that if there is sidewards movement in this case then this movement is greedy. In effect, we assume that the relation of a determiner like 'every' and a noun like 'man' is similar to the relation to a verb and its complement. This in effect encodes the DP hypothesis concerning nominal structure. What this derivation makes explicit is that the determiner assigns something like a θ-role to its nominal complement. This suffices to meet the requirements of GREED. The output of these operations is (63).

(63)   [$_{DP}$ every [$_{NP}$ man]] [$_{CP}$ wh-man [$_{TP}$ T^0 Bill [$_{vP}$ Bill [v [$_{VP}$ likes wh-man]]]]]

The next step is to merge these two expressions, i.e adjoin the CP to the DP, to form the RC. We derive a DP/DP structure, i.e. the RC is adjunct to the head DP. This matches the earliest proposals concerning RC structure which treated relative clauses as adjuncts to the NPs they modified. The modern version of this hypothesis given the DP hypothesis is a DP/DP structure. The rest of the derivation is quite standard. The derived phrase marker is provided in (64).

(64)   [$_{TP}$ Bill T^0 [$_{vP}$ Bill [$_{VP}$ likes [$_{DP/DP}$ [$_{DP}$ every [$_{NP}$ man]] [$_{CP}$ wh-man [$_{TP}$ T^0 Bill [$_{vP}$ Bill [v [$_{VP}$ likes wh-man]]]]]]]]]]

Option 2: The first part would be the same so start with (62). Next "promote" 'man' and adjoin it to CP. Note that this is a simple instance of raising. In contrast to the derivation outlined as option 1, no sidewards movement takes place here. To be licit, some feature must get checked as a result of this movement. Kim (1998) suggests that a Topic feature of C^0 is checked as a result of this. Let's assume that this is correct. The result is (65).

(65)   [$_{CP}$ man [C^0 [$_{CP}$ wh-man [$_{TP}$ T^0 Bill [$_{vP}$ Bill [v [$_{VP}$ likes wh-man]]]]]]]

Next, 'every' merges with this CP forming the relative clause.

(66)   [$_{D/D}$ [$_D$ every] [$_{CP}$ man C^0 [$_{CP}$ wh-man [$_{TP}$ T^0 Bill [$_{vP}$ Bill [v [$_{VP}$ likes wh-man]]]]]]]

Option 2 is structurally similar to the Det-N' analysis of old. The head noun and the CP form a constituent as in the Det-N' analysis and unlike the NP/NP theory sketched as option 1. The main difference with the older Det-N' theory is the categoricity of the nominal+clause. Here it is clausal (i.e. CP) whereas earlier it was nominal (i.e. an N'). We return to whether this is an important difference below.

Option 3 takes a page from each of the two earlier options. Start again with (62).

(62) $[_{CP}$ wh-man $[_{TP}$ T^0 Bill $[_{vP}$ Bill [v $[_{VP}$ likes wh-man]]]]]

Next copy 'man' and adjoin CP to it to yield (67). Observe that I am here assuming that copying 'man' is licit even though it may not immediately merge into a checking position.[72] Copying 'man' should be permitted if required for convergence. It is reasonable to assume that (62) is not interpretable as it stands. Further, if MOVE is not a primitive operation but is the serial application of COPY and MERGE then the steps just described should be fine.

(67) $[_{NP/NP}$ $[_{NP}$ man] $[_{CP}$ wh-man $[_{TP}$ T^0 Bill $[_{vP}$ Bill [v $[_{VP}$ likes wh-man]]]]]]

The next step is to merge (67) with 'every' to form (68).

(68) $[_{DP}$ every $[_{NP/NP}$ $[_{NP}$ man] $[_{CP}$ wh-man $[_{TP}$ T^0 Bill $[_{vP}$ Bill [v $[_{VP}$ likes wh-man]]]]]]]]]

Observe that (68) involves an operation akin to sidewards movement but not quite. Promotion in this case involves copying the nominal in Spec CP and adjoining the CP to it. This is not identical to earlier cases of sidewards movement used above as the nominal does not merge with some target (as e.g. in option 1). Nor is this raising as the nominal does not adjoin to the CP as in option 2. The derived structure (68) has the flavor of the old Det-N' analysis as the head noun plus the CP form a constituent. However, it also shares a feature with the NP/NP theory in that the promoted NP and the relative clause form an NP/NP adjunction structure. The hybrid nature of this structure has some interesting properties which I now turn to.

There are several kinds of data useful in diagnosing the structure of RCs. The first pertains to 'one'-anaphora; the process whereby 'one' goes surrogate for part of a nominal expression.

(69) John saw each tall man with short hair and Bill saw each short one

In (69), 'one' can be interpreted as "man with short hair." If we assume that 'one' can only substitute for a constituent, this argues that 'man with short hair' in the first conjunct in (69) is a constituent.

RCs function with respect to 'one'-substitution just like the adjunct 'with short hair' in (69).

(70)   John saw this man who Frank photographed and Bill saw that one

Thus, by parity of reasoning, 'man who Frank photographed' in (70) is a constituent. This argues against the treatment proposed in option 1 as it breaks the RC in (70) into two parts; 'this man' and 'who Frank photographed', the latter being an adjunct to the former (c.f. (63)).

The data also cause difficulties for option 2. Pronouns come in several varieties and go surrogate for distinct kinds of constituents. Pronouns like 'it' can stand for CPs and DPs. 'One' is restricted to NPs.[73] Option 2 labels 'man who Frank photographed' in (70) a CP (see (66)). Thus, we do not expect 'one' to be able to target this expression, contrary to fact. Second, we expect 'it' to be able to target the CP, which is false.

(71)   a.   This man, Frank photographed. Would you believe it?
      b.   *John saw this man that Frank photographed and Bill saw that it

Neither of these problems beset option 3 as this approach parses 'man who Frank photographed' as an NP constituent.

Relative clause extraposition offers a further probe into the structure of RCs. It is possible to separate the head of a relative clause from the clause that modifies it.

(72)   a.   Several men who Bill knew arrived
      b.   Several men arrived who Bill knew

RC extraposition has several interesting properties. First, it appears to interact with Principle C.

(73)   a.   I gave several spiders to Max_i that he_i loved
      b.   *I gave several spiders to him_i that Max_i loved

This follows if the underlying structure of these sentences is (74) with the head of the relative moving to provide the indicated surface order in (73).[74]

(74)   a.   I gave to Max several spiders that he loved
      b.   I gave to him several spiders that Max loved

If this is correct, 'several spiders' must be a constituent in (74a,b) for otherwise it could not move to form (73a,b).

Second, this process is limited to RCs headed by weak determiners. Diesing (1992; 75) observes that RCs with strong determiners like (75) are infelicitous.[75]

(75)   a.   *Most men arrived who were from London
      b.   *I gave each spider to Mary that was poisonous
      c.   *John's friends arrived who Bill met

The unacceptability of (75a) follows if 'most men' does not form a constituent. However, it is unclear how to square this with the facts in (73).

Option 3 allows these various facts to be reconciled as follows. Assume that strong determiners like 'each', 'most' and genitive nominals are in DP while weak determiners reside in NP (the most likely venue being Spec NP). This assumption gives the RC in (74a) the structure (76a) and the RC in (75a) the structure (76b).

(76)   a. $[_{NP/NP}$ $[_{NP}$ several spiders] $[_{CP}$ wh-$[_{NP}$ several spiders] $[_{TP}$ T^0 he $[_{vP}$ he [v $[_{vP}$ loved wh-$[_{NP}$ several spiders]]]]]]]]

   b. $[_{DP}$ most $[_{NP/NP}$ $[_{NP}$ men] $[_{CP}$ wh-men $[_{TP}$ wh-men T^0 were $[_{sc}$ wh-men from London]]]]]]

In effect the nominal head of the RC and the weak determiner form an NP constituent and hence are movable while the strong determiner and head noun do not form a constituent and so cannot be separated. This follows if we derive RCs along the lines of option 3 coupled with the assumption that weak and strong determiners occupy different positions.[76]

I believe these data support option 3. In what follows I assume this to offer the correct structure for restrictive RCs.[77,78]

If it is, there are further technical issues that need to be addressed. First, we must delete copies at PF to allow for convergence. Consider (68) once again.

(68) $[_{DP}$ every $[_{NP/NP}$ $[_{NP}$ man] $[_{CP}$ wh-man $[_{TP}$ T^0 Bill $[_{vP}$ Bill [v $[_{vP}$ likes wh-man]]]]]]]]

We want the copy of 'man' in the head to survive and all the other copies to delete. There are several ways of getting this result. Consider one that fits with the deterministic view of deletion advocated in earlier sections. We earlier assumed that A'-movement adheres to a strict interpretation of GREED and that all A'-movement is overt, i.e. elements only move to A'-positions in order to check strong features. This implies that 'wh-man' in Spec CP of (68) checks a strong feature. Thus, the copy that is object of 'likes' must delete. It is further reasonable to assume that this feature affects the 'wh-' in some way. In other words, it is a strong feature of the WH feature bundle that merged with 'man' that gets checked. Assume that this set of features cannot receive a phonetic interpretation if merged with a lexical noun. In short, the WH feature bundle that is the relative pronoun can only be phonetically realized if it is free standing. If so, there are two ways for (63) to converge; delete 'man' and spell out the WH features as 'which' or 'who' or delete the whole 'wh-man' complex. (77) lists the three legitimate PF outcomes.

(77)   a.   every man who Bill likes
       b.   Every man which Bill likes
       c.   Every man Bill likes

The assumption concerning the phonetic properties of the relative pronoun are tailored to this morpheme. However, it is hard to see how something analogous could be avoided by any other analysis given the distinctive characteristics of this morpheme. For example, unlike "real" WHs, this one deletes and cannot be stressed. Furthermore, whereas 'who' is a fine relative pronoun, 'what' and 'how' are decidedly odd.

(78) a. The book *what/which I read
     b. The way *how/which I fixed the car

I assume that these restrictions are idiosyncratic features of the relative WH pronoun which a promotion analysis packs into the PF interpretation rules for this expression. At any rate, this assumption suffices and seems to fit well.

What of the LF side of the derivation? Here too things work out well given standard assumptions. The copies in the adjunct are not c-commanded by 'man' in the head of the RC. The copy that is object of 'likes' has some unchecked features and so "deletes", receiving an interpretation as a variable. The copy in Spec CP is an operator, most likely a property forming expression, i.e. a lambda abstract. The whole adjunct can be interpreted as predicated of the head 'man'. Note, that we are not assuming a rule of predication as part of the grammar. However, this does not preclude endorsing the view that RCs are interpreted as predication structures at the CI interface.

To sum up. It appears possible to adopt a promotion analysis of RCs within MP. The resultant structures are similar to the traditional Det N' analysis of RCs.[79] The analysis derives RCs without using 0-operators. It further allows RCs to be interpreted as predication structures at the CI interface without invoking a grammatical rule of predication that annotates or otherwise changes the LF phrase marker. In short, it appears possible to offer a minimalist treatment to RCs that fits with the major assumptions above and that does so without postulating elements like 0-operators that have their own specific identification conditions and grammatical rules like predication.

8.2 'Tough'-Constructions

The analysis of relative clauses can be extended to other 0-operator constructions, though these require further bells and whistles if the full range of properties are to be accommodated. Consider first the properties of 'tough'-constructions.[80]

First, in (79) Moby Dick appears to bear a theta-role determined (at least in part) by a relation to the object position of 'read'.

(79) Moby Dick is easy to read

Second, the position that 'Moby Dick' occupies appears to be a non-theta-position as evidenced by the fact that expletive 'it' can be found there.

(80) It is easy to read Moby Dick

Third, extraction from the 'easy' clause results in a strong violation in the sense that even arguments cannot be moved out.

(81) a. This violin is easy to play sonatas on
   b. These books were easy to stack on the table
   c. *Which sonatas is this violin easy to play on
   d. *Which table were these books easy to stack on[81]

The standard GB analysis accommodates these properties by assuming that 0-operator movement interacts with the matrix adjective to form a complex adjectival predicate. For example, the structure proposed for (79) is (81).[82]

(82) Moby Dick is [$_{AP}$ easy [$_{CP}$ 0$_i$ [PRO to read t$_i$]]]

'Moby Dick' receives a θ-role by being the "subject" of this complex predicate, thereby becoming co-indexed with the 0-operator and the trace it binds. As in RCs, this indexing results in the antecedent assuming the θ-role of the variable it indirectly binds.

The 0-operator fills other important functions. First, by standing between 'Moby Dick' and the trace, it blocks Principle C from kicking in. Chomsky (1986b) states Principle C so that it fails to apply when an operator intervenes between the antecedent and the variable as in (82). Second, by plugging up the CP, it prevents further movement out of the clause. In this way, the 0-operator induces a WH-island violation.

Clearly, this analysis has many empirical virtues. It suffers from a few vices as well. As emphasized in Chomsky (1995: ch. 3), it does not fit well with the GB theory of d-structure. Moreover, it is not clear that the indicated account for the island effects is entirely satisfactory. The violations are treated as similar to WH island effects. However, the latter are typically rather weak, especially in constructions like relative clauses. However, the violations in 'tough'-constructions are quite a bit stronger and are redolent of the effects one finds in complex noun phrase violations rather than WH island configurations. For example, (83a,b) are quite a bit better than (84a,b) though both are assumed to be "mere" WH island violations.

(83) a. The book that I wondered who read was on display
   b. The book that I wondered when to give to Paul was . . .

(84) a. The sonata that violins are easy to play on is . . .
   b. The people that this book is easy to convince to read are . . .

Last of all, the status within GB of the complex predicate formation operation that forges the complex predicate from the adjective plus 0-operator headed clause is quite unclear. Note, that the analysis crucially hinges on this process as without it 'Moby Dick' receives no θ-role at all in these constructions.

In short, though quite successful, the analysis has clear problems even in its own terms. These failings, combined with those that a minimalist perspective supplies, motivate the search for a different analysis. Let's consider how an approach built on sidewards movement might be pressed into service here.

Let's make the following assumptions.[83] First assume that 'tough'-construction adjectives like 'easy', 'hard', 'tough' come with an internal argument whose thematic properties are met by a variety of expressions including DPs and clauses. This seems plausible given the acceptability of the examples in (85). The present assumption takes at face value the apparent linguistic fact that in (85a) 'the exam' is the subject of the predicate while (85b) has a sentential subject. In (85c) the subject appears in complement position and the syntactic subject position contains expletive 'it'. I assume that each argument is assigned the (internal) θ-role born by 'easy', 'hard' and 'tough'.

(85) a.   The exam was easy/hard/tough
      b.   To leave things alone would be hard/easy/tough
      c.   it is easy/hard/tough to leave things alone

Observe that this description of the examples in (85) carries with it the premise that if a D/NP occupies the grammatical subject position it could bear the internal θ-role of the 'tough' adjective. With this in mind, consider (79) once again with the derivation illustrated in (86).

(79) Moby Dick is easy to read

(86) [[$_{IP}$ Moby Dick is [$_{AP}$ Moby Dick easy]] [$_{CP}$ Moby Dick [$_{IP}$ pro to read Moby Dick]]]

The derivation leading to (86) goes as follows. First we form the adjunct CP: merge 'read' and 'Moby Dick'. This is a non-obligatory control structure, so I assume 'pro' is the subject. It merges into the subject position yielding an IP (irrelevant details omitted). Then 'Moby Dick' moves to Spec CP. I return to this step in a moment.[84] Next 'easy' is plucked from the array. 'Moby Dick' moves from CP to merge with 'easy'. This move is licensed in virtue of 'Moby Dick' checking the internal θ-role of 'easy'. 'Moby Dick' then raises to Spec IP to check case etc. Last, the CP from which Moby Dick moved out is adjoined to the IP.

Several features of this proposal are noteworthy.

First, 'Moby Dick' moves out of the adjunct sidewards to a θ-position. In this regard it patterns like a parasitic gap construction. In both cases the movement is from an A to an A' to an A position.[85]

Second, 'Moby Dick' first moves to CP in the adjunct prior to moving out. This too is similar to what occurs in PGs. There is a difference, however, between the two cases. Here, 'Moby Dick' does not bear any WH features. It is plausible that some sort of A'/WH features are required to permit movement through Spec CP (see appendix 1). This is available in PGs as the moved element is an expression that ultimately ends up in an A'-position. However, in these constructions the ultimate landing site of the moved D/NP can be an A-position. This suggests that the mechanism we find in 'tough'-constructions is similar to that in relative clauses. Promotion is the vehicle by which 'Moby Dick' leaves the infinitival adjunct. Let's assume that this is what happens. Then the derivation looks as follows:[86]

(87) [[$_{IP}$ Moby Dick is [$_{AP}$ Moby Dick easy]] [$_{CP}$ [[WH] Moby Dick] [$_{IP}$ pro to read [[WH] Moby Dick]]]]

Observe that the move to Spec CP is licensed by the WH features. The adjunct, 'Moby Dick' is then "promoted" out of the Spec CP to the θ-position of 'easy'.

Third, this derivation does not exploit any special licensing conditions for 0-operators. We assume that promotion is a viable grammatical option and that it meets the standard sorts of checking requirements on MOVE. Technically, this assumes that WH features of the "relative" variety can append to an expression to provide it an exit from its containing clause via Spec CP.[87] Observe, further, that I assume that this series of movements endows 'Moby Dick' with two θ-roles; one coming from its merger with 'read' and one obtained via the sidewards move to 'easy'.

Fourth, if we assume that A'-movements must be overt and always change the feature composition of the moved expression, then the copy of 'Moby Dick' in CP checks a strong feature in this position, e.g. a relative WH feature. Note too that the matrix copy checks its case feature as well. A consequence of this is that only the matrix copy has all of the relevant features checked. As such only this copy remains and the others delete (deterministically). These deletions allow the structure to linearize at PF and "scopify" at LF.[88]

Fifth, there is a natural interpretation that we can give to the adjunct. It acts like a circumstantial adverb parallel to the pre-sentential adverb in (88).

(88) As far as hockey is concerned, the Montreal Canadiens are the best club ever

The reading of (79) is roughly: As far as one's reading Moby Dick is concerned, Moby Dick is easy. The adjunct then acts adverbially. It is a "scene setter" like the adverb in (88). The copies of 'Moby Dick' in CP and inside the adjunct form a sort of topic structure that describes in what way ease is being evaluated; it's with respect to reading it that Moby Dick is easy, not necessarily with respect to memorizing it.

The proposal has the virtue of accommodating all the facts that the 0-operator analysis handled but without having to license 0-operators via indexing or predication. The θ-link to the object position in the adjunct follows from the fact that 'Moby Dick' in (79) checks the θ-feature of 'read' prior to moving out of the adjunct via CP.

The strong island effects witnessed in 'tough'-constructions follow in the same way that WH movement out of adjuncts in PGs is blocked. Recall, that movement out of an adjunct is licit just in case the movement is via a θ-position. Once the adjunct is merged with the rest of the tree, movement is blocked in terms, for example, of the standard *Barriers* account of islands.[89] The same technology works here. Assume that the infinitival adjunct adjoins to IP. Then movement to CP from the adjunct is blocked. This is illustrated in (89), with the relevant barriers highlighted.

(89)   [$_{CP}$ which sonatas [$_{IP}$ [$_{IP}$ this violin is [$_{AP}$ this violin easy]] [$_{CP}$ WH-this violin [$_{IP}$ pro to [play which sonatas on WH-this violin]]]]]

'Which violin' crosses two barriers in moving from the adjunct to CP. The CP is a barrier as it is not θ-marked due to its status as an adjunct. Moreover, given that Spec CP of the adjunct is filled by 'WH-this violin' and so prevents 'which sonatas' from moving via this position, the adjunct IP transmits barrierhood to the CP thereby reinforcing its barrierhood. The matrix IP inherits barrierhood from the CP adjunct. As such, two barriers are crossed and a strong subjacency violation ensues.

I observed above that the status of these violations was rather strong; stronger than expected if it were a "mere" WH island violation. The main difference between this approach and the standard one is that here the adjunct CP is a barrier. The standard analysis θ-marks the 'play'-clause as it is analyzed as a complement. This removes its barrier status and assimilates the unacceptability of extraction to that of WH islands. The clear difference in acceptability manifested in (83) versus (84) speaks in favor of the present approach.

Other data are accounted for as well. When there is no D/NP movement, the clause following the adjective is an internal argument. Thus, extraction should be fine and it is.

(90)   a.   It is easy for Bill to read Moby Dick
     b.   Which book is it easy for Bill to read

Chomsky (1981) observes that both expletives and idioms are blocked from 'tough'-constructions.[90]

(91)   a.   *good care is hard to take t of the orphans
     b.   *too much is hard to make t of that suggestion
     c.   *there is hard to believe t to have been a crime committed

These cases are all ruled out on the assumption that movement out of the adjunct is via a θ-position. These are all out, therefore, for the same reason that idioms and expletives are prohibited from control structures; they cannot move via θ-positions as they cannot support θ-roles. The standard account attributes the unacceptability noted here to a prohibition against having these expressions as subjects of predicates. However, at least in the case of idioms, this is dubious, at least if RCs are also predication structures. Note that (92a,b) are quite a bit better than (91a,b) despite involving "predications."

(92)   a.   ?It is hard to take care that is appropriate of the orphans
     b.   ?It is hard to make too much that is sensible of that suggestion

At any rate, the current proposal achieves at least as much empirical coverage and does so without invoking grammatical processes like predication or introducing additional entities like complex predicates.

Before exiting this section, let's address one obvious problem for an account that allows A-to-A'-to-A movement of the kind central to sidewards movement accounts. It is known that this sort of movement is barred in raising constructions.

(93)   a.   who does it seem that John likes t
     b.   *who t seems that John likes t

The question here is what prevents moving 'who' in (93b) via the embedded CP to the matrix Spec IP and then to Spec CP. May (1983) analyzes these cases of improper movement as Principle C violations; the variable in matrix Spec IP c-commands the one in the complement position of 'likes'. If this is a Principle C violation, then the derivation is ruled out.[91]

This can be adopted here as well. Recall, we have proposed that in MP variables be identified with case checked expressions that are immediately operator bound. At LF, (93b) has the structure (94).

(94)   who [$_{IP}$ who [seems [$_{CP}$ who [$_{IP}$ John [$_{vP}$ who [$_{vP}$ John v [likes who]]]]]]]

The copy of 'who' in the embedded CP deletes. The copy in matrix Spec IP is interpreted as a variable. The copy in the complement position of 'likes' has an unchecked case feature so it too deletes. The copy in the outer Spec of 'vP' cannot be interpreted as a variable as it is not immediately A'-bound. However, it is otherwise fine. This means that it cannot delete as it need not delete. But if so, it violates the SCA, not being a variable, and this causes the derivation to crash. In effect, improper movement from a *complement* leads to a Principle C violation and a non-convergent derivation.

This account relies on a central assumption: that movement in the case of complements cannot proceed via promotion. In short, complements cannot have the feature composition of relative clauses. This amounts to saying that verbs cannot select relative C⁰s. This does not seem like an exotic assumption.[92]

In the cases we have considered, however, movement is from an adjunct with a WH/relative head. This movement allows deletions that free the relevant expressions from LF "linearization" problems. Consequently, Principle C does not kick in to thwart the derivation. In short, Principle C blocks A-to-A'-to-A movement when the A'-to-A portion is from a complement clause but not (necessarily) if it is from an adjunct. Only the former instance is "improper," leading as it does to a principle C violation.

8.3   Purpose Clauses

Our proposal concerning these adjuncts is similar to the proposal for relative clauses and 'tough'-constructions.[93] (96) illustrates the derivation of (95).

(95)   John brought Moby Dick for Mary to read

(96)   John T⁰ [John v [[brought Moby Dick]] [$_{CP}$ WH-Moby Dick for [$_{IP}$ Mary to [Mary v [read WH-Moby Dick]]]]][94]

If we assume that purpose clauses hang adjoined to (the inner) VP, then the indicated movements are required for convergence. In fact, the derivation parallels the one outlined for RCs and 'tough'-constructions above. Note that there is a violation of procrastinate involved. The derivation moves 'Moby Dick' from the adjunct to the object position of 'brought' rather than merge 'John' there. As in PGs, procrastinate is violable as respecting it would lead to a Principle C violation. Note that purpose clauses with subject antecedents are unacceptable. (97) cannot be understood with the trace taking 'John' as its antecedent. This follows if 'purpose'-clauses with (A'-) gaps are adjoined to VP.

(97)   *John brought Moby Dick for Mary to admire t

In (96), 'Moby Dick' must be promoted before the adjunct is adjoined for otherwise it will be stuck there. This will crash the derivation. Because of this, movement is permitted prior to adjunction.[95]

There are some differences between PGs and purpose clauses. We observed in section 3 that PGs like (98) are unacceptable.

(98)   *Moby Dick was read after Frank reviewed

We chalked this up to a Principle C violation. In purpose clauses, the analogous construction is acceptable.

(99)   Moby Dick was brought for Bill to read

The acceptability of (99) is accounted for on the present analysis by assuming that purposives are formed by promotion rather than WH-movement. Promotion exploits a relative WH while PGs move a real WH. Both can move via Spec CP but they do so in different ways. Only the latter leads to a Principle C violation. This is a desirable distinction to make as neither purposives nor 'tough'-constructions prohibit licensing by an expression in an A-position.[96] Note that one role of the 0-operator in GB is to block Principle C from applying in cases such as this. Here this function is filled by distinguishing interrogative from relative WHs. The former use promotion to escape a containing adjunct, the latter do not.

I have suggested adjoining the purposive to VP. This would account for why only objects are generally acceptable, in contrast to PGs. Consider the contrasts in (100) and (101).

(100)   a.   Who did you show the book to t before Fred introduced t
          b.   Who did you talk to me about t right after Fred introduced t

(101)   a.   *I showed the book to Mary$_i$ for Fred to envy t$_i$
          b.   *You talked to me about Mary$_i$ for Fred to envy t$_i$

The sentences in (101) cannot have purpose readings. For example, they do not have paraphrases equivalent to (102).

(102)   a.   I showed the book to Mary so that Fred would envy her
        b.   You talked to me about Mary so that Fred would envy her

Note further that the problem is not with prepositions. Rather, it is objects which must license these constructions. In (103) the trace cannot be understood with 'me' as antecedent.

(103)   *John showed me the book for Bill to envy t

These considerations point to the generalization that only internal arguments are acceptable antecedents for the variable in infinitival purpose clauses. This fits all the data above including the passive case in (99). However, even this generalization is not perfect. One might expect unaccusatives to license these sorts of purpose clauses given their similarity to passives. This seems to be incorrect however.[97]

(104)   a.   John arrived at noon so that Bill could brief him
        b.   *John arrived at noon for Bill to brief t[98]

(104) suggests that purpose clauses have restrictions similar to the 'for' control cases discussed in section 6. They both only "fit" with 'v' constructions. This could be accommodated by adjoining purposives to VP and thereby putting them into the selection domain of 'v'.[99] In effect, this has 'v' select purposives of the promotion variety, i.e. ones with relative-WH C^0s.[100]

What of control purposives, i.e. those that do not contain an A'-gap? These appear to allow either subject or object control.

(105)   John brought Mary to the party PRO to impress Fred

(105) is ambiguous with either Mary or John the potential controller.

This PRO seems to be the OC variety. For example, it does not support an arbitrary reading and it forbids split antecedents.

(106)   *I brought Queen Elizabeth to introduce oneself to her

(107)   *I$_i$ brought Mary$_j$ to the party PRO$_{i+j}$ to present each other to the Queen.

This suggests that the adjunct with the control purposive can hang as high as vP and as low as VP. Note that the control purposive is not sensitive to the presence of 'v'. It can be used with unaccusatives.

(108)   John arrived to dress himself for the party

It can also appear with unergatives, in contrast with the (A'-) purposives.

(109)   a.   John$_i$ laughed PRO$_i$ to attract attention
        b.   *John$_i$ laughed for Mary to notice t$_i$

We can explain both facts on the assumption that the latter kind of purposives are confined to VP and are "selected" by 'v' while the former are not so restricted. If this is correct, then the adjunct in (109b) is frozen by the time the Spec v is available as a landing site as it has been adjoined. This is not so for the adjunct in (109a).

   This proposal makes a prediction. If we have two purposives, one a control adjunct and the other an A'-adjunct then they should appear with the former having outside position as it hangs higher. This seems to be correct.

(110)   a.   John$_i$ bought Moby Dick$_j$ for Mary to review t$_j$ PRO$_i$ to annoy Sam
        b.   *John bought Moby Dick PRO to annoy Sam for Mary to review t

Note as well that the interpretation of (110a) puts the A'-purposive in the scope of control purposive. That is: what John did to annoy Sam was buy Moby Dick for Mary to review. This scoping effect is typical of adjuncts on the right periphery, with adjunct further to the right scoping over those further to the left as in (111).

(111)   a.   I hit Bill twice three times
        b.   I hit Bill three times twice

   One last interesting feature. What about an A'-purposive with a PRO subject?

(112)   John brought Moby Dick PRO to read t

In (112) 'Moby Dick' is the antecedent of the trace, as expected. This being an A'-purposive, it should be adjoined to VP. This should make it impossible to move from the PRO position to the Spec vP. In short, this should be a non-obligatory control pro. There is some evidence that this is correct.[101] For example, one finds arbitrary readings here.

(113)   John brought these cookies to eat at one's leisure

And it seems to license split antecedents.

(114)   a.   John brought Moby Dick to Mary's house to read t together[102]
        b.   John brought Moby Dick to Mary PRO to knock heads over[103]
        c.   John bought Mary a book of love poems to read to each other

To end, a MOVE analysis can account for many of the intricacies of purpose clauses. I believe that the proposal is no worse off than standard GB analyses. The special assumptions required to cover the case of purposives have some independent motivation. Moreover, the analysis makes do without any special assumptions about 0-operator licensing conditions or predication. I conclude that the possibility of dispensing with these GB artifacts seems promising.

8.4 Conclusion

This section explored ways of extending the analysis of PG constructions to relatives, 'tough'-constructions and purposives. These are usually lumped with PGs as being 0-operator constructions. However, the two types of constructions are quite different in that the latter result in structures very like predicates while PGs do not. This difference is most clearly seen in the fact that PGs require A'-antecedents while these other constructions do not.

(115) a. *Moby Dick was read after Fred reviewed
       b. A book arrived that Frank reviewed
       c. Moby Dick is easy to review
       d. John bought Moby Dick for Mary to review

The above proposal has tried to accommodate these differences by distinguishing two ways of escaping a CP; via WH movement and via promotion. This correlates to the two kinds of WH elements; question WHs and relative pronouns. The latter allows one to finesse Principle C effects while the former does not. Because of this, PGs have Principle C obstacles that these other constructions do not. One question remains: why can't one promote out of adjuncts typical of PGs, e.g. out of an 'after'/'before'/'without' adjunct? I suspect the reason has to do with the presence of the overt preposition. The analysis has restricted relative-WH C^0s to positions where they are licensed, eg. by 'v' or 'easy'.[104] It is plausible that the C^0 escape hatch in PGs is not available because of the preposition that heads the adjunct. This hunch is confirmed when one considers one more brand of purposives.

(116) *John bought Moby Dick in order for Mary to review

These purposives are unacceptable with an A'-gap. We could attribute this to the fact that the relative-WH C^0 cannot be selected because of the intervening 'in order to' which blocks selection much like 'after' and 'before' would in PG adjuncts.

The aim of this section has been to make plausible the claim that the machinery developed in GB to deal with 0-operator constructions can be dispensed with and replaced by a sidewards movement analysis in terms of COPY and MERGE. The aim has been to do no worse than standard GB approaches that exploit these mechanisms. It is for the reader to judge how successful this exercise has been.

9   Conclusion

There is an ambitious reading of the minimalist program that aims to pare down grammatical mechanisms to the bare minimum. From a purely conceptual point of view, theories of UG that are lean and spare are methodologically superior to those that multiply entities and processes to meet the empirical exigencies of every novel construction. However, methodological parsimony can exact a high empirical cost against which its methodological virtues dim considerably. The aim of this chapter has been to argue that in a large range of cases we can adopt the minimalist program without sacrificing empirical coverage. Indeed, I suggested that there exist minimalist accounts that make do with less and that are at least as adequate (and often superior) to the standard more profligate GB accounts. The theoretical trick is to generalize MOVE in a radical fashion. If MOVE permits sidewards movement, A-to-A'-to-A movement and movement into θ-positions then we can (hope to) dispense with PRO, 0-operators, predication rules and the control module. Moreover, given the very tight restrictions that currently govern MOVE in the MP versions of UG, loosening MOVE in these ways seems to lead to very few problems of overgeneration. It appears that carefully (and radically) pursued, minimalism's methodological virtues can be attained without incurring serious empirical costs. This is an exciting conclusion if true.

Appendix 1   Features for Comp-to-Comp Movement

Comp-to-Comp movement raises problems for the idea that all movement is last resort, i.e. greedy. If such A'-movement is greedy a natural question arises: what features are being checked? The following is intended to show that it is possible to come up with a plausible feature checking scenario that does for A'-operations what case and φ-feature checking do for A-movement.

Assume that a WH-DP had to check some non-interpretable features *on itself*. Say this could only happen in a +WH C^0. Then a WH-DP in a −WH Spec CP would be ill-formed and would delete *deterministically*.

This proposal requires saying something about what the relevant features on a WH-DP are that must delete. It is not implausible that the relevant features are the WH features themselves or these WH features plus some analogues of case/agreement features relevant for A'-movement. The standard semantics of questions treats the WH-DP in Spec CP as simply an existential operator. The semantically important features are the ones in C^0, not the ones on the WH-DP. One might argue that to be interpreted as an operator requires stripping these features from the +WH-DP. For concreteness then, let's assume that WH-DPs (can) have WH features that are not interpretable and that these are matched by similarly non-interpretable features on a +WH C^0. This assumption largely makes copies in medial CPs defective in that they have unchecked features. These then will have to delete and will do so deterministically.

Note that this assumption concerning the feature structure of WH-DPs also handles another problem. It prevents movement out of a +WH CP to a higher +WH CP. The features that appear on the WH-DP disappear on being checked. This then renders irrelevant any further movement of the WH-DP to another +WH CP. The reason is that the non-interpretable features of the higher +WH C^0 cannot be checked by this moved WH-DP. In effect, once in a +WH CP a WH-DP is frozen in place, much like a DP in a case position.[105]

In sum, if we assume that WH-DPs and +WH C^0s bear uninterpretable features that require checking and these features are universally strong so that all A'-movement is necessarily overt, then we overcome both a problem for last resort movement as it applies to the A'-system and allow deletion to proceed deterministically.[106]

Another problem remains. What drives movement to a −WH CP? Is this movement also driven by greed? This is even less clear, I believe. Chomsky (1998) proposes that movement to a −WH CP comes from restricting inspection of categories that have already converged. In effect, one can only tamper with the "edges" of structure. He points out that this yields a strong version of subjacency.

Another option is that −WH CPs also have feature checking requirements. An analogy can be drawn between the CP system and the TP system. +WH CPs are like finite TPs and −WH CPs are like non-finite TPs. If the EPP is correct, then TPs in general require subjects. Finite TPs, in addition, are loci of case checking. A DP can move through successive non-finite TPs but is frozen in finite ones. Similarly, it is possible to move successively via −WH CPs but a WH-DP is frozen in a +WH CP. This suggests that WH-DPs might well check a feature of −WH C^0s in −WH CPs. There are well known cases of agreeing − WH CPs that track successive cyclic WH movement (Irish, Hausa, Chamorro). If this is correct, then the kind of feature one gets in +WH CPs and −WH CPs differ in precisely the ways that case and agreement differ for A-movement. Agreement can be checked on multiple heads. Case is checked once. All of this can be made explicit in specifying the feature structure of WHs. If case and agreement come together, then WH features are amalgams of A'-case and A'-phi-features. WH-DPs have A'-case and phi-features. +WH C^0s are akin to finite TPs with A'-case and phi-features. −WH C^0s have A'-agreement features but no case. In parallel to the A-system, we can treat A'-phi-features as interpretable on WH-DPs and A'-case as uninterpretable. Both sets of A'-features are uninterpretable on C^0.

It should be clear that the evidence for this set of features is not overly compelling. What I have done here is simply show how to extend the reasoning we typically make in the A-system to the A'-system to allow A'-movement to be greedy and to permit deletion in A'-positions to be deterministic. I have also assumed, following Hornstein (1995) that in contrast to A-movement, all A'-movement is necessarily driven by strong features and is always overt.

Appendix 2   Expletive Control into Adjuncts

Lasnik (1992: 244) observes that examples like (117) in which PRO would be controlled by an expletive are unacceptable.

(117)   a.   There was an investigation *PRO/there having been a robbery
        b.   There was a crime without *PRO/there being a victim

These structures do permit control by an argument, as Lasnik also notes.

(118)   a.   John aided the investigation PRO having witnessed the robbery
        b.   Harry was a witness without PRO being a victim

The cases in (118) are AC structures. They have been analyzed above in terms of sidewards movement. In what follows, I briefly outline how this account blocks AC in which the controller is an expletive.

The story developed above has as a consequence that control should be impossible in cases like (117). Recall that the following generalization was established for cases of sidewards movement.

(119)   Movement from the adjunct must proceed through a theta position in the matrix

In other words, sidewards movement from an adjunct passes through a theta position. The reason for this is that all other derivations either run afoul of (a) whatever accounts for island conditions or (b) the Extension Condition. Note that if (119) is descriptively adequate, then we can derive the facts noted in (117) for, *by assumption*, an expletive cannot ever occupy a theta-position. To see this in the case of expletives, consider the possible derivations of (117b).

One first forms the adjunct, eventually arriving at a structure like (120).

(120)   [without [IP there being a victim]]

The next step in the derivation is to form the matrix. One does this by Merging 'was' and 'a crime'. At this point, in order to get "control" movement must apply to move 'there' sideways to the matrix. Note, that being an expletive, it cannot move to a theta position. It in fact, moves to Spec TP. Thus the relevant structures at the point where movement could take place are (120) and (121).

(121)   [TP [VP was a crime]]

At this point, movement can occur from the adjunct to the Spec TP. However, the adjunct cannot then merge to VP (as it must) without violating the Extension Condition. The other option is to first merge the adjunct. This gives the structure (122).

(122)   [VP/VP [VP was a crime]] [without [IP there being a victim]]

We then merge Tns to (122) to get (123).

(123)   [TP T [VP/VP [VP was a crime]] [without [IP there being a victim]]]

However, once the adjunct is merged the CED restricts further movement from the adjunct. Thus, there is no licit derivation available in which the expletive moves from the adjunct sidewards to the matrix. The reason is that its target, Spec TP is "too high" to both permit movement and permit licit adjunction.

This case brings up an interesting detail. The argument assumes that with merging of the adjunct the CED becomes relevant. Note that it is not entirely clear why this should be so if CED effects are explained in terms of Barriers technology. The first barrier is the adjunct. However, it is unclear what the second one is. One might say that it is *VP/VP* or perhaps *TP*. However, it must be one or the other.[107] Note that treating either as a barrier is not particularly natural. After all, *TP* is the target of the operation so it is debatable whether one actually extracts from it. It is also very unclear within a barriers set of assumptions whether adjunctions ever form barriers and if they do whether the *VP/VP* is a barrier by inheritance or for some other reason. None of these technical problems have a minimalist flavor. Uriagereka's (1999) account seems less problematic here. Adjunction forces linearization which in turn freezes structure. This holds without the requirement of computing blocking categories, transmitting barrierhood or worrying about domination versus containment.

To recap, sidewards movement out of an adjunct is sensitive to where the adjunct must adjoin and the available landing sites generally available. As expletives cannot move via theta-positions, they must wait until the TP is constructed before being able to move. However, this prevents movement from an adjunct as these must be merged below TP. Thus, there is no licit sidewards derivation of an expletive from an adjunct and hence it is impossible for *there* to control a PRO in cases like (117).

Notes

1 To be more precise, the expression which will be the adjunct in the final structure is constructed first. It is not yet an adjunct. This is crucial as will become clear below. I will designate the phrase prior to its actual adjunction with scare quotes as the "adjunct."

2 By subject control into ACs being required I intend that intransitive matrix verbs' objects are not licit controllers.

(i)   *John saw Mary$_i$ [before PRO$_i$ leaving the party]

This does not prohibit I(nverted)-subjects from being controllers, however. Chomsky (1995: ch. 4) discusses examples like the following in which this is attested.

(ii)   There arrived three men$_i$ without PRO$_i$ introducing each other

We discuss these cases more extensively in chapter 6.

3 The commas indicate unmerged subtrees. The trace of V-movement is there for convenience in place of a copy, which is visually confusing. The present derivation is discussed in Nunes (1995), Uriagereka (1998), and Bobaljik and Brown (1997).

4 There is a way of so restricting movement and that is to replace MOVE with ATTRACT. In chapter 4 I argue against replacing MOVE with ATTRACT.

5 The account here depends heavily on the analysis of PGs developed in Nunes (1995). The implementation, however, is somewhat different from the one in Nunes (1995), though clearly the main lines of the analysis dog his every conceptual step. The notes track some of the relevant technical differences between the two accounts.

6 Note, the status of Comp-to-Comp movement in MP is unclear. I assume that whatever licenses it in standard cases will permit it here as well. For discussion see Chomsky's (1998) discussion of phases.

I also leave open whether the WH moves to Spec CP in this case or adjoins to IP. The reluctance to commit turns on the treatment of the adjunct PPs. Sentences within adjunct PPs are incompatible with overt complementizers in English. This suggests that perhaps they are in C^0. If so, the WH might be in Spec CP as in (i).

(i) ... [WH after [$_{IP}$ NP ......]]

As little seems to depend on how these issues are resolved I ignore them here.

7 Nunes (1995) tries to handle the observed island effects in terms of a semantic filter. He therefore does not move the WH to adjunct initial position. This is a problem for Nunes' analysis. Observe that the present proposal is identical to that provided by Chomsky (1986a). The main difference is not the movement but what drives it. For Chomsky (1986a) it is the requirement that subjacency holds at SS for composed chains. Here, it is the SMC that prevents movement out of the adjunct.

Nunes notes that one apparent problem for a sidewards movement analysis is that the WH that moves appears to check two case positions, the one inside the adjunct and the one within the matrix. How can one expression check two cases? Assume that the movement inside the adjunct proceeds as follows: the WH inside the adjunct moves to the adjunct internal CP position and then sidewards to the matrix theta position. The copies in theta-positions then check case at LF. As there are two copies each can check a separate case. As Nunes (and I) assume that copies are viable computational objects, this is a possible derivational option.

This is essentially what Nunes (1995) proposes. However, it seems to require that case be checked at LF. There is evidence that this might not be so (Lasnik (1995b) and Koizumi (1995)). Say that case does get checked in overt syntax. It is still possible to retain Nunes' basic proposal by assuming that the copy that "moves" to the CP inside the adjunct is the copy in the thematic position, rather than the one in the Spec vP (case checking) position ('C' = case).

(i) [WH [...... [$_{vP}$WH v [$_{VP}$ V WH]]]]
     +θ–C   +θ+C   +θ–C

This derivation is permitted if we assume that ATTRACT is *not* part of the definition of MOVE. For a fuller discussion see chapter 4 where I argue against incorporating ATTRACT into MOVE.

8 One must be careful about how one measures relative distance. Chapter 2 notes that one wants expressions that fail to c-command one another to be exempt from SMC considerations. This allows sidewards movement out of an adjunct to Spec vP across an object in the VP. This view of relative distance is consistent with the

proposal in the text given that the elements that might move are in a command relation even though their potential target does not command either expression. Note that superraising will also fall under the SMC as the candidate expressions for movement are in a command relationship.

9 See Aoun and Clark (1985), Cinque (1990), Weinberg (1988).

10 Nunes (1995) does not have an explanation for this as he assumes that Greed is not part of the definition of MOVE but part of a distinct rule FORM CHAIN. This permits adjuncts to move sidewards out of adjuncts. See Nunes (1995) for discussion.

11 It is likely that adjoined positions are not configurationally licit positions for feature checking at all. Only Specs and complements are feature checking positions. For empirical discussion of this issue see Chomsky (1995: 325ff).

12 Note that (13b) involves moving a selected adjunct; the manner adjunct in 'word' and 'phrase' is required. However, this does not improve the acceptability of PGs that use these selected adjuncts. This suggests that we must distinguish being an argument from being selected. See Schein (1993) and Hornstein (1995) for discussion of this point.

13 The fact that PGs are not licensed by PPs are another instance of the observation that it is overt syntax that is relevant for licensing PGs. At LF, the moved prepositions must reconstruct for semantic reasons. After this, there is no apparent structural difference between the unacceptable PG with a pied piped PP and one where the PP is stranded. However, the latter is acceptable while the former is not.

(i) This is a topic that you should think about t before talking about t
(ii) *This is a topic about which you should think t before talking t

14 Note that this assumes that copies are indistinguishable. Any copy can serve to "represent" an "original" in the array. This suggests that elements in the array do not have morphological or thematic features as copies can be distinguished from each other based on the features that have been checked. Chomsky (1995) observes that elements of the array can be thought of in two ways. Either they are "bare" and their morphology is added on the way to the computational system. Or they are counted in the array already morphologically encumbered. The presentation in the text relies on the former option.

15 For details see Nunes (1995). He assumes that there is a FORM CHAIN rule in addition to MOVE. Hornstein (1998) proposes the elimination of chains as grammatical constructs. If this is correct then the rule proposed by Nunes (1995) does not exist. In what follows, I try to technically modify Nunes' approach to the LCA to conform with the elimination of chains. The ideas presented here are close to Nunes in basic orientation if not in all the details.

16 This amounts to saying that the distinction between GREED as stated in Chomsky (1995, ch. 3) and GREED in the sense of enlightened self interest (Lasnik 1995b and Chomsky 1995: ch. 4) is often moot. The distinction actually only matters in two cases; multiple agreement and EPP. In the former case, on the assumption that phi-features are interpretable, they do not erase after being checked. This allows phi-feature agreement to occur via successive movement. The same holds for D-features. These too are taken to be interpretable and so indelible. The distinction between interpretable and non-interpretable features is not without problems. It is unclear, for example, that 'scissors' and 'trousers' are truly semantically plural in English, nor is it clear that tables and chairs are semantically feminine in

French or that little girls ('Mädchen') are semantically neuter in German. The problem compounds when D-features are considered. They are primarily exploited to account for EPP effects in ECM and raising constructions. However, the EPP is notoriously ill understood and it is likely that we do not fully understand what is going on here (see Chomsky (1998) where he dispenses with D-features). Chapter 2 noted some benefits of doing away with the EPP and D-feature checking (see Castillo, Drury and Grohmann (1999) for further arguments). The main conclusion of all of this is that it is quite possible that the original sense of GREED is the correct one in the sense that all cases of movement results in altering the feature composition of the moved expression. I discuss the virtues of this conception of Greed below.

17   For PGs the unacceptability of (16a) could be reduced to a prohibition against moving via this A'-position in the adjunct unless one proceeded to move to an A'-position in the matrix. If this A'-position is Spec CP, then this would say that movement via Spec CP is only licit for expressions that finish up in an A'-position. If A'-movement only holds only in overt syntax, then a derivation that finishes in overt syntax in an A-position is not grammatical. This suffices to block (16a). Recall, that movement via CP in PGs was motivated to evade a violation of the SMC. Without movement via the adjunct CP it is plausible that the derivation is blocked by the SMC.

Though this worked for PGs it is not clear that a similar strategy can be generalized to account for all cases of 0-operator constructions. Below, I discuss other cases of 0-operator constructions, in particular 'tough'-movement, that create problems for this assumption.

18   See Appendix for a possible feature theory for Comp-to-Comp movement. Observe that this version of Greed has one very desirable property: it allows all computational decisions to be very local. All one ever needs to consider in evaluating the well formedness of a structure is whether all the items that compose it are licit. Or, if a structure is ill formed, it is because some expression within it has an unchecked feature.

19   The relative unacceptability of these two sentences is different. (19b) is quite a bit worse than (19a). This suggests that the two sentences are out for different reasons. We return to this below.

20   In Chomsky (1982) there was no 0-operator in the adjunct. This allowed Principle C to be operative in cases like (19a). In the reanalysis of PGs in *Barriers* (Chomsky (1986a)) this was no longer tenable as there was a 0-operator at the head of the adjunct that would have blocked Principle C from applying, at least the version stated in *Knowledge of Language* (Chomsky (1986b)). As such, these cases were reduced to subjacency violations, a condition extended to composed chains. With the elimination of 0-operators, as proposed here, the original Principle C account can be revived.

(19b) was ruled out in Chomsky (1982) as a theta-criterion violation. The idea was that 'Moby Dick' headed a chain with two theta-roles as the PG was functionally interpreted as an NP-t. The reanalysis in *Barriers* had little to say about cases such as this. It is quite unclear why these derivations should be bad. There are various stipulations that one can make to accommodate these data but they do not follow from general principles. Once again, Principle C might be seen as operative if one is careful in how the principle is stated.

One last point. Nunes (1995) accommodates cases like (19b) in a way parallel to Chomsky (1982). He does not use 0-operators nor does he have anything in an A'-position inside the adjunct. He reduces the unacceptability of (19b) to the fact that one cannot form a well formed A-chain in these cases as the Minimal Link Condition is violated. Without a chain deletion is impossible and the LCA is violated.

21 See chapter 5 below.

22 Some modesty is called for at this point. Principle C appears to affect rather disparate sorts of relations: it applies to variable/variable, pronoun/variable, name/name (though not in all languages) and DP/bound epithet relations. This is a rather varied group of relations and it is not entirely clear what, if anything, unifies them. In what follows, I only consider the first case. It is plausible that the second case involves some sort of binding violation (roughly: a pronoun cannot have as antecedent an expression that it binds). I currently have no idea how to unify the two former cases with the two latter instances of Principle C.

23 Strictly speaking, the pg in (19a) is just a copy of 'which book'. This moves to Spec AgrO or the outer Spec of vP to check case at LF. This is the variable inside the adjunct, not the pg indicated in (19a). However, the details are irrelevant here so I ignore them.

24 I assume the following version of Principle C (see Chomsky (1986b)):

An r-expression must be A-free (in the domain of its operator)

Variables, defined below, count as r-expressions.

25 These are the minimalist analogues of the case marked A'-bound traces in GB.

26 Note that this use of Principle C to explain the absence of subject parasitic gaps returns to the proposal in Chomsky (1982).

27 This constitutes another reason for dispensing with PRO in MP. The view of PRO as licensed by null case in Chomsky (1995) and Martin (1996) would lead us to treat PGs and ACs on a par with respect to Principle C. The present discussion indicates that this leads to empirical inadequacies.

28 Within GB, this is meant to exclude traces in Comp which are A'-expressions but not operators and to include expressions that have been topicalized and focused as well as WH-operators. I here adopt analogues of the GB distinctions.

29 An early version of Nunes (1995) followed Kayne (1994) and assumed that the LCA applied to LF. I agree with Chomsky (1995) that the LCA makes more sense as a PF condition. However, what follows suggests that something very like the LCA holds at LF for scope. In this sense, what follows comports with what Nunes had in mind.

30 Whether this requires a process of LF deletion is addressed briefly in chapter 6.

31 Brackets indicate deletion.

32 Note, we cannot interpret the copy in the adjunct as a variable and the one in the matrix functionally. They require a parallel interpretation. The former possibility is unavailable because once we "reconstruct" the WH from Spec CP the copy in the adjunct is no longer operator bound and so cannot receive an interpretation as a variable.

33 This is similar in spirit to the functional definition of empty categories proposed in Chomsky (1982).

34 Observe, if variables were defined at SS rather than LF this problem would not arise given that QR applies covertly. However, minimalism does not recognize SS as a level and so doing things in this way is not available. Note that this fits with the suggestion above that A'-movement operations only hold overtly in MP. See Hornstein (1995: ch. 8) and Hornstein (1999) for further arguments against adopting QR in MP.

35   It is possible that variables should be identified with case checked operator
     (A'-)bound copies in A positions. This would prevent treating the copy in the
     A'-position within the adjunct as a variable.

36   There are cases that are surprisingly good however.

     (i)   ??Who did you visit Rome without meeting

     These contrast with examples like (ii) which are quite poor.

     (ii)   *Who did you read Moby Dick without meeting

     I have nothing to say about this contrast.

37   Observe that this proposal assumes a distinction between adjunction and sub-
     stitution as regards economy. Economy treats MOVE as more economical than
     MERGE as the former includes MERGE as a sub-operation. However, this would
     preclude sidewards movement out of adjuncts if taken to require adjunction prior
     to movement. There is an important difference between adjunction and substitu-
     tion; the latter does not involve any form of feature checking. As Chomsky (1998)
     notes substitution MERGE and MOVE are both GREEDY in that features get
     checked (if theta-roles are features). This provides a way of allowing MOVE to be
     as cheap as adjunction MERGE: it results in a checked feature. This cost account-
     ing should permit adjunction MERGE and MOVE to freely interleave.
         One last point. It was once observed (Chomsky 1982) that PG constructions
     were slightly "off." This was due to a proposed bijection violation. Since those
     early days, examples of PGs have been taken as nearly perfect and some have
     even argued that it is adjuncts with resumptive pronouns that are somewhat
     "off." Thus, (ia) is taken as less acceptable than (ib).

     (i)   a.   Which book did you read before Frank reviewed it
           b.   Which book did you read before Frank reviewed

     If is possible that the variants in (i) reflect the fact that movement and adjunction
     MERGE are equally costly operations. One gets the (ia) when movement precedes
     adjunction and (ib) when adjunction takes place. See Aoun, Choueiri and Hornstein
     (1999) and chapter 5 for discussion of resumptive pronouns and movement.

38   This does not mean it is uncontroversial. It rejects Larson's (1988) proposal that
     adjuncts are really syntactically "low," in positions similar to arguments. This
     assumption is incompatible with the above as it fails to distinguish sidewards
     movement from upwards movement. As such, it will treat all movement out of
     an adjunct on a par. For further arguments against the Larsonian treatment of
     adjuncts see Hornstein (1995: ch. 8).

39   In fact one exists. Uriagereka (1999) provides a way of reducing island effects to
     the workings of the LCA. In effect, he argues that the LCA should be interpreted
     in a way that results in adjuncts having to be linearized as they are adjoined. He
     further assumes that linearization precludes further movement. If this is correct,
     then these assumptions can serve to explain CED effects. What is crucial in the
     story above is that there be some locality condition that precludes extraction from
     adjuncts and that this condition not affect sidewards movement. Uriagereka's
     proposal has both features so it can adequately replace the barriers based
     Subjacency condition above.

40 Section 3 accounts for the absence of adjunct and PP parasitic gaps in terms of the condition that movement must be greedy. In effect, it proposes that adjuncts and PPs cannot check case or theta-features and so cannot move. Thus, they cannot move sidewards and so cannot license PGs.

There is another way of deriving these results in terms of the Barriers technology. Recall that barriers are defined in terms of domination. Thus an adjunct adjoined to VP has only the adjunct as a barrier if moving sidewards. Thus only one barrier intervenes between the moved expression and its landing site if movement is sidewards. Adjuncts cannot cross even a single barrier so they are prevented from moving out of the adjunct. Arguments, in contrast, can cross one barrier. There is evidence that PPs are also sensitive to single barriers:

(i) a. About who did John wonder why Mary talked
     b. Who did John wonder why Mary talked about

(ia) seems decidedly worse than (ib). If this is correct, then it can be explained in terms of the PPs being prohibited from crossing a barrier.

One problem arises however if this approach is taken. NP movement is generally taken to be prohibited across even one barrier. This would unfortunately prevent analyzing adjunct control in terms of movement. There are, however, Barriers-like theories that do not submit A-movement to ECP sorts of restrictions (see Aoun, Hornstein, Lightfoot and Weinberg (1987) and Rizzi (1990).

It is interesting to observe that what prevents sidewards movement from adjuncts in earlier GB theories is not the inherent islandhood of adjuncts but a combination of the theta-criterion and conditions on chains. If these are relaxed or dropped then sidewards movement is possible given conventional assumptions.

41 See Grimshaw (1990) and Williams (1982) (The NP cycle, LI).

42 This is proposed in Grimshaw (1990), Hornstein and Lightfoot (1987) and Zubizarreta (1987).

43 I take it to be the null assumption that all sentential complements are similarly positioned. There is evidence from 'one' substitution that this is correct. Recall that 'one' substitution distinguishes adjuncts from arguments in being illicit in the latter case.

(i) *This king of England and that one of France
(ii) This king from England and that one from France

It seems that this is generally quite acceptable with sentential complements.

(iii) This claim that Bill arrived early and that one that he arrived late
(iv) John's intense desire to leave early trumped Mike's weak one to stay until the bitter end

Observe that the verbal counterparts are complements if the VP ellipsis test (which functions very like 'one' substitution) is used.

(v) *John read a book and Bill will a paper
(vi) John read a book yesterday and Bill will tomorrow
(vii) *John claimed that Bill left and Frank will that Sam stayed
(viii) *John desires to stay and Bill will to leave

Other evidence for the adjunct nature of the non-finite clause is that "separation" is possible (see Dowty 1989).

(ix) John's desire is to leave the party early
(x)   John had one very intense desire. It is to be elected president.

44 Actually, the details are somewhat unclear given a Barriers-like framework. We must assume that the NP is a Barrier despite being a complement of D^0. This is not a natural assumption. A more congenial conclusion is to replace the Barriers approach to islands with one like that in Uriagereka (1999). Here islandhood is related to linearization. As all adjuncts are linearized *on adjunction* we need not worry about how and whether barriers are induced and transmitted. See Appendix 2 for further discussion.

45 See note 43 for empirical evidence supporting this different treatment of the sentential complements of nouns and verbs.

46 One can, for example, stipulate that 'desire' takes the non-finite clause as a complement and so allows movement from it while raising predicates take these as adjuncts and so prevent such movement. The problem is to motivate this difference on independent grounds.

47 For example, Williams (1980) concluded that nominals were not structures of obligatory control as they did not display the full paradigm of properties. Williams (1980), in effect, uses the obligatory presence of a controller as a defining property of OC. This is rejected here. It is not structures that are OC rather it is, to put things slightly misleadingly, PROs that are OC or not.

48 This is a problem for analyses like Martin's (1996) in which OC is a function of selecting the correct Inflection. On this view, it would appear that nominals do not select the same kind of inflections as their verbal counterparts given that they do not appear to force OC. If this is accepted there are two problems. First to explain why it is that when there is a controller the OC paradigm is fulfilled. Second, if nominal selection is different from verbal selection then, aside from complicating selection, we are left with no account for why "raising" verbs cannot have "control" nominal counterparts.

49 This assumes that barriers are computed in terms of dominance rather than inclusion. If inclusion is what is relevant then adjunction to TP is permitted. The main motivation for using dominance rather than exclusion in the Barriers framework was to allow movement out of VP by adjunction. However, this sort of movement is quite suspect in minimalist terms as it fails to be greedy. As such, domination can be replaced by inclusion for the bulk of the relevant cases.

One more point, analyzing things using Uriagereka's approach allows the adjunct to adjoin to TP and still leave it impermeable. See appendix 2 for additional reasons for adopting something like Uriagereka's approach to islands.

50 I assume that where adverbial adjuncts hang is determined by the sorts of expressions that they modify. Thus it is no accident that temporal adjuncts are located "near" Tense and that manner adverbials are lower, in close proximity to the verb. I have nothing to say about how "closeness" is measured here however. It is noteworthy however that expressions adjoined to a maximal projection XP dominated by a second projection YP are in the domains of both X^0 and Y^0 given the definitions in Chomsky (1995: ch. 3). This makes an adjunct adjoined to VP a potential modifer of both V and v. It is this sort of adjunct we examine here.

51 If we assume Uriagereka's approach to islands then once adjoined, the adjunct is frozen. As such, only W should be accessible to sidewards movement out of an adjunct that adjoins this low.

52   These cases were brought to my attention by G. Cinque (p.c.).

53   Note that all these sentences are fine with a "because" phrase, e.g.:

(i)   The boat sank because it ran the blockade

54   It is not possible to have 'for' phrases with unergatives.

(i)   *John coughed for being excited

If 'John' is the external argument here and the 'for' phrase hangs from VP or v'
the unacceptability of (i) follows.

55   See Chomsky (1993, 1995) and Nunes (1995).

56   Strictly speaking this is a derivation that would not converge on the assumptions
adopted here as the second merged copy would not have a theta-role. However,
given standard assumptions concerning chains like those in Chomsky (1995) the
derivation seems licit.

57   The difference in the two approaches is that one treats the making of copies as
strictly illicit if not used rapidly while the other treats it as an economy condition.
It is likely that the first approach is better as the second would suggest that
islands could be freely violated if convergence were at issue. I doubt that this is
true. If so the first option is preferred. This suggests treating (57) as part of the
definition of the COPY operation so that if not conformed to the derivation aborts.
Observe that this is consistent with the intuition that MOVE is a less preferred
operation than MERGE. If the copy theory of movement is correct then the problem lies with COPY; making them is subject to last resort considerations.

58   This is similar to Nunes and Uriagereka (forthcoming) principle of Maximizing
Minimal Resources.

59   If phrase markers are sets with labels this amounts to saying that there must be
more than just the copy in the set of terms. In Bare Phrase Structure terminology,
the set we get once we strip off the label must contain the copy and at least one
other member to be licit.

60   There may be another way to derive the benefits of (57) without making it an
explicit part of the theory of grammar. One might argue that COPY should always
be delayed until required. In other words, if one can continue a derivation (that
converges) by MERGE one should. This makes MERGE intrinsically preferable
to COPY. This would similarly prevent making copies until they are needed.
Why copying should be intrinsically more problematic than MERGE is discussed
below. See Chomsky (1995) for some speculations on this matter concerning the
conceptual necessity of MERGE but not of MOVE.

61   J. C. Castillo (p.c.) observes that this seems very close to reintroducing the operation MOVE as a primitive: why should the two operations be required to work so
closely together? Answer: They are subparts of a *single* operation. The empirical
payoffs of treating MOVE as a composite operation reside in the relative economy
issues discussed above. It is not clear whether these are sustainable if MOVE is
treated as a true primitive operation. This said, nothing here changes much if
MOVE is a single operation defined in terms of COPY and MERGE, i.e. it is a
bundling of two more primitive operations. There are some possible cases, however, in which COPY is not immediately followed by MERGE in the course of the
derivation. See the discussion of relative clauses in section 8.

62   This is reminiscent of the various parsing constraints that force rapid attachment
of terminals to trees.

63   The prohibition against movement out of adjuncts reduces to the prohibition of making copies of expressions in islands.

64   The locality restriction that this argument exploits is stated in terms of the Shortest Move Condition (SMC) rather than the Minimal Link Condition (MLC). The latter is defined over the output of the grammatical operations not on the process of construction. The MLC can be used to prevent the undesired operation in this case given that one ends up with interleaving chains regardless of how the derivation proceeds. Thus, the case above is only problematic if the SMC is assumed.

65   This general idea is very similar to the one proposed in Weinberg (1999) as part of a minimalist theory of parsing. It is interesting to see that the grammar and the parser exploit similar machinery to achieve computational efficiency.

66   This translates the notion of an island so that what is prevented from an island is not MOVE but COPY. In effect, elements within an Island are invisible to COPY. This view of islands fits well with the idea that islands are frozen expressions, along the lines of Uriagereka (1999).

Observe that this tacitly assumes that one cannot COPY anything in the adjunct and then adjoin the adjunct to some lower position in the phrase marker. This violates Extension and is prohibited.

67   There is some potential evidence that was noted above in the discussion of PGs. Adjuncts cannot form PGs. We attributed this to a failure of GREED. This suggests that adjunction does not check features. However, Jairo Nunes (p.c.) points out that this is consistent with adjuncts having featural requirements that once checked are not checkable again, much like case.

Another potential bit of evidence revolves around the variation between resumptive pronouns and gaps in PG constructions.

(i)   Which book did John read after Mary reviewed (it)

If (bound) pronouns are last resort expressions (see Ch. 5 and Aoun, Choueiri and Hornstein 1999) then this variation can be reduced to the order of the application of the rules of adjunction versus MOVE.

68   If ATTRACT is part of MOVE then similar results could be achieved if one assumed that COPY was dependent on ATTRACT (or AGREE). In other words, if COPY were restricted to apply only if ATTRACT or AGREE held then we would delay the COPY operation to apply when it must and no sooner. Note that restricting COPY to environments where ATTRACT/AGREE hold exploits the same intuition that (57) does. As I have reasons for rejecting ATTRACT based theories of movement (c.f. chapter 4) I prefer using (57) to incorporating ATTRACT/AGREE into MOVE. However, it is worth observing that the latter is likely adequate for reining in the COPY operation so that it does not overgenerate wildly. Note that like the present account that incorporates some version of (57) it would be nice to know why COPY awaits ATTRACT/AGREE. Presumably this is a reflection of the notion that superfluous operations do not apply if not needed to check some feature.

69   In fact, the account would not succeed were 0-operators an option, e.g. it would be impossible to explain given minimalist assumptions why it is that PGs are only licensed in overt syntax.

70   A recent proposal in Kim (1998) can be interpreted as saying that being adjoined to a WH is the only way to escape a CP and occupy myriad case positions. In effect, WHs function to permit two otherwise prohibited possibilities: (i) long movement to A-positions from finite clauses (ii) residence in multiple case positions

by one copy. (i) is made possible by transiting through A′-positions on the way to A-positions in neighboring clauses. This is accomplished by being adjoined to a WH expression whose distinctive property is to be able to move through Spec CP positions. (ii) is similarly made possible by this form of adjunction. The WH and its adjoined nominal can both be assigned case properties and so multiple cases can be checked. This is similar in the A′-domain to what is proposed in chapter 5 for reflexive 'self'.

71   Though not in general. For example, if there were a noun in the array such as 'woman' then at this point of the derivation merging it would be less costly than moving/promoting 'man'. However, it is not clear how serious this observation is. It is always possible to construct all the relevant DPs before creating the RC. In this case, MOVE will be the only option as all the relevant nominals will have been used in the construction of the other DPs. If this is so, the problem above reduces to the example at hand in which only 'man' can/need move.

72   Section 7 left open whether adjunction involved feature checking. If it does, then nothing further need be said as the operation conforms to GREED. If it doesn't, then clearly adjunction must be permissible in the course of a derivation as adjuncts exist. One way of allowing adjunction to apply in place of a feature checking operation relies on Extension as follows: The preferred option would have the promoted head merge with a V to check a theta-feature. However, this merger would prevent the RC from adjoining to the nominal it modifies without violating Extension. If the RC had to adjoin to the nominal to modify it (say this was a bare output condition regarding modification) and if adjuncts had to obey this condition, as argued above in section 4, then this would permit adjunction to intersperse with GREEDy operations.

73   See Hornstein and Lightfoot (1981). Here the discussion is carried out in terms of N′. The approach when revised to fit into a DP based theory will treat NPs as the target of 'one'-substitution.

74   See Kayne (1994) for such a proposal.

75   Chomsky (1977) observed that extraposition out of nominals with possessive determiners is unacceptable.

76   The idea that weak determiners are structurally akin to adjectives goes back to Milsark (1974). This is basically the idea exploited here. See Kim (1998) for further evidence for this assumption.

77   There is one further interesting property of RCs concerning the deletability of the complementizer. This is possible just in case the clause is proximate to the head of the relative. This has been treated as an ECP effect (c.f. Stowell 1981, Aoun, Hornstein, Lightfoot, and Weinberg 1987, Kayne 1984). How this is to be analyzed in minimalist terms is still murky. However, it is plausible that the head noun is "close" enough to license deletion in structures like (68). If deletion is actually incorporation of the complementizer as Pesetsky (1991) has argued, then what we find here is another instance of sidewards movement.

78   The structure of appositive RCs may well be different. Note that these appear to have a DP/DP structure and could be derived along the lines of option 1. It would appear, however, to require that names have (at least covert) determiners to license the required sidewards movement. See Longobardi (1994) for relevant discussion.

79   There is one bit of evidence in favor of treating RCs as of NP/NP form that I put aside here without explanation: it is possible to conjoin the heads of RCs.

(i)   Every man and several kids that I know

If conjunction is limited to constituents, (i) indicates that 'every man' and 'several kids' are such. This follows on an NP/NP theory but not on the 'Det-N' analysis.

There may, however, be a way of accommodating the cases in (i) with a Det N' analysis. It appears that when one conjoins a DP with a strong determiner with a DP with a weak determiner the preferred order is strong-weak. Compare (i) with (ii):

(ii)   ??Several kids and every man that I know

This carries over to cases in which there is no relative clause:

(iii)   a.   Most cars and a few boats have piston engines
         b.   ??A few boats and most cars have piston engines

We could account for this asymmetry by assuming two things: (a) Determiners begin in Spec NP and raise, if strong, to Spec DP; (b) as in many conjunctions, the left conjunct is more grammatically porous than the right conjunct, e.g. consider first conjunct agreement in Arabic.

With these assumptions, we could allow a strong and weak DP to conjoin while both were still NPs and then raise the strong one to a higher Spec DP when it was in the left conjunct. This operation would be illicit if the strong quantifier were on the right side. In effect, conjunctions like those in (iiia) would have structures like (iv):

(iv) $[_{DP}$ most $[_{NP/NP}[_{NP}$ most cars] [and $[_{NP}$ few boats]]]]

If this analysis proves feasible, we could allow conjunction if identical NPs in (i) with a similar kind of raising applying later. The decline in naturalness exemplified in (ii) could then be similarly explained. See Kim (1998) for additional arguments for assuming that determiners raise to Spec DP.

80   See Chomsky (1981: 310ff).
81   See Chomsky (1981: 310) for complications concerning these judgments that are glossed over here, in particular his discussion of the contrast between his examples (11)–(13).
82   See Chomsky (1981: 309 (3b)). He assumes that the 0-operator is identical to PRO. This implicitly treats 'tough'-constructions as complex control structures. If control is reduced to movement, as argued above, then this suggests that 'tough' clauses are movement structures as well.
83   The proposal made below bears a close resemblance to the position argued for in Williams (1983) and developed most fully in Jones (1985, 1991). In particular, Jones argues for the two assumptions most critical here: that the to-please clause in 'tough'-constructions functions very like a sentential adverb (and so can be adjoined high up) and that the subject in these constructions is in a theta-position.
84   I refrain from speculating whether 'Moby Dick' is adjoined to a WH that deletes later. See note 73 for some relevant discussion.
85   Brody (1993) also argues that A-A'-A movement is licit. He does not consider sidewards movement, however.
86   I assume, following Kim (1998) that the content phrase, viz. 'Moby Dick' adjoins to the WH relative.
87   I say of the "relative" variety for there is a well known difference between relative WH features and full blown question WH features. The latter, for example, are not deletable.

88   There are certainly details, perhaps non-trivial, to sort out. For example, in contrast to relative clauses, the WH is never expressed in these constructions. I leave these aside and assume that they can be accommodated. See the discussion on deletion of WH in relative clauses for some discussion.

89   Uriagereka's (1999) approach in terms of SPELL OUT "freezing" structure works just as well.

90   See Chomsky (1981: 309, (4)).

91   Brody (1993) also rules these cases out in terms of Principle C.

92   I leave it as an exercise to the reader to show that if verbs could take complements of the relative WH variety then this sort of illicit movement should be permitted. Jairo Nunes (p.c.) has observed that most of the data discussed in this section could be accommodated simply by distinguishing predicates like 'easy' from those like 'seem' in that the former select WH/relative C^0s while the latter do not. This makes a promotion analysis viable for 'tough'-constructions but not otherwise.

93   Jones (1985 and 1990) also treats these two cases as essentially similar structurally.

94   Note that I assume that 'for Mary' is not a constituent here. There is some evidence that this is incorrect. However, there is also some evidence supporting this view. For example, sentences like (i) are very poor.

(i)   ??For who did John hear that Mary brought a book to review

Moreover, in contrast to benefactive 'for', the one found here is non-strandable.

(ii)   a.   Who did Bill buy a book for
       b.   *Who did Mary bring a book for to review

95   Purpose clauses function as A'-analogues of the 'for' control adjuncts discussed in section 6.

96   The case of relatives is less clear. However, it is possible that the relative head is an A-position.

97   Purpose clauses seem to have restrictions similar to the 'for' control cases discussed in section 6. They both only "fit" with 'v' constructions. However, there are also interesting differences between the two construction types. It seems that the 'for' control cases are more sensitive to the content of the Vs they modify.

(i)   a.   I met someone to introduce to Mary
      b.   I saw someone to introduce to Mary

(ii)   a.   *I met someone for dating Mary
       b.   *I saw someone for dating Mary

This sensitivity to both the presence of 'v' and the content of V might be accommodated by assuing that the 'for' adjunct adjoins to VP. Kato and Nunes (1998) have noted that this puts the adjunct both in the domain of v and V given standard definitions of domain (Chomsky 1995). The purpose clause, on the other hand, could be adjoined higher, to vP for example, thereby making it sensitive to the presence of v, not V.

98   Note that examples such as (i) are not relevant for the 'for' clause is actually an extraposed relative clause as (ii) indicates. This sort of analysis is impossible for cases like (104) in which we use names.

(i)   A letter arrived today for Bill to read

(ii)   A letter for Bill to read arrived today

99   See Kato and Nunes (1998) for a development of this idea concerning adjunction and selection.

100   Note that selection does not imply complementation. See Schein (1993) for discussion.

101   See Chomsky (1982) for some discussion. I am not entirely convinced of this description of the PRO here.

102   It is unclear how good this test is however. It strikes me that sentences like (i) are worse than the one in the text.

(i)   John brought Moby Dick to Mary's house to read to each other

103   'Knock heads over' is an idiom meaning to argue about. It requires a plural subject:

(i)   *John knocked heads over Moby Dick

104   This suggests that relatives are actually licensed by something: perhaps Determiners as has often been suggested.

105   Lasnik and Saito (1992) argue that any expression overtly in an A'-position is frozen there. This is in line with the present proposal. See Aoun, Hornstein and Sportiche (1981) for some additional discussion.

106   Observe that these features may be PF troublesome but LF acceptable. If so, deletion of elements in CP might be required phonetically but not semantically. This might prove useful in 'tough'-constructions and 'purpose' clauses as it might allow the copy in Spec CP to remain at LF and function as an operator. See section 8 for discussion.

107   The same issue arose in section 5 as concerned blocking sidewards movement in raising constructions. Either the NP/NP or the DP had to inherit barrierhood to make account for the CED effects in terms of Barriers.

4

Attract and Sidewards Movement

Introduction

Chapter 3 argues that there are substantial benefits to allowing movement between subtrees. The advantages are both conceptual and empirical. Conceptually, sidewards movement is all but inevitable once (a) MOVE is resolved into COPY and MERGE and (b) the grammar builds structures in parallel. This does not mean to say that UG cannot be shaped so as to exclude sidewards movement. However, it requires complicating UG to do so. Sidewards movement's empirical payoffs are the accounts of adjunct control and 0-operator constructions (in particular parasitic gap phenomena) outlined in chapter 3.

This chapter proceeds on the assumption that generalizing MOVE so as not to preclude sidewards movement is well motivated. The aim is to see what this implies for approaches to movement that incorporate some version of ATTRACT as a sub-operation. My claim will be that incorporating ATTRACT into MOVE threatens the viability of sidewards movement operations. I conclude from this that MOVE does not involve an operation like ATTRACT. This conclusion, however, requires reanalyzing the favored current approach to multiple interrogative constructions which exploits the logic of ATTRACT to account for Superiority Effects. I examine these arguments and reanalyze the relevant data in terms compatible with permitting sidewards movement.

1   Two Views of MOVE

Every approach to movement imposes locality restrictions on the operation. Standard minimalist approaches incorporate some version of (relativized) minimality which prohibits moving an expression over another expression of the same type.[1] The intuition behind minimality can be implemented in at least two distinct ways. The first takes a target centered view of the MOVE operation. The second is launch based and focuses on the expression being moved rather than the position to which it moves. Consider each version in turn.

The target centered version of minimality measures the relative length of a movement from the perspective of the target of the operation. For example, in a structure like (1), where XP_1 c-commands XP_2 the distance between XP_1 and the target T is shorter than the distance between XP_2 and T so this blocks the movement of XP_2 to T.

(1)   T [. . XP$_1$ . . . XP$_2$ . .]

There are various ways to compute distance and we return to review these below. However, the thing to focus on here is the fact that whatever the metric for computing distance, the target centered approach anchors the measurement with respect to the target of the operation. In effect, (2a) is blocked because the span of the indicated movement, i.e. the length of the XP$_2$-chain, is longer than the equally available, but "shorter" XP$_1$-chain in (2b).

(2)   a.   XP$_2$ [T [. . . XP$_1$ . . XP$_2$ . .]]
       b.   XP$_1$ [T [. . . XP$_1$ . . . XP$_2$ . . .]]

A second implementation of the minimality idea centers on the expression moving rather than the position it targets. For a movement to be licit it must be greedy. Thus, some feature must be checked as a result of the MOVE operation. Say that (at least one of) the features that requires checking is on the expression being moved. Minimality requires that an XP's movement be the shortest possible to check this feature. For example, in configurations in which P^1 c-commands P^2, XP cannot pass over a position P^1 on its way to P^2 in which it checks feature F if F could have just as well been checked in P^1. Given this conception, the movement indicated in (2a) is perfectly licit so long as the feature on XP$_2$ could not have been checked in any position between XP$_2$ and T. The fact that XP$_1$ is closer to T (the position in which a feature is checked) is irrelevant so long as XP$_2$'s move is the shortest one possible *for XP2*.[2]

These different implementations of minimality have important consequences for sidewards movement. Consider why. Both conceptions define the metric of locality in terms of c-command. The target centered notion only compares the relative distances of expressions c-commanded by a target T. In other words, elements not c-commanded by T cannot be compared with respect to distance and so can be considered equi-distant from a given target. The second conception also invokes c-command but in a different manner. The only intervening positions relevant for computing minimality are the ones that c-command the expression that moves. In other words, if YP fails to c-command XP then its presence is irrelevant for computing shortest moves. This notion is also invoked in many target centered theories that incorporate ATTRACT into the definition of MOVE. We return to discuss examples below.

Of these two ways of thinking about minimality, the second is incompatible with sidewards movement for the target of movement can never c-command the expression that moves in cases where the movement is between subtrees. An illustration should help make the point clear. Recall that chapter 3 argued that adjunct control involves sidewards movement from the adjunct to a theta-position in a neighboring vP. This is illustrated in (3).

(3)   [DP$_1$ [v [V DP$_2$]]] [$_{adjunct}$ DP$_1$ . . .]

In (3), DP$_1$ moves from the adjunct to the Spec vP of a separate subtree. Two features of this movement are noteworthy in the present context. First, as it is a case of sidewards movement, the target, in this case v, does not c-command the adjunct and so fails to c-command the expression which has moved, i.e. DP_1, prior to movement. On the assumption that movement requires attraction and that attraction requires c-command, this sort of movement should be illicit. Second, DP_2 does not prevent the indicated movement. This would be surprising if ATTRACT were operative. The reason is that v does c-command DP_2 so one might expect the movement of DP_2 to v to be preferred to (and so block) the movement of DP_1 from the adjunct.

Note that the postulated sidewards movement operation is not problematic if MOVE is subject to the launch based conception of minimality outlined above. DP_2 does not c-command DP_1 so cannot block the movement of DP_1 to Spec vP. Moreover, this is the shortest move DP_1 can licitly make, e.g. that respects Greed. Thus, this case of sidewards movement respects the launch centered version of minimality.

Approaches to movement that incorporate ATTRACT are target centered in the sense applicable here and so are incompatible with sidewards movement. Thus, ATTRACT based approaches to movement are incompatible with the analyses outlined in chapter 3. As I am assuming that these analyses are essentially correct, this requires rethinking the arguments in favor of theories of movement that incorporate ATTRACT.[3] We proceed to this next.

2   Arguments for Attract

The principal argument in favor of a definition of movement incorporating ATTRACT is empirical. It is critical to most current analyses of Superiority Effects.[4]

(4)   a.   I wonder who saw what
       b.   *I wonder what who saw

The contrast between (4a) and (4b) can be explained if MOVE is understood as involving ATTRACT. Consider the details.

The structure of the sentences in (4) prior to movement to Spec CP is (5).

(5)   ... [C^0 [$_{IP}$ [$_{IP}$ who I^0 [$_{vP}$ who [$_{VP}$ saw what]]]]]

The C^0 has a strong WH feature that requires checking by a WH element. Both 'who' and 'what' can satisfy this need. The movement of 'who' is preferred for the distance it must travel is shorter than the distance 'what' must traverse to check the feature. More specifically, the set of nodes between the head of the A'-chain formed by moving 'who' is a subset of those formed by moving 'what'.

(6)   a.   ... [$_{CP}$ who [$_{IP}$ who I^0 [$_{vP}$ who [$_{VP}$ saw what]]]]
       b.   ... [$_{CP}$ what [$_{IP}$ who I^0 [$_{vP}$ who [$_{VP}$ saw what]]]]

The path traversed by moving 'who' is the set of nodes {CP, IP}. Moving 'what' yields the path {CP, IP, vP, VP}. As the former is a subset of the latter, moving 'who' is shorter and so is required. This accounts for the unacceptability of (4b).

This basic account of Superiority Effects can also account for a variety of apparent exceptions to the condition. For example, Superiority Effects are obviated when 'which' phrases are moved. Thus the relative acceptability of the sentences in (7) is roughly on a par.

(7)   a.   I wonder which book which man saw
      b.   I wonder which man saw which book

This follows if we are careful in computing the paths formed by the two movements.[5] Recall that what drives the movement in these examples is the requirement to check a strong WH feature of C^0. What is attracted, therefore, are WH features. These features reside in 'which' in the DPs in (7). The relevant structures of (7) are provided in (8).

(8)   a.   ... [$_{CP}$ [$_{DP1}$ which book] C^0 [$_{IP}$ [$_{DP2}$ which man] [$_{vP}$ [$_{DP2}$ which man] [$_{VP}$ saw [$_{DP1}$ which book]]]]]
      b.   ... [$_{CP}$ [$_{DP2}$ which man] C^0 [$_{IP}$ [$_{DP2}$ which man] [$_{vP}$ [$_{DP2}$ which man] [$_{VP}$ saw [$_{DP1}$ which book]]]]]

The 'C^0' attracts the WH features in 'which'. The relevant paths therefore are {CP, DP1, IP, vP, VP} for (8a) and {DP2, IP} for (8b). Note that neither path is a subset of the other. As such, either 'which' phrase may move to Spec CP as neither move is longer than the other.[6] Thus, on the assumption that 'which' phrases are complex DPs while simple WH phrases like 'who', 'what', etc are simplex, we can account for the lack of Superiority Effects with complex WH DPs.[7]

This general approach to Superiority has been very successful in accounting for the basic superiority data. Extensions have also been elaborated to account for a wide array of cross linguistic differences manifested by multiple interrogative constructions in a variety of languages.[8] In what follows I consider some problems for an approach to Superiority that relies on a target centered measure of distance. I will also offer an alternative way of accounting for these effects that dispenses with ATTRACT.

3   Problems for ATTRACT

There are various examples in the literature that raise problems for an ATTRACT based approach to Superiority Effects. I review these here.

First consider the following examples from Kayne (1984). Kayne observes that Superiority effects are mitigated when additional WH elements are added. He observes the contrast in (9).

(9) a. *John wonders what who saw then
     b. John wonders what who saw when

(9a) is a standard Superiority violation. What is curious, as Kayne observes, is that the effect seems to go away when we replace the pronominal adverb 'then' with the WH word 'when', as in (9b).

Observe that this is hard to account for if Superiority violations are analyzed in terms of Shortest Move based on ATTRACT. The distance that 'what' moves in (9a) and (9b) is the same. In both cases 'who' is closer to 'C⁰' than 'what' is. Thus, both sentences should have the same status. This is not what we find. (9a) is unacceptable while (9b) is fine.

Lasnik and Saito (1992) discuss a second problematic case.[9]

(10) Who wonders what who bought

(10) is ambiguous. The 'who' in the subject position of the embedded clause can be either paired with 'what' in the embedded Spec CP or with 'who' in the matrix comp. The former pairing leads to a structure in which we expect a standard Superiority violation and under this reading the sentence is indeed judged unacceptable. This contrasts with the acceptability of the sentence on the interpretation in which the embedded 'who' is paired with the matrix 'who'. An appropriate answer to this question would be: "John wonders what Bill bought and Mary wonders what Sheila bought." On this reading the sentence is fine.

Once again, this makes little sense given the standard analysis in terms of ATTRACT. Whether or not the embedded subject is paired with the matrix or embedded WH does not alter the fact that 'who' is closer to the embedded 'C⁰' than 'what' is. This should prevent moving 'what' over 'who' and should result in a violation of Superiority irrespective of the reading being considered. Let me put this another way. The analysis of Superiority Effects in terms of ATTRACT is purely formal. It identifies the shortest path to 'C⁰' and this alone is decisive in determining which WH element can move. Lasnik and Saito's case indicates that this is not sufficient. Rather, their example indicates that it is necessary to factor in interpretation in evaluating acceptability.

4 Another Approach to Superiority

It is interesting to observe that the cases discussed above are only problematic if one adopts a target centered view of minimality. If one adopts the perspective of the expression moved then the shortest (A'-) move that any WH can make is to its local Spec CP. Thus, in all of these cases, there is no violation of Shortest Move. The problem, however, is that this reasoning leaves Superiority Effects unaccounted for. In this section, I revisit an approach to Superiority first outlined in Hornstein (1995: ch. 7). It has the virtue of yielding an account of Superiority Effects without exploiting target centered conceptions of minimality based on ATTRACT. It also accounts for the data in section 3. The proposal in Hornstein (1995) is based on Chierchia (1992).[10] The basic idea is as follows. A WH *in situ* is interpreted functionally.[11] The idea is to treat functionally interpreted WHs as similar to bound pronouns within complex DPs. An example should make the core of the proposal clear.

Consider a sentence like (11) in which 'his' is understood as bound by 'everyone'. This sentence is true just in case there is a pairing of every relevant person in the domain with another individual, namely that person's mother, and the relevant individual loves the person he is paired with. In other words, one can understand a bound pronoun in cases such as this as establishing a function whose range is a set of individuals and whose domain consists of mothers of those individuals.

(11)   Everyone loves his mother

Assume that the same sort of relation is established in multiple interrogative constructions. In other words, assume that in (12) the 'what' in object position functions like 'his mother' in (11).

(12)   Who saw what

For concreteness, let's assume that a functionally interpreted WH actually resolves into a bound pronominal part and a nominal restrictor, i.e. a part corresponding to 'his' in (11) and a part corresponding to 'mother'. This provides (12) with a structure like (13).

(13) $[_{CP}$ Who$_i$ $[_{IP}$ t$_i$ saw [pro$_i$ thing](=what)]]

Given this much, it is possible to assimilate Superiority Effects to Weak Cross Over (WCO) Effects. For example, the unacceptability of (14a) can be analyzed as a Weak Cross Over violation. The indicated binding conforms to a Weak Cross Over configuration and the unacceptability of (14) is roughly on a par with that of (15), a standard WCO violation.

(14)   a.   *What did who see
       b. $[_{CP}$ What$_i$ $[_{IP}$ [pro$_i$ person](=who) see t$_i$]]

(15)   *Who$_i$ did his$_i$ mother see t$_i$?

Observe that the binding indicated in (13) is not of the Weak Cross Over variety and so (12) is fully acceptable.

Hornstein (1995: ch. 6) argues that the correct interpretation of pronoun binding is in terms of linking.[12] Assume that this is correct. The Weak Cross Over Condition can then be stated as (16).

(16)   A pronoun cannot be linked to a WH-t/variable to its right

The gist of the proposal then is that WHs *in situ* are analyzed as functionally interpreted expressions on a par with bound pronouns. Moreover, binding is understood as linking. We have seen how these assumptions suffice to account for standard cases of Superiority, e.g. (14) above. The same assumptions account for the cases described in section 2. Consider the details.

The Lasnik and Saito cases have the structure in (17) (irrelevant details omitted).

(17)   Who wonders [CP what$_i$ [IP who bought t$_i$]]

The current proposal says that the embedded 'who' must be functionally interpreted in a multiple question. It can be so interpreted with respect to the WH in the matrix or the embedded CP. The two relevant readings are diagrammed in (18).

(18)   a.   Who$_i$ [IP t$_i$ wonders [CP what$_j$ [IP [pronoun$_j$ person] bought t$_j$]]]
       b.   Who$_i$ [IP t$_i$ wonders [CP what$_j$ [IP [pronoun$_j$ person] bought t$_j$]]]

In (18a) the "functional" pronoun is linked to the matrix trace 't$_i$'. This linking is in conformity with the Weak Cross Over Condition (16) as 't$_i$' is to the left of the bound pronoun. Hence the structure is well formed and the sentence is acceptable.

In (18b), in contrast, the pronoun is linked to the trace/variable of the embedded 'what'. This trace/variable, 't$_j$', is to the right of the bound pronoun. This linking violates the Weak Cross Over Condition and so the structure is illicit. This is why the sentence under this reading is unacceptable.

Consider now the case discussed by Kayne (1984). He observes that the addition of WHs obviates the effects of Superiority in multiple interrogatives. The sentences, repeated here, have the structures in (19) with the indicated functional dependency of the WH *in situ*.

(9)   a.   *John wonders what who saw then
       b.   John wonders what who saw when

(19)   a.   John wonders [CP what$_i$ [IP [pronoun$_i$ person] saw t$_i$ then]]
       b.   John wonders [CP what$_i$ [IP [pronoun1$_i$ person] saw t$_i$ [pronoun2$_i$ person]]]

In (19a), the pronoun is linked to a WH-t/variable to its right, in violation of (16). The addition of an extra WH, which must also be functionally interpreted, allows the structure to conform to (16). Consider how. Assume that the following linking relations obtain: pronoun2 is linked to t$_i$ and pronoun1 is linked to pronoun2. This linking is perfectly legitimate. Moreover, the linkings conform to (16) as no pronoun is linked to a WH-t/variable on its right. If Superiority is simply an instance of the WCO effect then we expect the presence of additional WHs which require functional interpretations to ameliorate otherwise unacceptable sentences. Note that the same account extends to explain the improvement in (20b) when an additional bound pronoun is introduced. In (20a) the pronoun is linked to a WH-t/variable to its right. In (20b) it can be linked to the genitive pronoun in the 'mother'-DP, which is in turn linked to the WH-t/variable to its left. This multiple linking, which extra pronouns make available leads to the attenuation of the WCO effect in a manner parallel to that witnessed in (19). This parallel behavior of bound pronouns and functionally interpreted WHs in WCO and Superiority contexts supports the type of analysis proposed here.[13]

(20) a. *Who$_i$ did his$_i$ father talk to t$_i$ about Mary
      b. Who$_i$ did his$_i$ father talk to t$_i$ about his$_i$ mother

5   The Limited Scope of Superiority Effects

There is an additional argument in favor of the approach that assimilates Superiority to Weak Cross Over. It comes from considering the fact that most cases of multiple A'-movement fail to manifest Superiority Effects. Superiority Effects are absent in focus constructions and echo questions. Given the analysis in section 3, we only expect Superiority to appear in cases where a functional dependency among WH expressions is established. Where there is no such relation, linking does not obtain and the Weak Cross Over Condition should be inoperative. In this section, we review some recent analyses that suggest that this expectation is realized.

Romanian and Bulgarian are languages that require all WHs to front in multiple interrogative constructions. For example, the translation of (21a) in Romanian has the 'ce' (=what) overtly move to pre-sentential position.[14]

(21) a. who saw what
      b. Cine ce a vazut
          who what saw

Interestingly, this requirement carries over to echo-questions. Comorovski (1996: 59ff) observes that Superiority Effects are cancelled in echo questions. This is illustrated by (22).

(22) Despre ce cine ti a vorbit
      about what who to you has told
      "Who told you about what"

(22) is ill formed under a standard question intonation. This is expected given that Romanian displays Superiority Effects and in this case we are raising a PP containing a WH over a subject. In terms of the analysis presented in section 3, the problem with (22) as a standard multiple question is that it induces a Weak Cross Over Effect. The structure is that of (23) at LF.[15]

(23) what$_i$ [[pronoun$_i$ person] told you about t$_i$]

The pronoun in (23) is linked to a WH-t/variable to its right in violation of (16). Thus, the multiple interrogative is ill-formed as it violates Weak Cross Over/Superiority.

However, Comorovski notes that (22) is perfectly acceptable with an echo interpretation. She similarly observes that the English counterparts of (22) seem immune to Superiority in echo questions (Comorovski 1996: 59 (8)).

(24) a. It was a unicorn that Esmeralda saw
       b. *What* did *who* see (italics indicate stress for echo intonation)

Comorovski (1996: 60) makes a methodological point concerning these data with which I am fully sympathetic.

> The positive effect of echo intonation on the acceptability of a question shows that the unacceptability of the corresponding standard question is not due to a violation of a principle of syntax, but is rather related to semantic properties with respect to which echo wh-phrases differ from non-echo ones.

The absence of Superiority Effects is expected if the latter are simply the result of linkings in violation of Weak Cross Over. Echo questions do not establish functional relations between the WHs. There is no appropriate pair-list answer available to echo questions. Consequently, there is no linking and so no threat of a violation of (16). As such, Superiority should be, and is, inoperative.

Comorovski provides further evidence for the analysis in section 3. She notes that echo WHs are generally immune from Weak Cross Over considerations. She provides the following examples (p. 67, (20)–(22)).[16]

(25) a. His$_i$ mother saw *who$_i$*
       b. Mary said that his$_i$ mother yelled at *who$_i$*

If Superiority and Weak Cross Over both reflect the limitations that (16) imposes on linking, as proposed in section 3, then we expect to see this pair of effects swing in tandem.

Let me quickly recap. Given the analysis in section 3, the expectation is that Superiority Effects will arise in multiple interrogatives just in case the relevant WHs are functionally interpreted. The reason is that functionally interpreted WHs require linking and this linking is subject to (16). The hall mark of a multiple question with a functionally interpreted WH is the appropriateness of a pair-list answer to the question. Echo questions do not license such answers. Hence they do not (or need not) involve functionally interpreted WHs. Hence we predict the absence of Superiority and Weak Cross Over effects in echo questions. Comorovski (1996) shows that these theoretical expectations are fulfilled.

Bosković (1999) presents evidence from Serbo-Croatian (SC) that points to a similar conclusion as the one reached above. Following Stjepanović (1995) he argues that SC obligatorily focuses WH expressions. This is an instance of focus movement rather than WH movement, he argues, as there is no required pair-list answer in such cases. Rather it is possible to felicitously answer these questions with singleton answers (e.g. it is felicitous to ask 'Who bought what?' when the asker expects only a singleton answer like 'John bought a book' in reply). Only movement to CP, Bosković argues, forces a pair-list answer in a clause with multiply fronted WHs. Interestingly, these multiple WH constructions which allow singleton answers, do not exhibit Superiority Effects. If pair-list answers are taken as diagnostic of a functional dependency and only functional dependencies are subject to the linking condition (16), then we do not expect to find Superiority Effects in the cases discussed by Bosković. In effect, there is a complete parallel between the SC data and the Romanian data discussed above and we can treat them in an entirely parallel fashion.[17]

6   Conclusion

This chapter has attempted to make the grammar safe for sidewards movement. Doing this requires dispensing with Attract, as a prerequisite of Move. The reason is that sidewards movement and Attract based conceptions of Move fit poorly together. The intuition behind Attract based approaches to Move is that the target of movement guides the displacement operation. If locality is then executed in terms of c-command, the usual practice, this forces moved expressions to be in the c-domain of the positions they target. For movements within a single subtree movement conforming to Attract will be enforced by the Extension Condition. However, whereas Extension will permit movement between subtrees, Attract under the most straightforward interpretation will ban this sort of operation. Thus, if we are to adopt sidewards as a viable grammatical option we must reject the analysis of Move in terms of Attract.

The cost of doing this, I hope to have shown, is empirically negligible. The primary advantage to Attract based approaches to Move involves the analysis of Superiority Effects. This chapter has aimed to show that these data can be accounted for (as well if not better) without adverting to Attract. The linking/ Weak Cross Over approach to Superiority sketched above has two virtues. First, it is at least as empirically adequate as the alternative Attract based analyses. Second, it makes room for the possibility of sidewards movement. Given the utility of sidewards movement in accounting for adjunct control, parasitic gaps and other 0-operator constructions, it is reasonable to analyze Move independently of Attract and, perhaps, eliminate Attract entirely from the inventory of basic grammatical operations.

Appendix 1   On Tucking In

Richards (1997, 1999) offers a hybrid theory of movement which combines features of both MOVE and ATTRACT. This appendix makes a few critical observations concerning one particularly interesting application of his view to the case of multiple interrogatives in Bulgarian (and Romanian).

Rudin (1988) observed that there are many languages that front all the WH expressions in a clause. She argued that Romanian and Bulgarian did so by moving all the WH elements to CP. She contrasted Bulgarian and Romanian from Polish and Czech in that the latter two moved some WH elements to pre IP position but only one expression to CP. There were two kinds of evidence that Rudin used to distinguish these two languages. First, Bulgarian and Romanian, in contrast to Polish and Czech, displayed superiority effects. Second, the latter two languages allowed elements to intersperse with the fronted WH elements while Bulgarian and Romanian forbade this.[18]

Richards reanalyzed Rudin's superiority data for Bulgarian.[19] Richards' idea is the following. Consider a language like Bulgarian in which one finds multiple WHs at the front of the clause. These, he suggests, get there in the following two step process. On the first step, the highest WH is attracted to check the WH feature of the relevant C^0. Once checked, the other WHs move up as well.[20] However, they move in the shortest possible way to check a feature against C^0. This shortest possible movement has the expressions "tuck in" under the first attracted WH. Thus, a multiple WH construction in Bulgarian has the structure in (26) with the numbers on the WH elements indicating their order of movement. First, WH_1 is attracted to check a feature of C^0. Then WH_2 moves and tucks in under WH_1. Richards reasons that it tucks in, rather than extend the tree, as tucking in requires a shorter move than the one that derives (27).

(26) $[WH_1 [WH_2 [C^0 [WH_1 \ldots \ldots WH_2 \ldots]]]]$

(27) $[WH_2 [WH_1 [C^0 [WH_1 \ldots \ldots WH_2 \ldots]]]]$

Richards' analysis has the virtue of deriving the order of WHs in Spec CP in Bulgarian (and Romanian). Note that the analysis assumes that in these languages +WH CP can have multiple specifiers. In fact, tucking in is a necessary feature of multiple specifier constructions due to Shortest Move.

Why else assume that Bulgarian and Romanian have multiple specifiers in CP?[21] One reason is to accommodate the fact that Bulgarian and Romanian appear to violate the WH island constraint. This would be explained if CPs had multiple escape hatches, i.e. multiple Spec CP positions.

The interest of Richards' theory for current concerns is that it offers another argument in favor of ATTRACT. The empirical case that Richards makes is interesting, but, I do not believe that it is compelling. Here's why.

First, Richards observes that tucking in should only occur in multiple specifier structures. There are two bits of evidence for Bulgarian and Romanian having multiple specifiers. The first is the observed order of WHs in a multiple interrogative construction. The second is the claim that these languages violate the WH island constraint. Consider the second point first.

It is not quite correct that these languages freely violate the WH island condition. The reason is that only specific (d-linked) WHs are able to leave

WH islands, as Comorovski (1996) and Cinque (1990) have observed. This restriction is quite unexpected under a multiple specifier analysis. If there are multiple escape hatches for WH then any WH that can move long distance should be able to escape a WH island. However, this is apparently incorrect.

What could account for the restriction to specific/d-linked WHs? It has been observed that in these languages Topic nodes reside above CP. It is plausible that specific WHs are sufficiently Topic-like to be able to use this node as an escape hatch.[22] If this were so, we could explain the observed limitation on WH movement from WH islands. However, if this is what is actually going on, then the fact that WHs can escape WH islands in these languages is no longer evidence for a multiple specifier structure for CP in these languages.

What of the observed order of WH elements in multiple interrogative constructions? It is well known that in many languages, subjects are "default" topics. What this means is that in the absence of an otherwise specified topic, the subject functions as topic of the sentence. Say this were to hold in Bulgarian and Romanian as well. Then, in a multiple interrogative structure, where we have a bunch of non-(morphologically marked) specific, non-d-linked WHs we would expect the subject to function as the default topic. If topics move to topic positions, then we would expect these subject WHs to appear on the left periphery of the clause in multiple interrogative constructions.[23] The structures would look like (28).

(28) $[_{topic}$ WH$_1$ $[_{CP}$ WH$_2$ $[C^0$ [WH$_1$ . . . . . . WH$_2$ . . .]]]]

Observe that the derivation of (28) can proceed in the standard fashion, progressively extending the phrase marker. Note, however, to so derive (28) requires *violating* ATTRACT. *WH$_2$* moves over *WH$_1$* on its way to Spec CP.[24] This is a possible derivation given a mover based view of minimality, but not a target centered approach.[25]

Note, that this proposal gains support from the fact that one can find WH expressions that move over the subject in Bulgarian and Romanian. We observed above that echo questions freely violate superiority. Moreover, if the leftmost WH in a multiple interrogative structure is specific, then sentences with the configuration in (27) are fully acceptable (see, for example, Comorovski (1996: 152–3)).

So, if we assume that specific WHs can move to topic positions in multiple interrogatives and that subject WHs are default topics in such constructions, then we accommodate the key evidence that the multiple specifier theory adduces in its favor.[26]

We also make an interesting prediction concerning such languages. We have noted that it is possible to move out of WH islands in languages like Bulgarian. What happens if we have multiple WHs inside a WH island?

(29) C_{+WH} [. . . . . . $[_{CP}$ C_{+WH} [WH$_1$ . . . . . WH$_2$ . . .]]]

In (29), *WH$_1$* is a subject WH.

According to the multiple specifier analysis, WH_1 should move to the lower CP and there check the WH feature. If, like English, checking a +WH feature "freezes" the element in place, much like checking case (see chapter 3, appendix 1), then the only well formed sentence should have the structure (30) in which WH_1 is attracted by the lower +WH C while the upper +WH C attracts WH_2.[27] Note that (30) assumes that WH_2 moves via Spec CP from a "tucked in" position.[28]

(30) $[WH_2 \ [C_{+WH} \ [\ldots \ldots \ [_{CP} \ WH_1 \ WH_2 \ [C_{+WH} \ [WH_1 \ldots \ldots WH_2 \ldots]]]]]]$

In contrast, if the formation of multiple interrogatives proceeds by moving through a topic position (above the CP position) then we should see a different pattern of possible movements. It will depend on which of the WH elements is able to move via the Topic position. We should expect to see the following pattern. In the absence of clearly marked d-linked WHs the subject WH will function as the topic. Thus we should find a structure like (31) as the preferred option. In cases where the WH elements are potentially topics (i.e. are like 'which' phrases in English), then we should find that either structure in (32) is well formed.

(31) $[WH_1 \ [C_{+WH} \ [\ldots \ldots \ [_{Topic} \ WH_1 \ [_{CP} \ WH_2 \ [C_{+WH} \ [WH_1 \ldots \ldots WH_2 \ldots]]]]]]]$

(32)   a. $[WH_1 \ [C_{+WH} \ [\ldots \ldots \ [_{Topic} \ WH_1 \ [_{CP} \ WH_2 \ [C_{+WH} \ [WH_1 \ldots \ldots WH_2 \ \ldots]]]]]]]$
       b. $[WH_2 \ [C_{+WH} \ [\ldots \ldots \ [_{Topic} \ WH_2 \ [_{CP} \ WH_1 \ [C_{+WH} \ [WH_1 \ldots \ldots WH_2 \ \ldots]]]]]]]$

The evidence suggests that the latter set of predictions is correct.[29] The following appears to be what occurs in Bulgarian.[30]

There is a distinct contrast in the examples in (33) with (33a) clearly superior to (33b).[31]

(33)   a.   Koj se chudish   kakvo si e kupil
            who refl wonder-2sg what refl is bought
            "Who do you wonder what bought"
       b.   Kakvo se chudish koj si e kupil
            "What do you wonder who bought"

Note that (33) uses "simple" WH expressions that correspond to the English *who, what* variety. In this case, if we assume that subjects are "natural" topics, then only the WH corresponding to 'who', viz. *koj*, should be able to escape the embedded WH island. Interestingly, the only case that should be acceptable on the multiple specifier approach, i.e. (33a), seems to be comparatively unacceptable.

When d-linked WH expressions are employed, the empirical landscape changes as well. In this instance, both WH expressions can extract and there is no real difference between the two cases.[32]

(34) a. Koj covek   se chudish   koja   kniga si e kupil
         which person refl wonder-2sg which book refl   is bought
         "Which person do you wonder what book bought"
     b. Koja kniga se chudish koj covek e kupil
         "Which book do you wonder which person bought"

Note that this is precisely what the second account predicts.[33]

In sum, the above indicates that there are empirical problems for the multiple specifier analysis of multiple interrogatives in Bulgarian and Romanian. As the mixed ATTRACT/MOVE analysis in Richards (1997, 1999) is based on this sort of approach, there is reason to believe that his arguments for ATTRACT can be reanalyzed. This would allow us to dispense with ATTRACT and stick to a MOVE based account of dislocation. This would, in turn, leave sidewards movement as a viable grammatical operation.[34]

Notes

1 See Rizzi (1990: ch. 1).
2 As David Lightfoot (p.c.) points out this version implies that the locality of V movement is due to minimality. It has been observed independently that this is likely to be so as it is finite Vs that are at issue in most cases and the lack of movement of non-finite Vs can therefore be independently ruled out.
3 Note that such theories are more complex in the following sense. Virtually all current minimalist theories adopt some version of the copy theory of movement. Thus, they all analyze MOVE as involving at least COPY and MERGE as suboperations. Approaches differ as to whether in addition to this one ought to have a suboperation of ATTRACT. Clearly adding ATTRACT in this way makes the operation more complex.
4 There are some conceptual arguments advanced in Chomsky (1995) for treating MOVE in terms of ATTRACT. However, I consider them weak reasons at best. Chomsky (1998) seems to agree as this paper drops ATTRACT on conceptual grounds. However, his AGREE operation has many of the features of ATTRACT and is subject to many of the objections outlined below against target based conceptions of MOVE.
5 This is suggested in Koizumi (1995).
6 This argument relies on the non-counting property of grammars. Note that in computing distance via subsets we need not count the number of nodes traversed.
7 This assumption is somewhat controversial. It is semantically reasonable to treat 'who' and 'what' as semantically composite including both WH features and phi-features. The only question is whether there is syntactic complexity as well. Tsai (1994) and Wu (1999) provide arguments that even these WHs have internal structure. If so, the analysis presented above is empirically threatened. See below for an alternative analysis that does not rely on the assumption that 'who' etc. are syntactically simplex.

   Joseph Aoun (p.c.) points out that this analysis implies that in languages in which the WH can move independently of the DP it is a part of that it should be possible to have structures like (i).

   (i)   Whi [[WH NP] . . . . . [t$_i$ NP] . . .]

The French example (ii) exemplifies this structure.

(ii) Je me demande combien$_i$ quelle fille a lu t$_i$ de livre
      I   me ask   how many which girl has read of books
      "I wonder how many books which girl read"

Unfortunately, contrary to expectations, (i) is unacceptable. Cedric Boeckx informs me that similar sorts of sentences are available in Serbo-Croatian with equally unacceptable results. This suggests that this way of dealing with the cases in (7) is empirically incorrect. For purposes of further discussion, however, I assume that these problems can be resolved.

8 See, for example, Bosković (1999), Grohmann (1998), and Richards (1999) for some recent applications of this reasoning to multiple interrogatives in Serbo-Croatian, Bulgarian and German.

9 This case is also discussed in Reinhart (1995).

10 I do not go into great detail here as the proposal is extensively discussed in Hornstein (1995). What I observe here is that this approach has certain virtues when considered against the backdrop of sidewards movement. In addition, it has the empirical virtue of handling a range of data that are problematic for an ATTRACT based theory of MOVE.

11 This idea is independently developed in Comorovski (1996) and Reinhart (1995). Comorovski observes that treating the dependent WH in multiple interrogatives as having a functional interpretation has considerable independent motivation. For example, it accounts for why the interpretation of a singular interrogative phrase in multiple questions involves universal quantification. For a discussion of these and other relevant issues concerning the functional interpretation of WHs see Comorovski (1996, esp. ch. 2).

12 This is first proposed by Higginbotham (1983).

13 See Hornstein (1995) for additional arguments in favor of this approach to Superiority Effects.

14 The same is true for Bulgarian. For discussion see Rudin (1988). For additional review of this material see Hornstein (1995: ch. 7).

15 I translate the relevant sentence into English. The structures are the same.

16 The b example is from Postal (1971).

17 Bosković (1999) accounts for the absence of Superiority in Focus constructions by assuming that in this case the focus head must attract *all* the focused elements. Thus, there is a difference between attracting a single feature F and all instances of a feature F. When only one feature is attracted then Superiority is expected. When all features are, it isn't.

There are two problems with this approach to the absence of Superiority Effects. First, the issue is entirely featural. Thus, if Bosković is correct, nothing prevents a language just like SC but with C attracting all +WH expressions while focus would only attract a single focused expression. Thus he predicts the existence of a language in which focus is subject to Superiority but multiple interrogatives are not. Boskovic's analysis predicts this because his analysis treats the asymmetry in purely formal terms unrelated to the kind of reading or dependencies that one finds in these construction types. I suspect that this prediction is incorrect and that this option is never realized. Note the analysis presented in section 3 ties the presence of Superiority to the specific functional interpretation present in certain multiple interrogatives. Where this is absent we have no reason to expect Superiority at all.

There is a second feature of Boskovic's account that is problematic. He claims that if a head selects all instances of a feature F then, from the point of view of economy, there is no advantage to moving some F laden expressions before others. As he puts it:

Regardless of whether the wh-phrases move in 1-2-3, 1-3-2, 2-1-3, 2-3-1, 3-1-2, or 3-2-1 order, the same number of nodes will be crossed to satisfy the Attract all focused elements inadequacy of the relevant head. Hence by economy, he argues, all orders should be possible. Boskovic thereby accounts for the lack of Superiority effects with focus-movement.

This reasoning, however, only holds if one takes a global interpretation of economy. By the 'end' of the derivation the same number of nodes in total will have been crossed. However, the net effect of all these movements is irrelevant if it is 'local' economy that is relevant. For at any given point in the derivation, movement of the closer WH should be preferred on this conception. As such, an ordering should be imposed with the highest WH moving first, then the next highest etc. until the lowest WH is moved up. This, at least, is how things should proceed if economy is taken in the way that Chomsky (1995) takes it in his discussion of raising. He observes that "there seems a man to be in the room" is blocked by "there seems to be a man in the room" but only if it is local economy that is relevant. Globally, both sentences exploit the same total numbers of Merge and Move operations. What makes the latter sentence preferable is that it Merges *at a point in the derivation* where the other moves.

I take these two problems to cast doubt on Boskovic's analysis.

18 See Rudin (1988) for further discussion. The status of this last fact is unclear. Z. Boskovic (p.c.) informs me that the status of this contrast is quite unclear as the relevant languages do not contrast as clearly as Rudin suggested. Rudin accounted for the lack of interspersed elements by having all the WH elements in Bulgarian and Romanian form one large WH by adjoining to each other. This plausibly explains why nothing can intervene between any two. The more modern accounts based on her work deny that a "giant" WH is formed. Rather multiple specifiers are recruited. However, multiple specifiers do not account for the lack of interspersed elements without further stipulation. In what follows, I drop discussion of this second phenomenon.

19 He does not discuss Romanian but I assume that the analysis should extend to it as well.

20 Richards does not say what feature is checked by this movement. However, it is not necessarily a WH feature as this movement can serve as an escape hatch for further WH movement. See below. Bosković (1999) allows focus movement to this position. Thus perhaps a focus feature can be checked by the secondary WH movements. I leave aside what the precise mechanics ought to be.

21 Richards provides another sort of argument using the "subjacency tax." I do not discuss these here. I have tried to verify the rather subtle data that Richards uses to make his argument but have been unable to do so. My one Bulgarian informant agreed with none of the judgments. The various Romanian informants I consulted claimed that none of the judgments held for them in Romanian.

22 Wu (1999) and Grohmann (1998) provide evidence that some WHs function like topics.

23 That they move there in general need not be required. Hornstein (1995), following Chierchia (1991), notes that functionally interpreted WHs need generators to produce the observed interpretations. If we assumed that in these languages a generator resided in Topic position, then the relevant movement to Topic could be restricted to multiple interrogative constructions.

24   One could argue that WH_1 moves first to Spec CP, then WH_2 tucks in under WH_1 and then WH_1 moves to topic. I assume that this sort of derivation is illicit as it allows the WH that has checked the +WH feature of C^0 to vacate Spec CP. See below for further discussion.

25   Given the analysis above, the LF structure would be derived by reconstructing the WH in Spec CP and interpreting it relative to the WH in Topic which functions as the generator. For details see Hornstein (1995: chs. 6 and 7).

26   Observe that it is not clear on Richards' account why single answer questions, echo questions and multiple focus constructions fail to observe superiority.

27   There is empirical motivation for treating the checking of a +WH feature along the lines of checking case. In both instances further movement of the WH element is barred. Thus, the unacceptability of (ib) can be directly accounted for in terms of the assumption that checking the the +WH feature of C freezes the *who* in place, thus blocking the derivation in (ia).

(i)   a.   [Who [you wonder [who C_{+WH} [Bill saw]]]]
      b.   *Who did you wonder Bill saw

28   Given standard definitions of locality, the movement of WH_2 over WH_1 does not violate Shortest Move. See Chomsky 1995 for the relevant definitions of locality for a multiple specifier theory.

29   I owe these Bulgarian data to R. Izvorski and Milena Petrova (via R. Izvorski).

30   Essentially the same facts hold for Romanian. In particular, in an embedded +Wh clause with multiple Whs any Wh can be extracted so long as it is capable of receiving a d-linked interpretation. What is critical is that there is no apparent preference for moving the subject so long as the moved Wh can be interpreted as d-linked. I am indebted to Ileana Comorovski (by way of Kleanthes Grohmann) for this information.

31   Observe that this is the opposite of the standard judgments for English in which (33a) violates the ECP while (33b) is a "mere" subjacency violation.

32   More precisely, as R. Izvorski reports (p.c.): "When both WHs are d-linked, the preference for subject first largely disappears (maybe it's better to have the subject in the matrix, but the difference is really very subtle)."

33   It is unclear what the multiple specifier story predicts as there is little said about the difference between d-linked and non-d-linked expressions.

34   Dispensing with tucking in has an added benefit: it would allow the derivation of the Extension Condition in terms of a derivational view of c-command along the lines of Kawashima and Kitahara (1996). See chapter 6 for further discussion.

5

Is the Binding Theory Necessary?

Introduction

Chapters 2 and 3 have argued that the control module can be removed from UG at little or no empirical cost by treating control as a by-product of movement. If correct, this simplifies the internal structure of UG in a minimalistically pleasing way. This chapter continues this process. It aims to eliminate the Binding Theory (BT) from UG, more precisely principles A and B. Once again the theory of movement will be recruited to save the phenomena.[1]

The argument is based on three sorts of considerations. First, I argue that BT is suspect on methodological grounds given minimalist commitments.

Second, I suggest that Principle A is superfluous theoretically in both GB and minimalist terms and that it is empirically inadequate as well. The locality restrictions Principle A concerns itself with are more adequately accounted for in terms of MOVE. My particular proposal is that anaphors are the residues of overt A-movement.[2]

Third, if there is no Principle A then Principle B should be eliminated as well on conceptual and empirical grounds. I propose that pronouns are not true lexical expressions but are grammar internal "elsewhere" formatives which are costly to use but licensed if needed, i.e. when a derivation cannot converge through movement alone. This take on pronouns owes a great deal to the earliest proposals which viewed them as transformationally introduced objects (Lees and Klima 1963). In what follows, I dust off this position and restate it in MP congenial terms.[3]

The chapter is organized as follows. Section 1 discusses methodological objections to BT. Section 2 discusses Principle A and ways of doing without it. I here outline an overt A-movement approach to local anaphora. Section 3 discusses some technical issues of implementation that come with this proposal. Section 4 raises and tries to address some possible empirical problems that the theory proposed in sections 2 and 3 might be thought to have. Section 5 addresses the status of Principle B and the distribution of pronouns in light of what was done to anaphors in section 2. Section 6 is a brief conclusion. The chapter ends with an appendix suggesting how this approach could be extended to accommodate reciprocal constructions.

1 Minimalism and the Binding Theory

BT has several problems when viewed through a minimalist lens. These include the following.

First, BT uses the notion "domain" to account for the distribution of anaphors and pronouns. Anaphors are "near" their antecedents as they must be bound within their domains. Pronouns cannot be too "close" to potential antecedents since pronouns must be free in their domains. As the domains relevant for computing the binding requirements of anaphors and pronouns are largely identical, BT also derives (the largely accurate observation) that anaphors and pronouns are in complementary distribution.[4] Domains, in short, are the key to adequately describing the locality requirements that anaphors and pronouns display with respect to their antecedents. This is evident in the version of BT outlined in Chomsky (1986b) displayed in (1) and (2).[5]

(1) α is a domain for β iff α is the smallest complete functional complex in which β is governed

(2) A: an anaphor must be bound in its domain
     B: a pronoun must be free in its domain

Though empirically very successful, the definition of domain is minimalistically problematic. One problem is that it uses the notion "government" and this is a suspect notion in MP. There is a second problem. MP already has a notion of local domain, i.e. "minimal domain," as part of its theory of movement. This notion is critical for translating relativized minimality notions into "least effort/shortest move" terms.[6] Standard considerations of theoretical parsimony would favor eliminating one of these locality notions. Given the centrality of the latter variety to the MP theory of movement, this suggests that the one exploited in BT be dispensed with.

One might retort that such parsimony considerations are inappropriate here as the two notions of domain concern themselves with different kinds of operations; binding domains with rules of construal and minimal domains with movement. However, this rejoinder invites another objection: BT invokes an additional variety of rule. GB has two distinct ways of coding interpositional dependencies; via movement and via construal. Methodologically, it is preferable to have only one. On the assumption that displacement operations are ineliminable, this casts a methodological shadow on construal rules. In the best of all possible worlds, these should not exist. UG should contain one type of rule only: MOVE.

Observe that this argument gains force in the context of the reanalysis of control phenomena in terms of movement in chapters 2 and 3. As we note below, there are significant parallels between local anaphora and obligatory control that suggest that they should be handled by the same grammatical mechanisms. Thus, if the analysis of control as movement is correct, then it suggests that the binding theory should be reanalyzed in these terms as well.

Methodological objections to the binding theory get stronger when considered in the context of the most recent versions of BT. Chomsky (1986b, 1993) follows Lebeaux (1983) in assuming that anaphors move to their antecedents at LF. In effect, the locality requirements on anaphors imposed by Principle A in GB based theories are supplanted by locality conditions on abstract movement. Anaphors and their antecedents are proximate because conditions of movement forbid a more distant relation between the two.[7] Chomsky (1986b) proposes the ECP as the relevant locality condition.[8] The point worth noting is that once locality is handled by conditions on movement, Binding Principle A becomes idle and conceptually redundant. This argues against the existence of Principle A. However, without Principle A, the construct "binding domain" only operates to account for the distribution of pronouns. In short, we are left with only one construal rule – Principle B – and a very cumbersome module of the grammar whose only object of interest is pronouns. Moreover, the only remaining binding principle states an *anti*-locality requirement on nominal expressions. This smells very fishy.

In fact, as some might say, things are worse than this. Assume that we eliminate Principle A and account for the distribution of anaphors via movement. This has the effect of making the (near) complementarity of pronouns and anaphors a complete accident. Note that it is no longer possible to explain these distributional data in terms of the conflicting requirements on anaphors and pronouns imposed by principles A and B if there is no Principle A. So aside from being methodologically suspect, what's left of BT after anaphors are removed from its purview is empirically inadequate as well.

In light of these considerations, what is the best attainable result we can hope for? The best methodological result is if the distribution of both anaphors and pronouns reduces to the theory of movement. This is desirable for many reasons. If BT is eliminated from UG we can simplify the class of grammatical operations by dispensing with rules of construal.[9] We can also remove "binding domains" from UG. This furthers the minimalist agenda of removing government from the core inventory of grammatical relations.[10] Lastly, UG gains significant generality. The Binding Theory concerns itself with the distribution of very specific morphemes. This contrasts with a theory of movement based on a rule like 'Move α' where α can be anything at all. A worthwhile minimalist goal is to eschew morpheme specific principles of grammar whose aim is to regulate the distribution of specific lexical expressions. This project has one immediate goal: the elimination of BT as a module of the grammar. In the next two sections I suggest that anaphors are related to their antecedents by MOVE and that pronouns are also related to MOVE but more indirectly. If correct, this removes the need for BT and allows its elimination from UG.

2   Principle A

Principle A regulates the distribution of anaphors by requiring that an anaphor be in the same domain as its antecedent. This locality restriction has generally been applied indifferently to all anaphoric expressions. However, Lebeaux (1984–5) demonstrates that not all anaphors behave similarly. He distinguishes local anaphora from more long distance varieties manifested in picture NPs for example. Lebeaux shows that obligatory control (OC) PRO and locally bound reflexives behave identically and contrast with non-obligatory control (NOC) PRO and non-locally bound reflexives. The OC/NOC contrasts are discussed at length in chapter 2.[11] Consider their reflexive analogues.

(3) a. *John arrested herself
     b. *John's mother arrested himself
     c. *John thinks that Mary arrested himself
     d. *John told Mary about themselves
     e. John likes himself and Bill does too
     f. The unfortunate remembers himself receiving a medal
     g. Only Churchill remembers himself giving the speech

(4) a. pictures of myself are on display in the gallery
     b. John's campaign said that the nude pictures of himself were fabricated
     c. John thinks that it is unlikely that pictures of himself will be found
     d. John asked Mary whether pictures of themselves had been recently sold
     e. John said that pictures of himself were on sale and Bill did too
     f. The unfortunate believes that pictures of himself are flattering
     g. Only Churchill remembers pictures of himself being taken at the famous speech

The contrasts between the unacceptable (3a–d) and the (relatively) acceptable (4a–d) is clear. The data show that the local reflexives in (3) need antecedents, that the antecedents must be local and c-commanding, and that split antecedents are prohibited.[12] The ellipsis structure in (3e) only has the sloppy interpretation while the non-local analogue in (4e) can be interpreted strictly. (3f) only has a 'de se' reading. This contrasts with (4f) where a non-'de se' interpretation is available.[13] In (3g) no one other than Churchill can have the required memory. (4g), in contrast, admits a reading in which many people recall the photo-op. In short, (3) and (4) display virtually the same range of contrasts as displayed by OC and NOC pairs. Note, furthermore, that the non-local reflexives in (4) all have adequate paraphrases with pronouns in place of the reflexives. This stands in contrast with the examples in (3) where the standard Principle A/Principle B complementarity holds.

The empirical parallels between local reflexives and OC PRO argue for parallel theoretical treatments. Chapter 2 argues that OC PRO is equivalent to an NP-t, the residue of overt A-movement. Let's assume that local reflexives are similarly the residues of overt A-movement while non-local reflexives are emphatic pronouns or logophors (c.f. Reinhart and Reuland 1993).[14] For concreteness, assume *for the time being* that local reflexives are spelled out NP-traces. This may not be strictly correct and I will outline another implementation of the main idea later in this chapter. But for now, assume reflexives just are NP-ts. This supposes that the relation between a local reflexive and its antecedent is similar to that between an OC PRO and its antecedent, viz. a coupling established via movement. In chain terminology, an anaphor and its antecedent form an A-chain.

This assumption suffices to account for all the paradigm in (3). Consider some details. (3a,b) indicate that an anaphor, in this case a (local) reflexive, requires a c-commanding antecedent. This follows if we assume that reflexives are what "antecedents" leave behind when they overtly move. In effect, anaphors have c-commanding antecedents/binders for the very same reason that NP-traces do. They are formed by A-movement.

The locality requirement between anaphors and their antecedents exhibited in (3c) similarly follows from constraints on MOVE, in this case the Shortest Move/Minimal Link Condition. The derivation for (3c) would move 'John' across a potential landing site, the position filled by 'Mary', which is prohibited by minimality.

(3d) illustrates the prohibition against split antecedents. This also follows if reflexives are the residue of movement. Two expressions cannot both move from the same position, i.e. cannot be merged into the very same position from the very same position.[15] Consequently, local reflexives cannot support split antecedents any more than NP-traces or OC PROs can.

It is worth noting that the prohibition against split antecedents for anaphors is usually stated as an *extra* stipulation (see Lasnik and Uriagereka (1988: 131–2)). It does not follow from other interpretive facts about anaphors, such as their interpretation as bound variables for example. Pronouns interpreted as bound variables do not share the restriction against split antecedents as (5) indicates.

(5)   Someone$_i$ persuaded every kid$_j$ that they$_{i+j}$ should tell each other a story

The other interpretive facts are similarly explained. If reflexives are formed from overt movement we expect them to behave like raising constructions.[16] These too require a sloppy reading under VP ellipsis.

(6)   John seems to like bagels and Bill does too

In fact it is quite unclear what a non-sloppy reading would be in (6). VP ellipsis is only licensed under a parallelism requirement (see Chomsky 1995). The remnants of the process of ellipsis (as well as the elided expressions) must play similar logical roles. Assume that this means that they must (at least) have parallel thematic structures. Then, if local reflexives are semantically parallel to OC structures, the chain involving a reflexive has at least two θ-roles. The parallelism condition then forces the subject of the second conjunct to have the same roles as the remnant in the first conjunct. This suffices to license the mandatory sloppy reading under VP ellipsis.[17]

The obligatory *de se* reading of (3f) follows as well. The overt structure of (3f) is provided in (7).

(7) The unfortunate [T⁰ [$_{VP}$ the unfortunate v [$_{VP}$ remembers [$_{IP}$ *the unfortunate*
     [ing [$_{VP}$ the unfortunate receive a medal]]]]]]

The matrix copy of 'the unfortunate' has two theta-roles, one from 'receive'
and one from the 'v' associated with 'remember'.[18] To say that one and the
same expression has two theta-roles is identical to saying that it has the reflexive logical form displayed in (8).[19]

(8) The unfortunate λx [x expects x to receive a medal]

As this is what one necessarily gets by movement from one θ-position to
another, this is the interpretation that must arise if reflexives are formed via
movement.[20]

The reading that one has in (3g) is similarly accounted for. If reflexives are
residues of movement, then the only derivable reading is the one indicated.
The constituent 'only Churchill' moves from the position occupied by 'himself'. This expression (or chain that it heads) bears a pair of θ-roles and the
logical form is the one presented in (9). This only allows the reading in which
'himself' acts as if bound by 'only Churchill' not by 'Churchill' alone.

(9) Only Churchill [λx [x remembers x giving the BST speech]]

The upshot is that if we assume that local reflexives are the residue of
movement then all of the interpretive properties of sentences that contain
them are straightforwardly derived without additional stipulations and the
locality conditions described by Principle A can be reduced to the locality
conditions on movement such as the Shortest Move/Minimal Link Condition.
Assume therefore that this sort of conclusion is roughly correct. There remain
several technical issues that must be resolved. We address some of these now.

First, note that on the account above, reflexives *per se* make no semantic
contribution to the interpretation of the sentence. They are not (co-)referential
expressions, or bound expressions or operators that change the additicity of
predicates.[21] They are semantically inert. In this regard the above treats reflexives
entirely on a par with PRO and identifies both as simply NP-ts at LF. What
then distinguishes reflexives from OC PRO?

There is an important difference between OC PRO and reflexive constructions that is case based. Reflexives arise when case must be checked. Consider
an illustrative derivation.

(10) a. John dressed
      b. [$_{IP}$ John [I [$_{VP}$ John [dressed John]]]]
      c. John dressed himself
      d. [$_{IP}$ John [I [$_{VP}$ John [dressed John(=himself)]]]]

(10a) and (10c) both contain a three membered chain in overt syntax that
bears two θ-roles. I here assume that the verb 'dress' is distinctive in that it
optionally bears an accusative case feature. If inserted with accusative case, this

case must be checked. What checks it? The idea outlined above is roughly that a copy of 'John' checks this case at LF. The copy that checks this case is phonetically realized as 'himself'. This implementation of the basic proposal will be gussied up below so as to be more technically acceptable. But for right now assume that the copy checks case.[22]

Most verbs are mandatorily inserted with accusative case features. Thus, most require overt objects as in (11).

(11) John saw/heard/criticized *(himself)

The same analysis extends to more traditional examples of control in embedded clauses. Consider (12).

(12) a.   John expects himself to be elected
      b.   John expects PRO to be elected

The only relevant difference between these two sentences, on the current proposal, is that 'expects', an ECM verb, is optionally marked with an accusative case feature. If so marked, (12a) surfaces. If not we get (12b). Note that some ECM verbs are mandatorily inserted with case and so only the first variant appears well formed. The present proposal treats (13b) as a case theory violation.

(13) a.   John believes himself to be handsome
      b.   *John believes PRO to be handsome[23]

The basic facts concerning the distribution of local reflexives follow from this analysis. This is not surprising for it basically encodes the binding theoretic approach from Chomsky (1982) into a movement theory of reflexives. In Chomsky's (1982) theory, NP-ts and reflexives are grouped together and required to meet Principle A of the binding theory. The current theory groups them as well by insisting that NP-ts and reflexives are essentially one and the same object modulo case theory. Echoes of this earlier LGB proposal are found in Reinhart and Reuland's (1993) chain condition. They use this condition to account for the unacceptability of sentences like (14).

(14) Mary expects himself$_i$ to like John$_i$

On the present account, this sentence is underivable. Recall that 'himself' is the residue of overt movement. Thus, at LF it is simply a copy of 'John', the antecedent. To derive (14) would require lowering 'John' to the object-of-'like' θ-position (in overt syntax) leaving 'himself' as the residue of movement. Such lowering in overt syntax, however, violates the Extension Condition (or whatever subsumes it) and so is illegitimate.

Note that the same reasoning rules out cases like (15).

(15) *John thinks that heself/himself is here

'John' cannot raise from the subject of the embedded IP as it is a case checking position. In effect, checking nominative case on 'John' "freezes" 'John' in place. This prohibits the indicated raising. If reflexives are the residue of raising, then this reflexive cannot appear here any more than PRO or an NP-t can in (16).

(16)   *John thinks PRO/NP-t is here

This approach to examples like (15) has some technical advantages in MP accounts. It is generally accepted that reflexives move at LF (see Chomsky (1986b, 1995) following Lebeaux (1983)). This permits the ECP to account for the unacceptability of (15). This LF movement approach, however, does not easily carry over to MP for two reasons. First it is unclear what blocks movement of the reflexive at LF within the MP given the elimination of head-government from the grammar. Second, it is unclear what motivates LF movement of the reflexive to its antecedent in the standard GB account. The usual assumption is that the movement is required to check phi-features of the reflexive. However, it is unclear why these features need to be checked given their interpretability. These technical problems are finessed if one assumes that reflexives are the residues of overt movement which appear when case must be checked on some head. This obviates the need to raise the reflexive to its antecedent at LF. A movement relation between the reflexive and its antecedent already holds without recourse to this sort of LF movement. If the reflexive moves at all, it moves simply to check the accusative case feature. It need not move to check phi-features or establish a (semantic) relation between itself and its antecedent.

The basic idea, I hope is clear. Now it is time to address some technical issues that arise in implementing it.

3   Some Technical Issues of Implementation

3.1   *Another Implementation of the Main Idea*

The principal technical hurdle is to explain (i) how it is that a copy can check case and (ii) why a copy has the phonological shape of a pronoun.[24] The problem is illustrated in (17).

(17)   a.   John likes himself
         b. $[_{IP}$ John I $[_{VP}$ John [likes [[John]self]]]]

(17b) is the phrase marker underlying (17a). The derivation starts with merging 'John' with 'self' then merging this into the object position of 'likes' thereby providing 'John' with the object θ-role. Then 'John' raises to Spec VP where it gets the subject θ-role of 'likes'. Afterwards it raises again to Spec IP where it checks case and EPP features. Note, for this to work we need to assume that 'John' has nominative case features. And this is where the problem comes in. The upper copy of 'John' in (17b) must have had nominative features. But this implies that the bottom copy has nominative features as well. How then can the copy check accusative case features on 'likes' by movement?

Several technical solutions suggest themselves. Consider one way of getting around the indicated case problem.[25] Assume that what checks the case of the predicate 'likes' in (17) is not the copy but the reflexive element 'self'. Assume, in other words, that 'self' is a nominal expression that gets generated into the derivation with case features.[26] If it can be generated as having accusative case while the D/NP it is adjoined to carries nominative, then the derivation of (18a) could be done as in (18b).

(18) a. John likes himself
      b. [$_{IP}$ John I [self [$_{VP}$ John [likes [[John]self]]]]]
         −nom −acc +nom   +nom +acc

The derivation illustrated in (18) proceeds as follows. 'John' with nominative case merges with 'self', which-bears accusative case. This complex then merges into the object position of 'likes' allowing 'John' to assume the internal θ-role.[27] 'John' then raises first to Spec VP where it receives the external θ-role and further to Spec IP where its nominative case feature is checked, as are the relevant features of Infl. At LF, 'self' raises to check the accusative case features of 'likes'.[28] Note that the key assumption here is that what makes the reflexive morphologically accusative are the case features of 'self' not the features of D/NP it is adjoined to.

Let's assume that this proposal solves the problem of how the case of the predicate is checked. There still remains the fact that what surfaces is not 'Johnself' but an expression which has 'self' adjoined to a pronoun, viz 'himself'. How does this happen? There are two problems. The first, is how to get rid of the copy left behind, i.e. how to delete 'John'. The second is to say where the pronoun comes from. Let's concentrate on (18b) for concreteness.

The deletion of the lower copy of 'John' follows from whatever it is that requires copies to delete prior to the A(rticulatory)-P(honetic) interface. Nunes (1995) argues that this is required for the LCA to successfully apply.[29] Roughly speaking, if all copies are maintained, the expressions cannot be linearized consistently. Thus, all but one copy must delete. The derivation in (18b) indicates that the only copy of 'John' that has had its case features checked is the one in Spec IP. If this copy survives to the AP interface the derivation converges. The other copy crashes the derivation as it has an unchecked (nominative) case feature. Thus, the LCA requires the deletion of all copies but one and interface conditions pick the top copy as the required survivor. This implies that the bottom copy must delete. This line of reasoning, in short, solves our first problem as it leads to the deletion of the copy to which 'self' has adjoined.

Now for the second step. Observe, that in English, 'self' is a bound morpheme. In other words, it cannot stand alone. This is what lies behind the unacceptability of (19).

(19) *John likes self

I propose that the pronoun is inserted after the copy is deleted to provide morphological support for the bound morpheme 'self'. In effect, the pronoun fills the same function here that 'do' fulfills in 'do'-support configurations.[30] The steps of the process are indicated in (20) (parentheses indicate "deletion").

(20) a. [$_{IP}$ John I [self [$_{VP}$ John [likes [[John]self]]]]]
           −nom   −nom   +nom+acc
    b. [$_{IP}$ John I [self [$_{VP}$ (John) [likes [[(John)]self]]]]]
    c. [$_{IP}$ John I [$_{VP}$ (John) [likes [[HIM+self]]]]]

(20b) is the LF structure of (18a) and (20c) is the structure fed to PF.

I assume that the pronoun agrees in case with the adjunct it supports. The pronoun is there simply to support the morphological requirements of the unbound morpheme 'self' which is left without a morphological crutch given the required deletion of the copy for convergence. I return to a fuller discussion of pronouns below where the logic deployed here is more fully generalized.[31]

The upshot, then, is that English reflexives are the residues of movement, that the reflexive is an unbound morpheme that needs support and that all copies but one of a chain must delete for LCA reasons. The last two suppositions are quite standard. The first is the hypothesis investigated here that reflexives are formed via overt A-movement.

3.2 A Possible Problem for this Implementation

This implementation differs from the earlier one in assuming that what checks case in reflexive constructions is the 'self' morpheme rather than the copy. I motivated this proposal by noting that typically there would be a case clash that would prevent one expression from checking two separate cases. However as the discussion in note 27 indicates, this motivation is not decisive. Consequently, I would like to briefly consider a problem with the current implementation.[32]

The argument motivates 'self' as the case checker by considering examples like (17a) repeated here.

(17) a. John likes himself

The problem, recall, is that *if* 'himself' is simply the morphological realization of a copy that has checked case then it suggests that copies of 'John' can bear realize multiple cases.

(21) [John   [John likes   John]]
    −Nom/+θ+θ +Nom/+θ+θ +Nom/+θ

If the structure of (17a) is (21) prior to LF movements, we have the following problem: the lower copy cannot check accusative case as it is nominatively marked (recall that the 'John' in object and subject are copies). We used this to motivate the claim that 'self' is actually the accusative case checker and that *John* is inserted with nominative case. Given this reasoning, one can think of *self* as inserted to prevent case clash.

However, *if* this is why we have *self*, then we expect that in examples like (22), where we only need to check accusative cases, well formed derivations do not need *self*. The reason is that all copies of *John* will have accusative case and so there will be no case clash if the lower copy moves to check the accusative case of *like*. To see this more explicitly, consider (23), the phrase marker underlying (22).

(22)   *I expect John to like

(23)   [I [John [I expect [John to [John   [John like   John]]]]]]
       −acc+θ+θ   +acc/+θ+θ −acc/+θ −acc/+θ/+θ +acc/+θ

The derivation at issue is the following. In overt syntax 'John' merges with 'like' assuming a θ-role. Say it has accusative case features. We then move 'John' to Spec vP and it gets a second θ-role. This copy continues to move, first to Spec IP in overt syntax and then to Spec of the matrix ECM verb 'expect' (perhaps at LF) where it checks its accusative case. At LF, the copy left in the object position of 'like' or even the one in Spec vP still has an unchecked case feature. One of these copies moves to the outer Spec of the lower VP to check case.[33] Note that we still have LCA considerations. So let's assume that in order to meet the LCA (at PF) and its scopal equivalent the SCA (at LF) we delete all copies but the highest one.[34] This derivation converges as (22) and this should be a perfectly fine reflexive sentence. It clearly isn't. Why not?

Chapter 3 proposes that deletion rules, like all other grammatical operations, apply deterministically in the sense that they can only apply if they must apply, viz. to delete an expression that is ill-formed in the sense of being capable of crashing the derivation if not removed. Note, that, so construed, determinism effectively prevents the deletion of an interpretable expression (i.e. one whose uninterpretable features have all been checked and that bears a theta-role) simply because its deletion would permit convergence. Putting this positively, determinism allows an expression to be deleted only if it is defective in some way.

With determinism in mind consider the derivation in (23) once again. It requires deleting copies at PF and LF to meet the LCA and SCA. However, not all the copies that must be deleted are defective. For example, the copy in the outer Spec of the lower vP has its case checked and bears a(t least one) θ-role. It is perfectly well-formed and interpretable. Thus, it cannot delete given determinism. If accusative case is checked in overt syntax, this will leave two perfectly well-formed copies at PF and result in a violation of the LCA (as Nunes has shown). If accusative case is checked at LF, then we will have at least two copies of 'John' at LF and so prevent the SCA from applying. Either way, convergence is blocked and the derivation is illicit. This is the desired result.[35]

To sum up. 'Self' is required in reflexive constructions not to avoid case conflicts but to allow a derivation to licitly converge. Copies can, in principle, check case but if they do they will likely prevent either LF or PF linearization. By virtue of being perfectly interpretable the copies become undeletable given determinism. The surviving multiple copies then prevent linear and scope orderings at PF and LF.[36]

3.3   The Interpretation of 'Self'

To this point the analysis assumes that reflexives are semantically inert. They are not coreferential to or bound by their antecedents nor are they predicate operators whose semantic function is to change the additicity of the predicates they saturate. Reflexives are present simply for case reasons. Adjoining 'self' to a nominal allows it to bear more than one case. In effect, reflexives are a means by which nominals can be multiply case marked and this allows movement to obtain between case positions, an option that Greed normally prevents. At LF, a sentence with a local reflexive is structurally identical to one with an obligatory controlled PRO; both are formed by movement and involve chains with multiple θ-roles. It is these chains alone that are the active semantic units.

The idea that 'self' is an adjunct that bears case but is otherwise semantically inert has some additional benefits. Consider two.

First, it has long been observed that reflexives can be topicalized.

(24)   Himself, nobody hates t

Such sentences are not perfect but they appear to be far better than they should be given that they appear to induce both Principle A and Principle C violations. One way out of this conclusion is to insist that reconstruction is required in these cases. However, the present approach suggests another reason for their relative acceptability: the movement violates no condition at all. What makes them odd is that one has topicalized a semantically inert expression and this is pragmatically an odd thing to do. However, the indicated movement has no binding theoretic consequences.

Second, there is some evidence that the reflexive actually moves like an adjunct.[37] Consider the following contrasts:

(25)   a.   It's himself that I said that Bill amuses t with card tricks
      b.   ?It was John that I wondered why Bill amuses
      c.   *It was himself that I wondered why Bill amuses

(25a) involves long movement of a reflexive and it seems relatively acceptable. (25b) is a weak WH island violation. Its acceptability is lower than (25a) but still tolerably fine. The interesting contrast is with (25c) where there is a further decrease in acceptability. This decrease can be attributed to the fact that reflexives are adjuncts and so cannot be extracted out of weak islands.

The same effects can be seen with questions. One can answer (26a) with 'Bill' but it is quite unacceptable to answer it with 'himself' in contrast with the question in (26b) where both answers seem acceptable.

(26) a.   Who did you wonder how John amuses t
      b.   Who did you say that John amuses t

These data support the conclusion that 'himself' is structurally an adjunct, as assumed above.

The complete assimilation of local reflexives to OC PRO is probably too extreme. It is known that English reflexives historically derive from expressions with an emphasizing function (Keenan 1994). Recently Lidz (1997) has argued that reflexives divide into two types; pure-reflexives and near-reflexives.[38] Descriptively speaking, the former identify the same entity in the world that their antecedents do while the latter are slightly more liberal in that the referent of the reflexive must be similar to, but not identical with, that of its antecedent. An example will make the point clear.

Consider the following context first discussed in Jackendoff (1992). A famous person, say Ringo, goes into the wax museum which contains his statue. He goes to see it. We can describe this appropriately using (27).

(27)   Ringo saw himself today (at the museum)

Here Ringo sees his statue, what Jackendoff called I(mage)-Ringo. Assume, further that Ringo decides to scrub this statue down and make it sparkle. Then, I think, we can describe this using (28).

(28)   Ringo washed himself today (at the museum)

This same reading however is not supported by (29).

(29)   Ringo washed today (at the museum)

Why is this interesting in the present context? We have assumed in chapter 2 that in (29) 'Ringo' has two θ-roles (or heads a chain with two theta-roles). The analysis of reflexives above assumes that this is also true of (28). However, it seems that this can't be the whole story as (28) has a reading absent in (29). In short, 'self' does affect the meaning of local reflexive constructions by loosening the identity requirements between the reflexive and its antecedent.

Can these intriguing observations be incorporated into the present analysis? I believe so. Consider (18) again reproduced here for convenience.[39]

(18) a.   John likes himself
      b.   [$_{IP}$ John I [self [$_{VP}$ John [likes [[John]self]]]]]
               −nom −acc   +nom   +nom +acc

'Self' here is an adjunct to 'John'. 'John' bears the object θ-role. In effect, the expression denoted by 'John' bears the logical object role of 'like'. Typically, this gets cashed out semantically as the individual that 'John' names is the likee. What 'self' does is say that it need not be the individual John that bears the likee-role but some object suitably "similar" to John, in particular his image. In other words, 'self' can alter the set of satisfiers relevant to the evaluation of 'John', not only the individual John can count as a legitimate satisfier but so can his image. Without 'self' modifying the θ-recipient, only the object itself, i.e. John, is a satisfier of 'John'. The difference between (28) and (29) can be tracked back to the modificational role of 'self'.

This fits well with the assumption that 'self' is an adjunct that has modificational powers. Changing the relevant set of satisfiers for an expression is what adjuncts do. It should be observed, however, that the potential impact of adding 'self' is very narrow. The relevant similarity is of the kind discussed by Jackendoff, the image relation. To see how narrow consider the following context. Ringo goes to lunch and orders a sandwich. The order is delayed. Finally Ringo complains and the short order cook yells to the waiter "Ringo has been waiting here for your pick-up for the last ten minutes". In this context 'Ringo' can refer to the sandwich. However, in this same context one cannot say "Ringo saw himself on the counter waiting" meaning he saw the sandwich. At any rate, the relevant similarity is very narrow and likely restricted to images of objects as discussed by Jackendoff.

It is restricted in a further interesting way. It is the satisfier of the object θ-role that is affected not the others. Consider the following story. There is a Ringo fountain. The real Ringo goes near the fountain and gets sprayed. We cannot describe this as (30).

(30)   Ringo sprayed himself

This can mean that Ringo sprayed the statue. But not the statue sprayed Ringo. In other words, 'self' modifies not the set of 'Ringo' satisfiers but the set of 'Ringo' satisfiers that bear the relevant θ-role.

This fits with the present analysis. Consider (18) once again. The expression that is merged into the θ-position of 'likes' is the expression '[[John]self]'. This enables us to restrict the powers of 'self' to the expression with the correct θ-features, i.e. the likee John, not the liker John. Another way of saying the same thing is that 'self' allows the satisfiers of the likee θ-role to be the objects that satisfy the bearer of the θ-role or the image of that bearer.

3.4   Conclusion

The proposal above has two separable parts. The first is the intuition that the properties of (local)-reflexive constructions are due to the formation of multiple θ-marked A-chains whose head is the "antecedent" of the "reflexive." In effect, the canonical characteristics of reflexives follow from the fact that they are formed by overt A-movement. The heart of this proposal is the treatment of reflexives as essentially the residues of this overt movement. The second part proposes an implementation of this idea in terms of treating 'self' as an adjunct that is introduced to bear an extra case if one is required. I have only outlined the major features of such a proposed implementation. There are, I am certain, many further technical issues that must be resolved for this implementation to be fully successful. I leave discussion of some of these further issues to Appendix 2 (p. 188).

In sum, it appears that 'self' can contribute to the interpretation of local reflexives. Its contribution appears consistent with the assumption that 'self' is an adjunct that modifies the D/NP to which it is adjoined.[40] This resolves the primary technical problems that arise with treating reflexives as the residues of overt A-movement without affecting the properties that lend this approach its empirical appeal. The next section deals with some additional empirical problems that surround this approach and suggests some ways of dealing with them.

4   Some Further Empirical Problems Considered

The above analysis collapses obligatory control (OC) with local reflexivization. Both are the product of overt A-movement. The principal difference between the two constructions is that the latter involves a nominal adjunct with case features and this adjunct is absent from the former. However, the core interpretive and distributional properties of both constructions are traced to the fact that both involve A-movement of a D/NP through several θ-positions. The result is a single A-chain formed by movement. The locality restrictions follow from the fact that (A-) movement is subject to locality restrictions such as Shortest Move/Minimal Link Condition and the interpretive properties follow from the fact that a single (A-)chain with multiple θ-roles results from this movement.

Unfortunately, OC and local anaphora configurations are different in some respects. This potentially threatens the current proposal that treats them as essentially parallel configurations. The aim of this section is to show that most (and perhaps all) of these differences can be accommodated without undermining the basic proposal. The relevant text for this exercise is Lasnik (1992). Consider the data he presents.

First, Lasnik (1992) observes that there are many cases where one can get reflexives but not PRO and vice versa. Consider some examples. (31) illustrates that some verbs allow both control and reflexive objects.[41]

(31)   a.   John washed/shaved/dressed
      b.   John washed/shaved/dressed himself

In section 1 above, this alternation is derivable by assuming that these verbs may optionally join the derivation without accusative case features. Given this optionality, two derivations can arise. If the verb is inserted with case features, these must be checked and the reflexive is required. If no case features are appended to the transitive verb, then the OC option obtains and sentences like (31a) are derived. The LF configurations of these sentences is offered in (32).

(32) a. [John T^0 [$_{vP}$ John v [$_{VP}$ wash John]]]
      b. [John T^0 [$_{vP}$ self[$_{vP}$ John v [$_{VP}$ wash [[John]self]]]]]

In (32a) John has two θ-roles derived from merging into the complement position of 'wash' and moving to the Spec position of 'v'. 'John' bears nominative case and so moves to Spec IP to check this case and the case of 'T^0'. We assume that the outer 'v' of 'wash' or 'v+wash' does not have an accusative case feature that needs checking in this derivation. This contrasts with (32b) where an accusative case feature on the predicate must be checked. 'John' once again has nominative case and checks two θ-positions and so bears two θ-roles. Note that the copy of 'John' in the object of 'wash' cannot check this accusative case feature for the reasons discussed above. However, 'self' can be inserted with case and it can check the case on the verb. Both derivations converge with the indicated assumptions.[42]

Observe that this optionality is presumably marked. In other words, most transitive verbs *must* enter the derivation with an accusative case feature that needs checking.[43] Thus, for most verbs, we expect to see the paradigm illustrated by (33).

(33) a. John injured himself
      b. *John injured PRO

The same logic applies to embedded clauses. Thus, 'believe' is an ECM verb that is inserted into the derivation with an accusative case feature which must be checked if the derivation is to converge. This contrasts with 'try' which is unexceptional in that when it takes a sentential complement it does not come carrying a case feature. This difference suffices to produce the following contrasts.

(34) a. John believes himself to be cool
      b. *John believes PRO to be cool
      c. *John tried himself to be cool
      d. John tried to be cool

The reflexive is required in (34a) so that the accusative case can be checked. 'Self' being a nominal can carry case. If it does then 'John' can check the nominative case of the matrix 'T^0' while 'self' checks the accusative case of 'believe'. If there is no 'self' in the derivation then the accusative case of 'believe' remains unchecked and the derivation crashes.[44] Note that 'John' alone cannot check both the case of the matrix tense and that of 'believes'. The reflexive is forbidden to surface in (34c) as 'try' does not have an accusative case feature. As such, the case of 'self' cannot get checked and the derivation crashes. If 'self' is not inserted the derivation converges and a fine sentence results. In (34d), the case of the matrix 'T^0' is checked by 'John'.

The same reasoning extends to cover examples like (35). Lasnik notes that one cannot account for the distribution of PRO simply by saying that it cannot appear in case marked positions. The position after 'sincerely' in (35a) is not a case position as the unacceptable (35b) indicates. Thus, one might expect 'PRO' to appear here.

(35)   a.   *John believes sincerely Mary to be clever[45]
       b.   *John believes sincerely PRO to be clever

Note that the present analysis does not lead one to expect a PRO in (35b). PRO is simply the residue of A-movement. However, 'believes' is an ECM verb and its accusative case must be checked. This is impossible in (35b) as there is nothing that can check this case and the others that require checking as well.[46]

One can generalize this line of reasoning further still. Lasnik notes that 'belief', the nominalization of 'believe', does not permit OC either – (36b) – despite the subject position of the complement infinitival not being a case marking position – (36a).

(36)   a.   *My belief [Harry to be intelligent]
       b.   *My belief [PRO to be intelligent]

This is accommodated if we assume that nominals bear the lexical properties of their corresponding verbs. Thus, 'belief' has the lexical requirement that it bear an accusative when coupled with an infinitival argument. If we assume that nominalization "buries" the accusative so that it cannot get checked, then there is no way for this case to be discharged and the derivation necessarily crashes. In short, the problem is a lexical one. The nominalization of 'believe' has the same lexical properties as the verb but its nominal outer structure prevents the case from being checked.[47]

Consider another asymmetry between OCs and reflexives. The antecedent of a reflexive is often optional while that of a PRO is not. Thus, in (37) 'himself' can have either 'John' or 'Bill' as antecedent.

(37)   John told Bill about himself

This optionality follows if 'about himself' can adjoin to several positions. Thus, when 'Bill' is the antecedent 'about himself' hangs low while if 'John' is the antecedent it hangs higher. The logic of this response is similar to what one says about secondary predicates, which may involve PRO, e.g. (38).[48,49]

(38)   John painted the model nude

Consider a final discrepancy between the two construction types. Lasnik notes that a controller can impose requirements on the controllee. A particularly dramatic instance of this comes with verbs like 'serve'.[50]

(39) a. The ice melted
   b. *The ice served to melt
   c. The ice chilled the beer
   d. The ice served to chill the beer

Higgins accounted for these data by observing that here the subject of the complement infinitival clause must be interpretable as an instrument. In short, these verbs impose a thematic requirement on the embedded subject position. Lasnik provides further evidence that the requirement is indeed thematic and not structural. He observes that mere transitivity is insufficient to license 'serve' constructions.

(40) *Edison served to invent the light bulb

In terms of control theory, the requirement is that in configurations like (42), the controllee 'PRO' must have the instrument θ-role.

(41) NP serve [PRO to VP]

The asymmetry alluded to consists in the fact that there are no analogous cases in which bound reflexives have similar θ-restrictions placed on them.

Before addressing the asymmetry, it is interesting to consider how these data are to be accommodated given standard assumptions. Lasnik suggests that these facts are the province of the control module. However, it is not at all clear how this is to be technically executed given the usual assumptions. Selection is a head/head relation. As such, verbs like 'serve' in which the embedded subject is selected or the embedded verb is selected should not exist. Furthermore, selection is generally thought of as a very local head to head relation. Thus, Vs can select the embedded 'I^{0}' of a complement clause but not the embedded 'V^{0}' as the latter is simply too remote to be selected. Unfortunately, given the VP internal subject hypothesis, the relation relevant for stating the θ-restriction 'serve' imposes is between 'serve' and the embedded 'V^{0}'.

There are some ways out of this conclusion. One could argue that the control module is not limited to the selection environments other modules are restricted to. However, this is an undesirable weakening of UG. A second option would be to abandon the idea that control complements are actually IPs. This would allow that matrix to directly select the embedded VP. However, this is not compatible with the general view that 'PRO' is licensed in Spec IP.[51] A last move would be to have the embedded 'I^{0}' require that its subject be instrumental when selected by 'serve'. This, in effect, treats θ-roles as features that can be checked in the course of the derivation. This option fits poorly with the current MP view that strongly distinguishes features like case from θ-roles, the latter being treated as structural properties rather than features. However, given the approach to control outlined in chapter 2 this is a viable analysis. I return to this option in a moment.

There are likely more technical options out there. However, it seems fair to say that given standard GB or MP assumptions, the observations surveyed above are difficult to fit into current theory.

These difficulties, however, dissipate if we treat θ-roles as features, as required by a movement theory of OC and local reflexivization. Observe that this approach *requires* that θ-roles serve to license greedy movement. Thus, they are features. If, so, it is reasonable to suppose that they function as features in ways similar to the third proposal mooted above. Furthermore, if θ-roles are featural in the way this approach requires, then the 'serve' case can be described by simply observing that its 'external' θ-role can only be checked by a D/NP with an instrument θ-role. This is akin to stating that 'T^{0}' can only be checked by a D/NP with nominative case and phi-features. Though an idiosyncratic property of 'serve' it is a *locally* dischargeable idiosyncracy.[52]

What now of the contrast with reflexives? Why do the latter not impose similar restrictions? The most direct answer is that reflexives might do so if they appeared in similar constructions. However, case seems to bar phonetic expressions from the subject of the complement of 'serve'. Lasnik argues that similar restrictions to those found in 'serve' are imposed in verbs like 'try' and 'persuade'. Here the subject must be an "agent."

(42) a. John tried PRO to visit Bill
      b. *John tried [PRO to resemble Bill]
      c. John persuaded Mary [PRO to visit Bill]
      d. *John persuaded Mary [PRO to resemble Bill]

Note, that these restrictions, however, seem to be independent of control. (43) seems about as odd as (42d) with the indicated reading.

(43)   John persuaded Mary$_i$ that she$_i$ should resemble Bill

This suggests that the indicated restrictions have little to do with control. It also suggests that it is not unreasonable to suppose that were reflexives allowed in configurations analogous to obligatory control configurations, then similar restrictions would hold on these reflexives.[53]

This section aimed to outline an approach to local reflexivization based on overt A-movement. This movement creates A-chains with multiple θ-roles and this fact accounts for the similarities between local reflexivization and OC structures. The differences come down to a simple matter of case. Reflexives appear where case features on predicates must be checked. They are absent when this is not required. Otherwise, the constructions are largely identical. The next section moves on to discuss the distribution of pronouns on the assumption that this approach to (local) reflexives is essentially correct.[54,55]

5   Principle B

5.1   *The Basic Idea*

The previous sections have argued that there is considerable utility to treating (local) reflexives as the residue of overt A-movement. Technically, this requires treating 'self' as an expression that carries its own case and can be adjoined to a D/NP. The immediate payoff is that Principle A, so far as it regulates the distribution of anaphors, is superfluous as are many stipulations concerning the interpretation of local anaphors e.g. its *de se* semantics and the inability to support split antecedents. There is a more remote payoff as well: another construal rule has been eliminated from the grammar furthering the program of reducing the inventory of grammatical operations. This "success," if it proves to be real, leads immediately to the question of what to do with Principle B. This section offers a proposal. Just as the above analyzes local reflexivization along the lines of obligatory control structures, this section proposes that pronouns obey roughly the same principles as regulate the distribution of Non-Obligatory Control (NOC) configurations.[56] Here's the story.

Chapter 2 observes that NOC must be the elsewhere case, i.e. that OC must be preferred if it is available. Were this not so, the signature properties of OC configurations would be invisible since OC clauses display a proper subset of the properties manifested by NOC configurations. Thus, were NOC and OC structures allowed in the same context, the former would blot out all traces of the latter.

What drives this complementarity? If OC PRO is the residue of (A-)movement, then the complementarity could be made to follow if movement were cheaper than whatever licenses NOC structures. The properties of NOCs follow if (small) 'pro' inhabits NOCs. Thus, the complementarity of OC and NOC follows if movement is preferred where available and 'pro' is inserted just in case movement cannot take place.

The logic is essentially that of *do*-support. Recall, that *do* can be inserted only if movement in the guise of affix hopping is prohibited from applying.[57] This accounts for the unacceptability of (44); as affix hopping is possible in (44), (unstressed) *do* cannot be inserted.

(44) *John did kiss Mary

In short, where *do* is not required, it is prohibited. Another way of saying this, is that if the derivation can converge without the use of *do*, its use is forbidden.

How can this be stated in an MP context? Arnold (1995) argues that this requires excluding *do* from the numeration. If *do* were part of the numeration and a necessary condition for comparing derivations is that they have common numerations, then unless *do* is excluded (45) could not serve to block (44) as the numerations would differ.

(45) John kissed Mary

Thus, in an MP context, the elsewhere property of *do*-support requires treating *do* as a non-lexical expression. This, in effect, returns us to the intuitions behind the earliest analysis in generative grammar where *do* was treated as an expression introduced by the transformational component (via the *do*-support transformation), rather than an item inserted from the lexicon by lexical insertion.

Let's assume that this line of reasoning is correct. In particular, assume that the correct way to model these sorts of elsewhere relations is by identifying lexical elements that do not originate in the "lexicon" (and so are not part of the array) and can be added to a derivation but only at a cost (and, thus, only if required). This can be applied to the case of NOC by assuming that *pro* is akin to *do* and so only usable if required. In what follows I propose that the distribution of other pronouns can be similarly modelled.

So here's the proposal: certain expressions/morphemes are inherently grammatical in that they are not part of the lexicon and cannot be used unless required for convergence. Among such expressions are NOC *pro* and lexical pronouns; and, as we shall see in a moment, *self*. Note once more that this is a modern incarnation of very traditional views, ones that invoked transformations to introduce reflexives (i.e. via Reflexivization) and pronouns (i.e. via Pronominalization).

The main virtue of this approach is that it immediately accounts for the complementary distribution of (local) anaphors and pronouns.[58]

(46) a.   Everyone likes himself
      b.   *Everyone$_i$ likes him$_i$

If (46a) is formed by overt (A-)movement and pronouns can only be used if a derivation fails to converge by movement alone, then (46b) is blocked by the convergence of (46a).[59]

This explanation requires making explicit some technical assumptions. First, this is an economy argument. It says that the reason that (46b) is unacceptable is that (46a) is a more economical derivation than (46b). This must mean that both (46a) and (46b) have identical arrays. This in turn implies that *self* is not part of the array of (46a) and *him* is not part of either array. The array of both derivations is (47).

(47) {everyone, likes, assorted functional material}.

In other words, on the assumption that *self* and pronouns are not lexical elements and so not part of the numeration, combined with the view that local reflexives are the products of movement and that pronouns are only used if convergence by Merge and Move alone is otherwise impossible, we can derive the complementary distribution of anaphors and pronouns. The first assumption, to repeat, is a contemporary incarnation of the older view that reflexives and pronouns are transformationally introduced items. The second assumption is the conclusion of the earlier sections. The last assumption is the proposal being considered here.

5.2   Bound Pronouns in Islands

There is further evidence that pronouns are related to movement in this way. First, note that relation of reflexives to pronouns is identical to that pointed out between OC and NOC structures. This is what we expect if PRO is actually the residue of movement (an NP-t) while *pro* is a null pronominal. The latter should only occur where movement is prohibited. Chapter 2 argued that this is indeed the case.

Second, the interrelation of movement and pronouns shows up in movement out of islands in English. Consider the paradigm in (48).

(48) a. Which person is it that John met a man who likes *(him)
      b. Which person is it that John denied the claim that Mary likes *(him)
      c. Which person is it that John wonders why Mary likes *(him)
      d. Which person is it that reports about *(him) implicated Bill in the crime
      e. Which person is it that John read Moby Dick before Fred compared *(him) to Ahab
      f. Which person is it that you said that Fred likes (*him)

(48) has two relevant properties. First, (48a–e) indicate that 'which person' can only be related to a pronoun, not to a trace. That a trace is forbidden is not surprising as extraction from the pronoun's position would violate island conditions. What is interesting is that a (bound/resumptive) pronoun in place of the trace results in an acceptable sentence. (48f) displays the second interesting property: a pronoun is prohibited in this case. In other words, the trace is preferred to the resumptive pronoun. This is what we expect if pronouns are only permitted where movement is barred. In other words, (48a–e) require the pronoun because movement cannot extract a WH from these islands. (48f) forbids a pronoun because WH can move in these cases. The logic simply recapitulates that of *do*-support but with pronouns in place of *do*.

To recap, (48) indicates that pronouns are in an elsewhere relationship to WH-movement as follows: movement only converges if island conditions are respected. Consequently, pronouns can "resume" WHs outside islands – (48a–e) – precisely because movement from islands is prohibited. When movement is possible, pronouns cannot resume WHs because pronouns "cost," i.e. the derivation that eschews pronouns is cheaper – (48f).[60]

5.3   Expletive 'It' and Economy

There is a third place where this approach to pronouns proves useful, especially within a minimalist context. Consider a case such as (49).

(49)   *It seems (that) t was told John that Bill left

Why is (49) unacceptable? Given the array of derivational options in Chomsky (1995) there appears to be a convergent derivation for this sentence. The apparent problem with (49) is that the case of the matrix I^0 cannot be checked. *It* was inserted into the position marked by *t*. Here it checks its case features and those of the medial I^0. Once checked this case is no longer available for further use. Hence, when moved to the matrix I^0, *it* cannot check the matrix inflection's case. Thus, the derivation crashes.

However, this argument is incomplete.[61] This derivation should converge if at LF *John* or its case features raise to the matrix I^0 and check the case of the matrix inflection. Given the assumptions in Chomsky (1995) this movement should be licit and the covert movement should save the derivation. In other words, (49) should be perfectly well formed.

One way out of this problem is to say that (49) is blocked by (50).[62]

(50)   It seems (that) John was told t that Bill left

However, given standard MP assumptions this option is unavailable. The reason is that the derivation of (50) violates the preference of Merge over Move and is thus less economical than the derivation that yields (49). This would not be a problem if (49) did not in fact converge, as Chomsky (1995) in fact assumed. For violations of procrastinate are allowed to permit convergence. However, as noted above, there is a licit way to generate (49) without violating anything and this should suffice both to block the derivation of (50) and to allow the derivation of (50) to block the derivation of (49).

This issue is resolved however if pronouns are only allowed into a derivation at a cost, if we assume that pronouns are "elsewhere" expressions that can be used to permit convergence but not otherwise. This assumption serves to remove *it* from the arrays of (49) and (50). This simple step has an interesting property. Consider the derivation of (49) and (50) at the point where the medial I^0 is reached. It looks like (51).[63]

(51)   Array: {seems, that}
       partial structure: was told John that Bill left

The next step moves *John* to check the features of the medial Infl; in particular, case and agreement features of I^0 are checked and the case features of *John* are checked. Observe that if pronouns are not part of the array, *it* is not available for merger from the array. Thus, there is no violation of economy if *John* raises. Thus the next step of the derivation must be (52).

(52)   Array: {seems, that}
       partial structure: John was told John that Bill left

The derivation then continues by merging *that* and then *seems* and the matrix I^0. At this point we can insert a pronoun, *it* for if we do not insert one the derivation fails to converge. Note that raising *John* will not suffice given that its case feature has already been checked and so cannot check the case feature of the matrix Infl. Using a pronoun, however, allows convergence and so is permitted.

This derivation has two interesting properties. First, (50) turns out to be derivable. Second, its derivation is optimal. This second fact serves to block (49) which turns out to be more costly. The greater cost arises from the fact that deriving (49) requires using a pronoun *before* the other options are exhausted. In short, (49) is a case of premature pronominalization. If this is correct, it bolsters the view that economy is locally computed as Chomsky (1995) has proposed. Pronouns can be used at that point in the derivation where they are needed to permit convergence *and not before*. This assumption presupposes local economy and, what is important here, the assumption that pronouns are non-lexical "elsewhere" expressions that do not form part of the array.

Consider another example where this reasoning proves useful. Bosković (1994) considers (53).

(53)   *It believes John to like Mary

It has the LF structure (54).[64]

(54)   [$_{TP}$ it T [$_{AgrO}$ John [$_{VP}$ John believes [$_{IP}$ John to [$_{AgrO}$ Mary [$_{VP}$ John like Mary]]]]]]

The derivation proceeds as follows. *John* merges with *likes Mary* and receives the embedded θ-role. It then raises and checks the EPP feature. *It* inserts in the matrix Spec TP to check case and θ-features of the matrix inflection. At LF, *John* raises to the Spec VP of *believe* and receives a second θ-role. It then checks its case in the matrix Spec AgrO. This derivation should converge on our assumptions as, contrary to Chomsky (1995), we allow a nominal to receive multiple θ-roles.[65]

The derivation, however, can be ruled out if we assume that pronouns can only be used if they are required. In (54), *it* is not needed for convergence. This is attested by the fact that (55) is well formed.

(55)   John believes himself to like Mary

It has been argued above that the reflexive in (55) is, in effect, the residue of overt movement of *John*. If movement is preferred to the use of pronouns then (54) involves premature pronominalization in that there is a convergent derivation that can be attained without using *it*.[66] This suffices to block (54) and rule out (53).[67]

5.4   Deictic Pronouns

This proposal has an interesting implication for deictic pronouns. The approach makes the derivation of (56) impossible if 'him' is simply a pronoun.

(56)   John likes him

(56) should be blocked by (57) in which 'John' saturates both θ-positions and 'self' is added to permit convergence.

(57)   John likes himself

This is clearly an undesirable result. However, the conclusion is evaded if we assume that deictic uses of the pronoun are not the same as expletive 'it' or bound pronouns. This is a defensible assumption. It is well known that in English deictic pronouns are stressed while "regular" pronouns need not be. If we take this stress fact to indicate a featural difference, then what permits 'him' in (56) is the need to support the stress/deixis feature. In effect, deictic pronouns are treated as analogous to stressed 'do' in emphatic sentences. In the latter cases 'do'-support is required, presumably to support the emphatic feature as suggested in Chomsky (1957).

(58)   John DID leave

Deictic pronouns, then, are nominal analogues of emphatic 'do'. They are available to support a stress/deictic feature. Note, that we have seen pronouns function to support features before. It was used in section 3 to get 'him' into 'himself'.[68]

5.5   *Bound Pronouns and Weak Cross Over*[69]

It may be possible to extend the idea that pronouns are last resort expressions to constructions that manifest WCO effects. The idea above is that a pronoun can be inserted into the derivation just in case convergence cannot proceed without use of the pronoun.[70] A particularly interesting example of this is the case in which a pronoun goes surrogate for an element that cannot move from a given position. In other words, pronouns can function to establish a relationship between two positions that cannot be established through movement. More concretely, let's assume that a pronoun can get a bound interpretation if and only if it goes surrogate for a (syntactic) variable that could not licitly be formed by movement.[71] Note, we here retain the idea that pronouns are "elsewhere" elements in the sense that their use is pre-conditioned by the prior *non*-convergence of a movement derivation. We add the hypothesis that pronouns are interpreted as bound just in case they enter a derivation in this way: as proxy for a variable that would have appeared were the movement licit. This amounts to treating bound pronouns as shadows cast by failed attempts at movement. Consider an example which illustrates the point.

(59)   Everyone loves his mother

The claim here is that (59) is acceptable with the bound reading because (60) isn't. Pronouns are interpreted as bound if and only if they occupy a site from which movement has been tried and have as antecedent the nominal that movement would have established had it been licit. In (59), 'his' occupies the position of 't_i' in (60).

(60)   Everyone$_i$ loves [t_i mother]

Three assumptions concerning pronouns are required to encode the "last resort" nature of pronoun use within the grammar: pronouns are (i) costly to use, (ii) introduced by the computational system and (iii) not items of the lexical array. These three assumptions permit a comparison of derivations with and without (bound) pronouns and favor the latter.[72] To illustrate the logic of these three assumptions, consider a derivation of (59).

The derivation of (59) at the point where movement could apply is (61).

(61) loves [everyone's mother]

The next step is to copy 'everyone' and merge it with 'loves [everyone's mother]' to obtain (62).

(62) Everyone MERGE loves [everyone's mother] YIELDS
       Everyone loves [everyone's mother]

'Everyone' has merged into Spec vP getting the external θ-role of 'loves'. However, this derivation will not converge as this step is illicit. For example, it violates the Left Branch Condition.[73] And so the indicated structure is ill-formed. Because of this, we are permitted to consider the alternative derivation in (63).

(63) Everyone MERGE loves [pronoun mother]

(63) is formed from (62) by targeting copies of the expression that "moves" and replacing them with pronouns and merging the intended movee in the position at which (the unsuccessful) movement aimed. If this maneuver yields a licit step in the derivation then it is permitted and the inserted pronouns are grammatically licensed with a bound variable interpretation. If convergence is possible without use of the pronoun, its use is not permitted.[74]

The above "derivations" informally illustrate the logic of assumptions (i)–(iii). Pronouns are introduced into derivations to "save" them just in case movement has failed to suffice for convergence.

How are we to concretize assumptions (i)–(iii) in minimalist grammatical machinery? There are several ways of implementing these assumptions. Given a minimalist framework roughly like the one in Chomsky (1995), less economical operations become available just in case derivations that are more economical fail to converge. In the case under consideration here, this implies that resumptive pronouns become an option just in case convergence is blocked without their use. For the case of (59) above, we have assumed that derivations that violate island conditions (such as the Left Branch Condition) do not converge. How do islands "block" convergence? They can do so in one of two ways in a minimalist context. Islands conditions either reflect Bare Output Conditions (BOC) of the C-I interface or they characterize restrictions on the computational system that bar the application of movement for formal reasons. These interpretations of island restrictions each suggest a way of implementing the above assumptions. Consider a version of each.

Assume that islands reflect a BOC that characterizes what constitutes a well formed chain. This would make something like the "minimal link condition" (MLC) part of the specification of well formed LF chains. Note that treating the MLC as a BOC means that though island violations are derivable by MOVE, the structures created are not interpretable at the C-I interface as they are not legible objects. Thus, this version of the MLC blocks convergence and so allows the use of (bound) pronouns. On this view, (bound) pronouns allow a structure to evade the MLC requirement on legible chains by creating a formal object that the C-I interface can interpret. For concreteness, assume that what a resumptive pronoun does is "cover" a copy inside an island that would otherwise be interpreted as part of an illicit chain. We understand "covering" a copy as composed of two sub-operations: deleting the copy and merging a pronominal into the position of the copy.

In the illustration above, this set of operations takes (62), deletes *everyone* in the DP *everyone's mother* and replaces it with a pronoun *his*. This yields (63).

(62) Everyone MERGE loves [everyone's mother] YIELDS
      Everyone loves [everyone's mother]

(63) Everyone MERGE loves [pronoun mother]

There are several points worth noting about this implementation of (i)–(iii) above. First, the mechanism encodes the fact that establishing a relationship between an antecedent and a resumptive pronoun is more costly than relating an antecedent to a trace/variable. It encodes this by making the structure with the pronoun the output of more operations than the one with the trace (i.e. Copy). Thus, if one measure of derivational cost is the number of operations required to generate the structure, those that have bound pronouns require more operations, and hence are more costly, than those simply derived by movement. Second, the feature that allows the proposed mechanism to encode this cost accounting is that the pronominal structure is derived by manipulating a phrase marker obtained by prior applications of movement. Thus, pronominal structures presuppose those involving movement and hence should be expected to be more costly. This is illustrated in the derivation of (63) from (62) by a pair of operations that "cover" the copy. Third, the assumption that makes this all viable is that bound pronouns are not lexical elements and so not part of the numeration, i.e. no pronouns are listed in the array/numeration underlying (59). Rather, pronouns are part of the computational system and serve to "repair" otherwise "illegible" non-convergent derivations.

There is a second way of implementing the three assumptions listed above. This one starts by treating island conditions as reflections of limitations on the form of computations rather than as a species of BOC. For concreteness, let's assume that islands are manifestations of the shortest move requirement.[75] Thus, movement is impossible from islands because movement is defined so that "long" moves are not legitimate operations and that moving out of an island counts as a long move. This approach contrasts with the prior implementation in the following way. The first approach generated a structure by moving out of an island and then repairing the phrase marker. This second implementation cannot generate the illicit (62) as the movement operation is defined so as to prohibit its generation. Thus, we cannot simply use (62) as input to the derivation of (63). Nonetheless, we can mimic the effects of the earlier implementation as follows.

Let's define the Non-Movement Alternative (NMA) to a derivation D. Let's further assume that NMAs are what license pronouns. In specific, bound pronouns can be used to generate a sentence S via derivation D′ iff D′ is the NMA(D) (read: non-movement alternative to D), D cannot converge and NMA(D) can.[76] (64) defines how NMA(D) is obtained from D.

(64)   D′ is the NMA(D) iff$_{def}$ D′ is formed from D as follows:
    (i)   D is a phrase marker that does not converge.
    (ii)   D′ is obtained from D by demerging an expression E, substituting a pronoun for E and merging E at the relevant point in the derivation.

(64) defines a process that allows one to (a) unmerge a previously merged expression E (b) merge a pronoun into the position E occupied and (c) remerge E into another position that allows the derivation to continue to convergence. The use of NMAs as defined in (64) is quite costly as it involves several instances of Merge Copy and delete as well as the use of non-lexical elements. NMAs are to be avoided if possible. As NMAs introduce pronouns, the use of pronouns is to be avoided if a derivation can converge without their use.

Note that this implementation of the 'last resort' logic is very similar to the prior implementation. Like the earlier procedure, NMAs are parasitic on phrase markers that fail to converge without their use. Moreover, as in the previous implementation, bound pronouns are not treated as lexical items but are introduced via NMAs. Thus, only structures that cannot converge without the use of bound pronouns are permitted to exploit them derivationally.

In the example above, (63) is derived from (62) by *de*-merging *everyone* from the DP, merging a pronoun into that position and then merging *everyone* into the Spec vP of *loves*.[77] The pronoun so introduced is interpreted as bound. Observe that (63), the NMA(62), does not violate the Left Branch Condition (or any other condition). NMA(62) is fine and eventually converges yielding the acceptable (59) with a bound variable interpretation for the pronoun.

For current purposes either of the two interpretations above serve equally well. However, I believe that of the two interpretations of conditions on movement, it is more natural to think of island effects as reflecting properties of the computational system rather than interpretive features of the C-I interface. Thus, I prefer the second approach in terms of shortest move and NMAs. I will, therefore, use the NMA formulation in what follows.[78]

This approach has an interesting descriptive consequence. It is (roughly) correct that bound pronouns must be c-commanded by their antecedents. This is encoded in current theory as the Bound Pronoun Condition.[79]

(65)   Bound Pronoun Condition:
>   A pronoun P can be interpreted as a bound variable iff P is bound (i.e. c-commanded and co-indexed with) its antecedent

As Aoun (1982) noted, it is curious that a binding requirement should be part of (65). Aoun suggests deriving this fact by analyzing bound pronouns as spelled out traces, i.e. the residues of movement. We know why traces are in c-command relations with their antecedents. They are formed by MOVE. The proposal here endorses Aoun's intuition with a twist. To accommodate the last resort nature of pronouns, bound pronouns are not treated as the spell out of traces but as the residues of failed attempts at movement. However, given that a NMA(D) relies on D in the way indicated in (64), the relation between an antecedent and the pronoun it binds is expected to be similar to that between a moved expression and its trace.[80]

Consider now a sample derivation of a sentence with a WCO violation.

(66)   his$_i$ mother loves everyone$_i$

Given the reasoning above, this sentence with the indicated bound reading cannot be licitly derived. If pronouns (interpreted as variables) are introduced in NMAs then the derivation relevant for computing the NMA of (66) is (67).

(67)   [everyone's mother loves] MERGE everyone

This derivation violates at least two conditions: (a) the Left Branch Condition (or case theory) as in derivation of (59) and (b) the Extension Condition due to the fact that 'everyone' merges at the bottom of the structure rather than at the top.

NMA(67) is (68).

(68)   [pronoun's mother] loves MERGE everyone

(68) no longer violates the Left Branch Condition (or case) but it still violates Extension as *everyone* is merged at the bottom of the tree and so does not extend it. In short, (68), the NMA of (67) does not converge. This prohibits a bound variable reading for the pronoun in (66).[81]

This approach to WCO has some interesting properties. It treats WCO effects as violations of the process of sentence construction. It also relates WCO to movement phenomenon. The specific problem with WCO sentences is their construction violates the Extension Condition. Second, the analysis relates the possibility of a bound variable interpretation for pronouns to the fact that they are introduced into derivations as surrogates for copies that would be interpreted as variables were they licit. Thus, there is a rationale for why pronouns have this interpretation and there is a reason for why "leftness" should make a difference to their binding properties.[82]

5.6   Binding Without C-Command

Before ending this section, let's consider some other cases of pronoun binding that are possibly related to this derivational approach in terms of NMAs. There are a number of cases in which binding seems possible without c-command. Three prominent examples of this are displayed in (69).

(69)   a.   I will drink no wine$_i$ before it$_i$ is ready
      b.   Nobody's$_i$ mother loves him$_i$
      c.   Someone from every city$_i$ hates it$_i$

These have standardly been considered problems for the Bound Pronoun Condition and various proposals have been made to accommodate them.[83] The approach to bound pronouns in terms of NMAs suggests another possibility. These constructions are acceptable because they can be licitly derived via NMAs that are parasitic on failed instances of sidewards movement. Let me elaborate.

Overt movement within a connected tree results in chains in which the head c-commands all the other links. This is because any other form of movement violates the Extension Condition. With sidewards movement a possibility, however, there are licit derivations in which the moved expression may not c-command the position from which it moves. For example, in cases of parasitic gap constructions or adjunct control discussed in chapter 3 the move from the adjunct is sidewards to the VP and this landing site within the VP does not c-command the adjunct either when the movement takes place or when the subtrees combine to form a single structure. If Move includes sidewards movement, then it need not require c-command. Furthermore, as NMAs track "attempted" movements it should be possible to find cases of non-c-commanding pronominal binding.[84] With this as background, let's consider some possible derivations of the examples in (69). Let's start with (69a).

The derivation proceeds as follows. We construct the adjunct with 'no wine' merged into the position of the pronoun. We then take 'drink' out of the array. The situation is depicted in (70).

(70)   drink [before [no wine is ready to drink]]

Consider the next step in the derivation. Something must merge with 'drink'. The move from 'no wine' to the object of 'drink' is not allowed as it violates several conditions, including the case filter (there is no A-movement from a case position).[85] As such, we have an instance of failed movement here. The NMA (70) is (71).

(71)   [drink no wine] [before it is ready]

To derive (71) the copy of 'no wine' in (70) is replaced by a pronoun and 'no wine' is merged into the position where 'no wine' would have moved were the movement licit. (71) is well formed and has been licitly derived. If bound pronouns are introduced by NMAs then the relation established between 'no wine' and the pronoun 'it' becomes interpreted as a bound variable. In effect, we have derived a bound pronoun configuration without c-command between the antecedent and its bindee, the pronoun.[86]

Consider now (69b). Here too we can have a derivation via a NMA that "links" 'nobody' and 'him'. The derivation proceeds as follows. We first merge 'loves' and 'nobody'. We then take 'mother' from the array. What we have at this point is (72).

(72)   mother [loves nobody]

If we try to move 'nobody' sideways to 'mother' we will end up with a derivation that does not converge. The reason is that 'nobody' bears some case, either accusative or genitive. Say it is accusative. Then it cannot check genitive case within the DP that comes to be formed. Say that it is genitive, then the accusative case of 'loves' cannot be checked. Either way, their derivation does not converge.[87]

(73)   [nobody mother] [loves nobody]

If movement does not converge, we are allowed to consider the NMA of (72) as in (74). At the point where movement would apply we would be faced with a violation of case. Thus, we are allowed to consider the NMA of this derivation. It does converge licitly. This licenses the bound pronoun reading.[88]

Consider the final example of binding without c-command:

(69c)   Someone from every city$_i$ hates it$_i$

The same reasoning as applied to (69b) can be applied here. The underlying derivation is one in which there is movement of 'every city' from the object position sidewards to the adjunct – (74). This is blocked by case theory. As such the NMA – (75) – is considered and this derivation converges. Hence the bound reading is allowed.

(74)   [from every city] [$_{vP}$ every city [$_{vP}$ someone v [$_{VP}$ hates every city]]]

(75)   [from every city] [$_{vP}$ it [$_{vP}$ someone v [$_{VP}$ hates it]]]

This example does have problems however. It is unclear what blocks (76).

(76)   Someone from every city hates itself

In contrast to (69b) genitive case is not at issue (see note 90). I have no convincing account for what prevents (76). One possibility is that 'from' assigns inherent case to 'every city' and this sort of case cannot be assigned to copies, i.e. to expressions that already have some feature be it case or θ-role. If this is correct, then movement to the object of 'from' is blocked by Greed and a non-movement alternative derivation becomes an option.[89]

Cases of inverse linking have other intriguing properties worth considering.

First, it appears that these are acceptable only if the DP containing the quantifier which is antecedent of the pronoun is weak.

(77)　*Everybody/most students on every panel$_i$ hated it$_i$

Second, the inverse linking is only possible if the relevant quantifier is in an adjunct. It is blocked from a complement.

(78)　a.　A prince from every region$_i$ praised it$_i$
　　　b.　*A prince of every region$_i$ praised it$_i$

This particular fact makes sense in a minimalist context where phrases are constructed in conformity with Extension. Adjunction to a nominal expression can be accomplished while respecting the Extension condition. However, complementation will not respect Extension. In (79a) 'from every region' can be adjoined to the NP and Extension is followed. This is not so in (79b).

(79)　a.　[$_{NP}$ [$_{NP}$ a prince] from every region]
　　　b.　[$_{NP}$ a [$_{N'}$ prince of every region]]

Third, nominals with genitive determiners also block inverse linking.

(80)　*Someone's friend from every city$_i$ hates it$_i$

This too makes sense on the assumption that 'from every city' is adjoined to NP and that nominals headed by genitives are DPs. This prevents adjuncts from adjoining as, once again, their adjunction would violate the Extension Condition. In other words, if the structure of 'someone's friend' is (81) and 'from every city' must adjoin to NP after being formed, then Extension prevents this derivation in ways analogous to standard WCO configurations like (66) above.[90]

(81)　[$_{DP}$ Someone's [$_{NP}$ friend]]

This same reasoning extends to cover (77) if strong DPs have structures similar to (82).[91]

(82)　[$_{DP}$ every [$_{NP}$ student]]

Note that these explanations rely on the fact that bound pronoun configurations are constructed in the course of the derivation. The key assumption is that Extension regulates the construction of phrase markers. This is consistent with the approach proposed here in terms of NMAs.

This section exploits an intuition about pronouns advanced in Chomsky (1981). Chomsky proposed that there exists a preference against the use of pronouns which he dubbed the Avoid Pronoun Principle. This section makes two points. First, that the particular preference is for movement over pronoun binding and second that this "elsewhere" view of pronouns requires some technical adjustments concerning how one views expressions in the array. The concrete claim is that pronouns are not part of the array but can be introduced into a derivation just in case their introduction is conducive to convergence. They are last resort in that they cannot be used if convergence can occur without their use. I noted that this view of pronouns is very similar to the approach outlined in the Standard Theory in terms of rules like reflexivization and pronominalization. In this framework Reflexivization was an obligatory rule ordered before Pronominalization. The proposal above duplicates these requirements.[92]

As noted, the relation between pronouns and anaphors is similar to the standard view of 'do' in English. In fact, all this section has really done is extend to pronouns the approach to 'do' outlined in Arnold (1995). Generalizing the analysis of 'do'-support in this way has one additional pleasant consequence. It serves to make 'do'-support quite a bit less weird. There is nothing odd about English having a pro-V like 'do' while other languages do not.[93] This sort of variation is standard fare. What is odd, however, is that 'do'-support stands out as the only sort of rule of its kind in the grammar. With the extension of the logic of 'do'-support to pronouns, this isolation ends.

6   Q-float

Chapter 2 used q-float as a probe into the chain structure of certain derivations. In particular, we used the fact that single chains resist multiple quantifier structures as in (83).

(83)   ??The men both/all/each have both/all/each eaten supper

The oddness of (83) follows given the oddness of (84) and the assumption that floated Qs are the residue of movement (Sportiche 1988).

(84)   ??Both the men both have eaten supper

This chapter has argued that reflexives are formed by overt A-movement. This suggests that they should pattern with examples like (83) with respect to the q-float diagnostics as well formed reflexive structures involve a single A-chain. Moreover, these examples should contrast with ones involving (bound) pronouns. These latter are not formed by movement and thus involve separate chains. In this light, consider the examples in (85) and (86).

(85) a. ??The men both believe themselves (both) to (both) be winners
     b. ??The men all believe themselves to all be winners
     c. ??The men each believe themselves each to be winners
     d. ??The men both believe themselves to each be winners
     e. ??The men all believe themselves each to be winners

(86) a. The men both believe that they are both winners
     b. The men both believe that they both are winners
     c. The men all believe that they are all winners
     d. The men each believe that they each are winners
     e. The men both believe that they each are winners
     f. The men all believe that they are each winners

The reflexives in (85) resist modification with an extra quantifer, be it appended to the reflexive (85a,c,e) or floated off the reflexive (85a,b,d). This is to be expected if indeed reflexives are formed by overt A-movement as the structures involve a single extended chain. In effect, in cases like (85a) there is a single A-chain that spans from the lower VP to the matrix subject and includes the intermediate reflexive. The oddness of the cases in (85) follows if it is only possible to have a single quantifier per chain.

(86) contains multiple chains. These are acceptable under the reading in which the pronoun has the matrix subject as antecedent. In these cases the pronoun and its antecedent are not related by movement. Thus, there are multiple chains. Consequently, we expect multiple floated quantifiers.

7 Conclusion

This chapter began with a proposal to rethink principles A and B of the binding theory with an eye to reducing them to the theory of movement. The main empirical impetus for this comes from the parallelism between obligatory control and local binding on the one hand and non-obligatory control and pronoun interpretation on the other. Much of the technology introduced in this chapter could be revised and the main ideas still kept intact. The central contentions are the following:

(A) local anaphors (reflexives and reciprocals (See appendix 1)) involve structures formed by movement via multiple θ-positions (i.e. multiply θ-marked chains or multiply θ-marked expressions).
(B) Something like the Avoid Pronoun Condition is correct in the sense that the use of pronouns is costly. Pronouns cannot be used unless required for a successful derivation.
(C) Neither pronouns nor reflexives are lexical items. Rather both are grammatical formatives introduced by the computational system. They are, in this sense, like formal features that get added to lexical items before being computationally manipulated. This view of these morphemes returns to

the treatment of these expressions in earlier transformational treatments which introduced pronouns, reflexives and reciprocals transformationally rather than via lexical insertion.

(D) Pronouns interpreted as bound variables are grammatically related to "traces" that get interpreted as variables. In other words, something like Aoun's (1982) idea that bound pronouns are the spell out of traces is correct.

(E) Deictic pronouns (or the features that make them deictic) are lexical elements, members of the numeration.

If this line of reasoning proves successful it has one interesting consequence. It buttresses the idea that construal rules should be eliminated from the grammar. We return to discuss this larger theme in chapter 6.

Appendix 1   Reciprocals

The distribution of reciprocals closely resembles that of reflexives. Reciprocals, like reflexives, are subject to Principle A of the Binding Theory. Moreover, reciprocals come in local and non-local varieties with properties that match those of the analogous anaphors. For example, local reciprocals must have local antecedents – (87a,b), do not permit split antecedents – (87c) and only allow sloppy readings under VP ellipsis – (87d).

(87) a. *The men said that Mary saw each other
      b. *The men said that each other left[94]
      c. *The men$_i$ told the women$_j$ about each other$_{i+j}$
      d. The men like each other and the women do too (*The women like the men)

Non-local reciprocals allow all three.

(88) a. The men$_i$ were angry. Pictures of each other$_i$ in the buff had just been published in the NYT.
      b. John$_i$ told Mary$_j$ that rumours about each other$_{i+j}$ were spreading fast
      c. The men think that pictures of each other were just published in the NYT and the women do too

(88a) displays that non-local reciprocals need not be bound (within the sentence). (88c) shows that split antecedents are permitted and (88c) is acceptable with a strict reading, i.e. the women think that the men's pictures were just published.

This points to the conclusion that local reciprocals, like local anaphors and obligatory control structures, are also formed by overt movement and that non-local reciprocals are not. In this section, I outline an approach to reciprocals that has these properties.

I argued above that treating local reflexives in terms of movement results in the creation of complex monadic predicates. In effect, the accretion of θ-roles by an expression (i.e. the construction of a multi-θ-marked chain) has a specific semantic interpretation. It results in a complex predicate, one in which various argument positions are all satisfied by a single satisfier. In the simple two θ-role case, this says that the proposition that reflexives express contains a relation and a satisfier of that relation.[95] For example, (89a) has the LF (89b) with the propositional structure equivalent to (89c).

(89) a. Mary admires herself
      b. [$_{IP}$ Mary [$_{vP}$ Mary [$_{VP}$ admires Mary-self]]]
      c. <Mary, λx(x admire x)>

If reciprocals are similarly formed by movement, then they too should include complex monadic predicates as part of their propositional structure. I propose that (90a) has the LF structure (90b) and that its propositional structure is something like (90c).[96]

(90) a. The kids like each other
      b. [$_{IP}$ The kids [$_{vP}$ the kids [$_{VP}$ like the kids each other]]]
      c. <The kids, λX(X likes X), each other>[97]

The plural subject, 'the kids' in (90a) provide a (contextually specified) set of values for satisfying the variables of the indicated complex/polyadic predicate. 'Each other' can be treated in various ways. Here, I assume that it functions like an adverb and specifies, among other things perhaps, that the values of X λX(X likes X)' must be distinct.[98] Putting this together, the interpretation of (90) is that it is true just in case there are individuals drawn from the set of kids, say a and b, such that 'a likes b' is true and a and b are different. This yields the "weak" reciprocity reading.[99]

If this is correct then the syntax of reciprocals is very similar to the syntax of reflexives. I assume that like reflexives, reciprocals can check case. I also assume that, with reciprocals, the pronominal reading, the one that is non-local, is the elsewhere case and that movement is preferred where it is available. Thus, it follows that the properties of local and non-local reciprocals should pattern with reflexives and pronouns. They should be in complementary distribution where movement is possible and not otherwise.

The main difference between reflexives and reciprocals then is semantic. Reciprocals impose the condition that the variables of the polyadic predicate have distinct values. It is this condition that accounts for the unacceptability of (91). 'Each other' requires that the thematic variables of 'like' be satisfied by distinct entities provided by the set determined by the subject. As the subject in (91) is singular, only the singleton entity John is provided. This makes it impossible to meet the condition set by 'each other'.

(91) *John likes each other

The complexities of reciprocal constructions lie beyond the scope of this work.[100] The principal aim has been to show the plausibility of treating reciprocal constructions on a par with reflexives. It is critical to the present analyses that both involve movement between θ-positions resulting in multi-θ-marked structures. In both cases the reciprocal and the reflexive "check" case. Reciprocals also impose an interpretive requirement on the variables of the complex predicate formed via movement.[101]

This section has aimed at showing that movement is plausibly involved in the generation of (local) reciprocal constructions. Movement in these structures would account for why (local) reciprocals pattern like (local) anaphors with respect to binding, the inability to support split antecedents etc. I have suggested that it is plausible to treat the "antecedent" in a reciprocal as bearing multiple theta-roles which it receives by movement through multiple θ-positions. There are many further details to be worked out to fully vindicate this approach. However, this I leave for another time.

Appendix 2   Nominative Reflexives

It is well known that languages generally do not possess nominative reflexives even in cases where reflexives can occur in the subject position of finite clauses. Icelandic provides examples of the relevant contrast. Whereas nominative reflexives are barred from the subject positions of finite clauses, quirky case marked reflexives are not. Woolford (1999) has recently reviewed this phenomenon cross linguistically and has concluded, that Rizzi (1990) was essentially correct in attributing this effect to restrictions on agreement rather than nominative case per se. She observes that nominative reflexives can occur in the absence of agreement and that non-nominative reflexives are barred when there is, for example, object agreement. She provides substantial evidence that the following generalization proposed by Rizzi (1990) is correct.

(92)   Anaphors do not occur in syntactic positions construed with agreement.

With a minor refinement to the theory of reflexives developed above, it is possible to derive the generalization in (92). Before outlining the precise details, consider a possible derivation which places a reflexive in a position where there is agreement, say the subject of a finite clause. If the account outlined above is roughly correct, then the reflexive must be the residue of overt movement. Thus, in a structure like (93) (I use "English" analogues of the relevant cases), the derivation involves the movement of 'John' from the Spec TP of the embedded clause to the Spec vP of the matrix and, eventually, to the Spec TP of the matrix.

(93)   [John Tns [John [said [John-self Tns [John-self left]]]]]

Note that A-movement from the embedded Spec TP of a finite clause is usually barred. The reason is that a DP in this position checks the case and agreement features of the embedded clause. Thus, when the expression moves to the matrix Spec TP it can no longer check the features there and the derivation crashes. However, the analysis outlined above has assumed that *self* can bear case and check it. The relevant question for examples like (93) then is why *self* cannot check the features of the embedded *Tns* and *John* move up and check those of the matrix *Tns*.

Two assumptions suffice to prevent this. First, we assume that *self* can bear case but not phi-features. This is a standard assumption in the literature. Second, assume that if an expression checks *any* feature it must check *all* the features that it can check. This means, for example, that if an expression E checks the case of some head and it can also check the phi-features of that head then it must check the phi-features as well. This seems like a natural assumption on feature checking and plausibly follows from some economy condition as it applies to the feature checking operation.[102]

With these two assumptions, we can account for why the derivation in (93) is illicit. Consider what happens at the embedded Spec TP. The *Tns* has case and phi-features that need checking. The *self* can check the former, but not the latter. *John* can check both. Given that for the derivation to converge, *John* must at least check the phi-features of *Tns* it must, by the second assumption, check the case features as well. But this then essentially freezes *John* in place. For were *John* to move up to the matrix, it could no longer check the case features of the matrix *Tns*. Note that both assumptions are critical: *self* cannot alone check enough features of *Tns* for the derivation to converge and once the DP adjoined to *self* has to check any features it must check all the features it can, in particular, case. However, once it checks the case feature the DP is essentially frozen in the position it is in. Thus, there is no licit derivation of (93) where the embedded *Tns* has both case and phi-features.

Consider what happens if the embedded *Tns* only has case features. This is what we find in Icelandic quirky case constructions. If the embedded clause has a quirky case subject, the DP does not check agreement (rather there is default agreement). This means that *self* suffices to check the features of the embedded *Tns* as these are restricted to case features. If *self* checks these features, then *John* can raise up and check the case and phi-features of the matrix. This derivation, in short, converges and we should find reflexives in this situation, as we do.[103]

Three further points are worth observing.

First, the logic outlined here is not restricted to the Spec position of finite clauses. If *self* cannot check phi-features then anytime agreement must be checked the same logic kicks in and the derivation will crash. Thus, this analysis extends directly to the non-subject agreement cases discussed by Woolford.

Second, anytime nominative case is divorced from phi-feature checking we expect *self* to suffice to check the relevant features and the derivation to converge. This permits nominative reflexives just in case nominative need not require phi-feature checking. Woolford provides examples of these as well.

Third, the problems with the derivations above only occur if *both* case and phi-features must be checked against the same head. As indicated, if only case needs checking, there is no problem with the relevant derivations. Observe that if only phi-features need checking there should be no problem either if, following Chomsky (1995) we assume that phi-features are interpretable and hence do not disappear from a DP under checking. This is significant for Woolford (1999: 276, section 3.4) observes that the generalization in (92) breaks down in cases of past participle agreement. This is just what we expect if in these cases phi-features and accusative case are checked against different heads. Were this the case, then the DP adjoined to the reflexive could be used to check the relevant phi-features of the agreement head without having to check case. But this means that the case and phi-features of the DP would be available for later use. The accusative case of the construction would be checked by *se*. One could implement this by assuming that the complement of the auxiliary in a sentence like (94a) is a small clause with an agreeing participial head P^0 that takes vP as complement, (94b). This is essentially the structure that Chomsky (1991) proposes following Kayne (1989).[104]

(94)   a.   Marie s'était   décrit-*e* comme chaotique
            Marie refl-was described-Fem as chaotic
            "Marie described herself as chaotic"
       b.   Marie s'etait [Marie-se P^0 [Marie-se [Marie-se v [V Marie-se]]]]

In (94b), *Marie* receives a pair of theta-roles, *se* checks accusative case in the outer Spec of vP and *Marie* checks agreement features in Spec of P^0 before moving to the matrix to check case and phi-features of the matrix Infl. If this is roughly the derivation that obtains, then the fact that agreement and case are checked separately allows *Marie* to check both the participial agreement features and those of the matrix without being frozen in place. This proposal can survive a change in the specific details so long as the agreement witnessed in participials is not tied to the same head that checks case.

The present account contrasts with others in the literature in being a purely featural explanation. We need say nothing about referentiality or the binding theory or anything else.[105] All that is required is that *self* be bereft of phi-features and that feature checking be "efficient." This suffices to derive the generalization in (92).[106]

Appendix 3   A Few More Technical Issues

I will mention a few more technical problems with the current proposal concerning the structure of reflexives that have been brought to my attention. Here are three.

How does one prevent a derivation of (95)? Its problematic status was brought to my attention by Acrisio Pires and Juan Uriagereka.

(95)   Johnself loves

The derivation proceeds as follows: *John* and *self* merge. Then *Johnself* merges in the object of *love*. The whole expression then moves to Spec vP then Spec IP.

In Spec vP case and θ-role are checked, *self* checking the latter and *John* the former. Note this derivation assumes that case and θ-role can be checked in the same configuration. The whole complex then raises to Spec IP. To linearize, delete all the copies but the one in Spec IP. The derivation has the phrase marker in (96).

(96) $[_{IP}$ [[John]self] $[_{vP}$ [[John]self]   v $[_{VP}$ loves [[John]self]]]]
       +θ/+θ/−Nom −Acc +θ/+θ/+Nom −Acc   +θ/+Nom +Acc

The determinism hypothesis can be used to crash this derivation. Note that both copies of *self* in Spec IP and Spec vP have checked accusative case. As the only function *self* has is to bear a case that needs checking, both copies have met their full grammatical requirements. Thus, neither can be deleted. But if so it is not possible to linearize the output. So the very fact that *self* has checked case and then moved again is problematic if one assumes that deletion is deterministic, i.e. the assumption that only expressions that are somehow defective can delete.[107]

There is a variant of this problem with an alternative derivation that was brought to my attention by Jairo Nunes. Consider the derivation of (97a) in (97b).

(97)   a.   I expect himself to see John
       b.   I [expect [John-self [expect [. . . see [John-self   [John-   self
                 +θ/+θ/−C −C   +θ/+θ/−C +C +θ/+θ/+C +C
            see John-self]]]]]]
                +θ/+C +C

(97a) is intended to have the interpretation "I expect John to see himself." The derivation proceeds as follows. *John-self'* merges into the object position and gets the internal θ-role of *see*. The complex then raises to Spec v and receives the external θ-role. It raises and adjoins to the outer Spec v and *John* checks case. The complex moves again to Spec IP and *self* checks the case of *expect*. The derivation as stated does not converge for the same reason that (96) doesn't. We cannot delete either of the two higher copies of *John*. This prevents linearization at PF (or LF).

Another derivation would move only *self'* up to the outer Spec of *expect*. It would be possible to prevent this by observing that one is overtly moving a bare case holder. This is plausibly forbidden.

There is a second, simpler way, to prevent this derivation. Observe that it relies on allowing *John* to check the lower case and *self'* to check the upper case. I have assumed that *self* is a morpheme whose function is to "extend" the stem of an expression so that it can bear a second case. If this is correct, then the two cases are ordered, with the case on *self* higher than the case on *John*. If we assume that cases are checked from the outside in, i.e. from higher to lower, then one cannot check the case on *John* before checking the case on *self*. In the complex *John-self* the outer case of *self* must be checked first.[108] This assumption prevents the indicated derivation.

Consider a third problematic case brought to my attention by Jairo Nunes. What is wrong with (98)?

(98)   Which person$_i$ did John like t$_i$ after Mary introduced himself$_i$

The derivation would proceed as in the case of a standard PG (see chapter 3) but *which person* would have *self* adjoined to itself. This *self* would then check case of *introduced*. The phrase marker would look as follows.

(98)   Which person [John [[John like which person] [after which person [Mary [self [Mary introduced which person-self]]]]]]

Note that given standard assumptions the lowest copy of *which person* is case marked. This would seem to make the marking of an extra case via *self* redundant. In the case of PGs, we have assumed that the lower copy checks the lower accusative case of *introduced* while the higher copy in object position checks the case of *like*. If this is correct, then adding *self* with an extra case is redundant and possibly barred for this reason, i.e. for standard economy considerations.

This proposal relies on the (possibly erroneous) assumption that the object copy that checks case inside the adjunct does so at LF. This permits *which person* to leave the adjunct with its case features unchecked.

This, however, might be incorrect. Another possible reason for the redundancy of *self* might be the presence of Wh features which are also able to carry case. If this is correct, then one does not require *self* to bear additional case as the WH features that are added to permit movement via Spec CP are already able to fill this function. If this is correct, then (at least some) WH expressions might already be able to bear multiple case and so the addition of *self* would be redundant.

These remarks are very speculative and should be treated as such. For the nonce, I will assume that these remarks can be fleshed out sufficiently to make the particular implementation adopted here viable.

Notes

1   Some aspects of Principle C are discussed in chapter 3.

In contrast to some suggestions by Chomsky and Lasnik (1993) the project undertaken here does not aim to eliminate binding operations from the grammar by relocating them to the interface and treating them as purely non-grammatical interpretive operations. Rather the aim is to keep binding facts within the purview of the grammar (not the interface) and reanalyze binding operations as the manifestation of grammatical operations that are very different from the construal rules approach of GB.

Just a word on the Chomsky and Lasnik approach. Their approach and the proposal made here agree that the Binding Theory should be reconsidered in light of minimalist concerns. However, their approach, I believe, downplays the properties that suggest that binding effects are reflections of grammatical (rather than interface) properties. For example, the binding theory exploits locality effects similar to those used in constraining movement and the binding principles crucially exploit c-command. These are hallmarks of a grammar internal process. Consequently, it seems best to try to reanalyze binding effects as grammar internal processes rather than interface properties, in my opinion.

2 Uriagereka (1988) argues in detail that Principle A of the binding theory is suspect even in GB terms and should be reduced to movement. He similarly suggests that Principle B should be reanalyzed. What follows below is motivated by many of the same concerns, strengthened in part by additional minimalist commitments.

3 This view of pronouns is also developed in Aoun, Choueiri and Hornstein (1999) to deal with resumptive pronoun constructions in Lebanese Arabic. A similar view of pronouns as last resort expressions in developed in Reuland 1996. The general intuition these approaches shore can be traced to the Avoid Pronoun Principle in Chomsky (1982). See also Lidz and Idsardi (1998).

4 For a recent defense of the essential accuracy of this complementarity see Safir (1997).

5 This version of BT is adapted from Chomsky (1986b). "A complete functional complex" is a clause or nominal with a subject. Chomsky (1986b) frames the BT in terms of BT-compatibility but the added empirical coverage this affords is irrelevant to the points made here so I ignore it.

6 See Chomsky (1993; reprinted as ch. 3 in Chomsky 1995: 177–86) and (1995: ch. 4, 356–7).

7 What these conditions are has never been explicitly stated. The idea is that anaphors are essentially LF clitics that adjoin to I^0 at LF. There are problems with this view, however. First, it is not clear that anaphors are X^0s and so the analogy to elements like 'se' in Romance is not clearly appropriate. Second, many languages have both complex and simple anaphors. Nonetheless, they display very similar locality conditions. In fact, if anything, it is the simple anaphors which display long distance capacities, uncharacteristic of head movement, not the complex ones, e.g. Chinese 'ziji' versus 'taziji'. Third, in Romance, pronouns also move to Infl overtly. Does this imply that pronouns so move at LF in English? If so, it is not clear what is gained by making this assumption.

8 Curiously, the ECP only adequately covers cases of local anaphora. It is inadequate when extended to cases of non-local anaphora as it rules most such cases ungrammatical. Consider, for example, (i).

(i) John thinks that pictures of himself sold well

Movement of 'himself' to 'John' at LF violates all known locality conditions. The movement is from the subject of a finite embedded clause. It thus violates, the tensed S condition, the subject condition, subjacency and the ECP. Comparable overt movement is unacceptable

(ii) *Who does John think that pictures of t sold well

GB, then, only handles the distribution of local anaphors in terms of movement. Non-local varieties must be subject to other considerations. I mention this because this is the route pursued here. Lebeaux (1984–5) pioneered the distinction between local anaphora and non-local anaphora. It has recently also been endorsed in Reinhart and Reuland (1993). The idea that the local variety is tied to movement was first proposed by Lebeaux. Reinhart and Reuland advert to movement-like restrictions, their chain condition, though movement of local anaphors is not a feature of their analysis.

9   Earlier chapters try to remove other construal processes such as predication (that identifies 0-operators) and obligatory control (that binds PROs). If binding can be removed as well, it suggests that construal should be either a very costly or prohibited operation. We return to this in chapter 6.

10   Not all GB versions of BT used government in its definition of domain. Some substituted the notion SUBJECT (which included both subjects and finite T^0). Neither set of notions is particularly attractive on minimalist grounds.

11   See chapter 2, (21) for the OC paradigm and (23) for the NOC paradigm.

12   One can have third person reflexives that are tolerably good that are analogues of (4a) if there is a discourse antecedent.

(i)   John$_i$ is proud as a peacock. Pictures of himself$_i$ are on display in the gallery.

13   This contrast is more subtle than I would have liked. However, I think that a contrast exists.

14   It does not matter for present purposes what the exact nature of non-local anaphors turns out to be so long as they are pronoun-like. See section 3 for a more elaborate discussion of pronouns and Safir (1997) for a very interesting discussion of these non-local reflexives. I have very little to say about where these pronoun-like reflexives can appear. What is required for the viability of the following analysis is that they cannot appear in places where "real" reflexives are licensed. Thus, like pronouns, these pronoun-like reflexives are in complementary distribution with local reflexives. I assume that this is not the whole story. However, I have nothing interesting to add beyond this negative prohibition.

15   The way MERGE is defined, two different expressions cannot both merge into the very same position in a given derivation. See chapter 2 for a discussion of this point in the context of obligatory control.

16   This does not say what the correct theory of ellipsis is. The above, I believe, is consistent with both a deletion approach or an interpretive approach, though the details would greatly differ depending on which proves to be most adequate.

17   The theta-roles need not be identical actually. Rather, the second conjunct must have at least as many as the first, though it may have more.

(i)   John ate a piece of pie and Bill tried to

In (i), 'Bill' must have the eater role though it can also have the trier role.

18   I argue in Hornstein (1998) that the copy is actually marked with two roles however it is compatible with what follows if we assume that the chain headed by 'the unfortunate' bears two roles. In either case, the reflexive reading is the only one available.

19   For details see Salmon (1986 and 1992).

20   Salmon (1992) observes that his theory of reflexivization is compatible with a theory that treats anaphors as bound, rather than coreferential. He in fact prefers this to the complex predicate formation option that he takes to be proposed by Soames (1989/90) and that certain misreadings of his paper have engendered. However, if the text is correct, it suggests a mechanism for forming complex predicates in cases such as this. Moreover, as examples from Higginbotham (1992) indicate, bound pronouns need not carry *de se* readings, see (i). If so, analyses that tie reflexive interpretations to binding are inadequate.

(i)   Every unfortunate expects that he will receive a medal

Higginbotham notes that (i) can have a non-*de se* reading for every unfortunate. If so, pronoun binding and *de se* readings don't swing together. But if not, then it remains to be explained if *de se* readings are tied to binding alone why reflexive binding is different in requiring a *de se* interpretation.

21   See Salmon (1992) for discussion of these options.
22   We revise this assumption with the result that the copy is prohibited from checking case.
23   The same logic would extend to (i) under the assumption that here too the derived nominal retains the ECM case property of the underlying verb.

(i)   *John's belief to be handsome

Noun complement constructions like (i) are more fully discussed in chapter 3. The key here is that the genitive case marking on 'John' blocks checking the ECM feature on 'belief' so the derivation cannot converge.

24   The idea that reflexives are the overt residues of movement is developed independently by Idsordi and Lidz. Their analysis and the one outlined below are conceptually very similar. Both are reminiscent of the standard theory's approach to reflexivization. The standard theory postulated a rule of Reflexivization defined over identical NPs. Thus in a structure like (ia), the second 'John' would be transformed into a reflexive (ib).

(i)   a.   John$_i$ likes John$_i$
      b.   John$_i$ likes himself

There were several problems with this operation. The chief difficulty was that (iib) did not seem to have the same interpretation as (iia).

(ii)   a.   Everyone likes everyone
       b.   Everyone likes himself

It is possible to simply adopt the standard theory account here. We could claim that there is a rule like reflexivization that at PF changes the phonological structure of certain copies. It does this to comply with the LCA. Note that because we are dealing with *copies* the problem that arose for the standard theory does not arise here. The structure in (iia) involves a different numeration than the one in (iib). The former involves two selections of *everyone* the latter just one. This makes all the interpretive difference in the world. So, for current purposes, it would be feasible to adopt a rule of reflexivization that changes the phonological contour of copies under certain conditions. This rule would permit us to retain the assumption that reflexives are *literally* the residues of overt movement. The answer to the two questions is that reflexives are used by the grammar to change copies so that well formed outputs are derivable. The fact that there is agreement between the "antecedent" and the anaphor is plausibly the result of the fact that it is a copy that has been converted, i.e. the rule of reflexivization retains a residue of the altered copy in the agreement features. Why a pronoun form is used is plausibly related to the fact that pronouns are last resort expressions, as discussed in more detail below.

   In what follows I will examine an alternative implementation. However, it should be kept in mind that this more traditional alternative is a possible implementation of the basic idea and would serve almost as well.

25   I emphasize the qualifier *one*. There are others. Another option is to argue that
case features are not as finely differentiated as often supposed. In other words
they come marked simply as +case not as nominative, accusative etc. The realization on a given D/NP as accusative or nominative would then be treated as a
relational fact about the +case marked DP and the head that it checks this feature
against. If checked against an I^0 it is realized as nominative. If checked against a
V it comes out accusative (see Chomsky 1998 for such a suggestion). Note that
this suggests that in English accusative case is checked via overt movement given
the morphological difference between nominative and accusative pronouns in
English. This is argued for in Koizumi (1995) and Lasnik (1995). The conclusion is
not forced for the case of English as the default case in English is accusative.
Thus, one could argue that a case that has not been overtly checked in English
always surfaces as accusative morphologically.

   This more abstract approach to case has some conceptual support in MP
contexts. Consider what blocks the derivation of examples like (i) in which 'John'
is marked accusative and generated in Spec VP of 'saw' and 'Mary' is marked
nominative and generated in the complement of 'saw'. What then prevents this
underlying structure from surfacing as (ia) with the meaning that John saw Mary.

(i)   a.   Mary saw John
      b.   [$_{IP}$ Mary I [John saw Mary]]

Chomsky (1993) argues that this is prevented by some version of the MLC or
Shortest Move Condition. The problem then with the derivation in (ib) is that
'Mary' cannot move over 'John' to check case in Spec IP as 'John' could also check
this case and this movement is preferred as it is shorter. Note, however, that this
account presupposes that 'John' *could* check features of Infl.

   This presupposition makes sense under two assumptions. One is that case
features are not more finely differentiated into nominative and accusative and
thus either 'Mary' or 'John' are potential checkers of the case of I^0. Second, 'John'
and 'Mary' share features relevant to I^0 beyond case. Chomsky (1995) in fact
adopts the second option. He argues that the EPP should be analyzed as the
requirement that a strong D-feature of Infl needs checking. Both 'John' and 'Mary'
in (i) carry a D-feature and this is what triggers the shortest move violation. If we
drop the EPP (as suggested in chapter 2 above and others have recently urged
(see Martin 1999)), then the first option must be adopted. Recall, that this assumption suffices to get around the problem noted concerning (17b) above.

   There is yet one more possible implementation. Say that case is "assigned"
rather than "checked." Then there is no case prior to movement. But then there is
no case clash on copies. Note that the reason for assuming a checking theory
rather than a movement theory is empirical. It was assumed that accusative case
in English is checked by covert movement (Chomsky 1993). This assumption,
however, has been recently challenged (Lasnik 1995b and Koizumi 1995). Say it is
false. Then we can return to an assignment theory of case and the problem again
disappears.

   Note that either assumption can be adopted here. We note below that given the
LCA one of the two copies must still change its form.

   This said, let's continue, assuming that the technical problem indicated in the
text is real.

26   This was historically the situation. 'Self' was once an unbound nominal morpheme
that bore case and modified other nouns. See Keenan (1994) for discussion. Note

that this is rather similar to the view of reflexives proposed in Helke (1970). Helke assumed that reflexives were similar to bound pronouns in idioms such as (i).

(i) John lost his way

Note that both 'his' and 'way' are case expressions. Also 'way' is the head of the phrase. Similarly here 'self' is a case marked expression adjoined to another nominal that it modifies.

27 There is a tacit assumption that in an adjunction structure the phrase that heads the projection is marked with the theta-role that is checked on the verb. In other words, it is the DP that bears the role not the DP/DP.

28 It is actually irrelevant if the movement is in LF or overt syntax as argued by Koizumi (1995) and Lasnik (1995).

29 See chapter 3 for a discussion of Nunes' proposal.

30 See Lasnik (1981) and Arnold (1995) for discussion of 'do'-support.

31 I leave the question of how the pronoun gets the specific phi-features and case it reflects to one side. There are various possibilities consistent with the current approach. For example, it might get these features by agreement with 'self'. Adjuncts, like adjectives, typically agree with the DPs they modify in phi-features. This would then be another instance of this process.

32 The problem to be discussed was forcefully brought to my attention by Roger Martin.

33 Note that in chapter 3 we do essentially this, i.e. allow copies to check case, in PG constructions.

34 See chapter 3 for discussion of the SCA.

35 Note that this argument does not rely on the assumption that nominative and accusative case are distinguished on DPs. The problem above was motivated by considering case clash as the underlying reason for reflexives. However, the problem Martin raised arises even without case clash. The assumption that *self* checks case removes this problem.

The alternative approach in terms of a rule like reflexivization (see note 24) can be construed as a grammatical mechanism for permitting linearization when copies exist. By transmuting one of the copies into a reflexive, linearization can proceed without the problems noted by Nunes.

36 There is one more example worth considering given the discussion in chapter 3.

(i)   *Who does John believe likes
(ii) Who does John believe who likes who

Why can't (i) have the structure (ii) with the meaning 'who does John believe likes himself'. The difference between this example and the one in the text is that the 'who' copies would be case marked and so be read as variables. The SCA, recall, does not apply to variables.

Given the definition of a variable in chapter 3, however, the lowest case marked copy would not be a variable. Recall, variables are both case marked and locally A'-bound. The lowest copy would not be locally A'-bound. Thus it is not a variable and so would be subject to the SCA. This copy and the one in Spec CP could not be assigned consistent scopes.

37 I find these contrasts exist but they are far too subtle for my taste. I present the argument here without much confidence in the data.

38   The following assumes that what is responsible for the near reflexive reading is 'self'. However, another possibility is that this extra reading piggybacks on the pronoun+self, rather than the reflexive 'self' alone. Lidz observes that there is a contrast between 'zich' and 'zichzelf' constructions in that the former does not allow the near reflexive readings nor does it license sloppy identity under ellipsis whereas 'zichzelf' cases do. The same facts seem to hold in Spanish if one uses 'se' as the reflexive marker versus 'se mismo'. This suggests that the full pronoun+self construction is the relevant carrier of the additional information. This might suggest that 'pronoun+self' is the relevant adjunct rather than just 'self' as proposed above. I will put this possibility aside in what follows.

39   I find that the I-reading is most accessible when the pronominal part of the reflexive is not reduced. Thus there is a contrast between (ia) and (ib) in that the second cannot support an I-reading very easily (if at all).

(i)   a.   John bumped himself at the exhibit
      b.   John bumped'mself at the exhibit

This suggests that the pronoun+self is what is critical. This fits with the fact that reflexives have an emphatic use in English but only if stressed.

40   Things may be more complicated than this brief discussion suggests. Section 1 notes that reflexives support a 'de se' reading. Consider now a sentence like (i).

(i)   Ringo expects himself to be exhibited at noon

I find it difficult to understand this to mean that Ringo expects his statue to be exhibited in the contexts mentioned in the text. Rather, it means that Ringo expects the person Ringo, not I-Ringo to be exhibited.
   Similarly consider (ii).

(ii)   Only Ringo remembers himself singing "Yellow Submarine"

Imagine this said in a Disney studio where an electronic statue of Ringo sang the song. I find it hard to understand (ii) to mean that Ringo recalls I-Ringo singing the song. Rather the memory pertains to Ringo's own singing not the singing of any I-Ringo.
   I am unsure whether these judgments hold in general. Nor do I have an account for any of these data should they hold more generally.

41   These are often referred to as inherent reflexives. However, this cannot be a semantic categorization as these same verbs *all* have non-reflexive usages.

(i)   John shaved/washed/dressed Bill

This indicates that what it means to be "inherently reflexive" is simply that the verb without an overt object supports a reflexive reading.

42   One further premise is worth making explicit. I assume that in an adjunction structure either the whole constituent or its parts can freely move, at least out of this position, without violating Shortest Move requirements.

43   This would be consonant, for example, with Burzio's generalization which notes that an external argument is assigned iff the object is case marked. If this is understood as a markedness condition, it suggests that the option of having a transitive verb without accusative case is the marked option.

44 Or it gets checked by a copy and this leads to a violation of the LCA or SCA as discussed above. On either option, the derivation crashes.

45 This structure is not a case theory violation given a minimalist approach to case. For discussion see Chomsky (1995).

46 Note that this argues against treating OC as Chomsky and Lasnik (1977) do in terms of an implicit 'PRO-self' configuration. This structure would permit 'self' to check the indicated case.

47 This seems like a simple application of the lexicalist hypothesis which prevents the integrity of words from being broached by syntactic processes.

There is another way of explaining these data that does not rely on this assumption. It relies on the analysis of control in nominals discussed in chapter 3. I sketch it here.

Chapter 3 assumes, following Stowell (1981), that clausal complements in nominals are actually adjuncts to the nominal, despite bearing adjunct θ-roles rather similar to the verbal ones. Assume, further, that case is checked inside the DP not the NP. So, for example, the underlying structure of 'My belief [Bill to win]' is (i).

(i) [$_{DP}$ my [$_{D0}$ genitive [$_{NP/NP}$ [$_{NP}$ belief] [$_{IP}$ Bill to win]]]]

Assume now that 'belief' inherits the characteristics of its verbal form in that it bears an accusative case that must be checked. The question is where? If we assume that nominalizations are parallel to their verbal counterparts, then this case is checked in a second Spec DP projection. In effect, assume that 'D' is analogous to 'v' in the corresponding verbal structures. If this is correct, i.e. if both genitive and the lexical accusative case of 'belief' are checked in the DP projection, then (i) cannot be derived as it would violate the CED.

Chapter 3 argues that one can only escape a nominal by overt sidewards movement via a θ-position. To converge, 'Bill' would have to move to a case position. This movement is illicit on the assumption that the clausal complement is actually a syntactic adjunct of NP, as assumed in chapter 3. Consequently, the derivation crashes.

The problem with (ii) is different.

(ii) Bill's belief to win

Here 'Bill' could move out via the θ-position of 'belief'. However, it cannot check both genitive and accusative case. This makes (ii) entirely analogous to the unacceptability of "John believes [PRO to be nice]".

48 See Hornstein and Lightfoot (1987) for such an analysis of secondary predicates.

49 There is a way of testing this. Chuang (1997) argues that long distance reflexives in Chinese can be treated in roughly the terms outlined here. She argues moreover that it is very hard to get long distance reflexives that are bound by subjects over objects in 'persuade' type structures. If Long Distance Anaphors are indeed reflexives formed by movement, Chuang's analysis supports the view outlined here as this is precisely what is expected. Embedded subjects cannot "hang high" so they should not be expected to move over more proximate DP interveners.

50 Lasnik bases his discussion on Higgins (1973) which is in turn based on Kajita (1967). These constructions are also discussed in Lightfoot (1989 and 1991).

51 If these structures involve VP complements, it would strongly argue against the theory of case marked PRO. I personally have nothing against this conclusion.

52   Observe that the compatibility among theta roles that these examples appear to require can be stated quite directly on the theta requirements of the external argument of 'serve'. There is no need to assume that there is movement via the Spec IP of the embedded clause. In other words, this does not require adopting the EPP.

53   Lasnik (1992: p. 244, example 52) observes one further interesting property of control structures; PRO cannot be bound by an expletive.

(i)   There was a crime without *(there) being a victim

For discussion, see appendix 2 of chapter 3.

54   At a high level of abstraction this approach resembles others in the literature. So, like Reinhart and Reuland, it distinguishes local cases of reflexivization from non-local cases. They try to assimilate the latter to logophoric cases (see Safir (1997) for interesting discussion). However, the intuition behind these two approaches differs in an important way. They essentially treat reflexivization as a lexical process; which manipulates co-arguments. They run into difficulty with ECM constructions so they extend this essentially lexcial process to "syntactic predicates". The current approach starts from a very different intuition. It relies on the idea that reflexives are the creatures of (A)-movement. They are not lexical processes any more than control is.

55   See Chuang (1997) for an extension of these ideas to long distance anaphors in the East Asian languages.

56   And perhaps non-local reflexives as well. This leaves many issues regarding non-local reflexives and the details of their interpretation unresolved. The current wisdom is that these are pronoun-like in their interpretations and the data canvassed in section 2 support this. However, more needs to be said as these non-local reflexives are not interpretively identical to pronouns. These reflexives are 'logophoric' but this names the problem. It does not solve it. I have nothing to say here on these issues. What I do assume is that logophoric reflexives cannot appear where local reflexives do. In this sense they pattern like pronouns in being in complementary distribution with local reflexives. See Safir (1997) for discussion.

57   Whether affix hopping is actually movement is irrelevant to the main thrust of the argument.

58   Observe that we are considering the *bound* pronoun here.

59   The earlier analyses not only postulated morpheme introducing rules like Reflexivization and Pronominalization but also ordered the former before the latter and made both rules obligatory. This had the effect of putting local reflexives and pronouns in complementary distribution. In what follows this line of reasoning is implemented by assuming that the operations that underlie reflexivization are cheaper than those that underlie pronominalization.

60   This paradigm can become considerably more complex in languages with a rich resumptive pronoun system. Arabic is one such language. Essentially the same logic can be applied in these cases. For an analysis of Arabic resumptive pronouns see Aoun, Choueiri and Hornstein (1999) where this elsewhere logic is deployed.

61   This was brought to my attention by Jairo Nunes and Juan Uriagereka. It apparently was first noticed by Eduardo Raposo.

62   The statement of the problem relies on several ancillary assumptions. One of these is that the trace of *it* is not visible to block the movement. If it were, then the

move might violate shortest move or minimality. Chomsky (1995) assumes that the foot of a chain is invisible so the trace of *it* cannot block this operation. Note, if one assumed that movement was driven by attraction, then the trace of *it* does not have features relevant for checking the matrix Infl. As such, it might well be invisible even if all links in a chain were potentially visible.

Chomsky (1998) rules this sort of derivation out in terms of phases. The complement of a v or a C is grammatically opaque. As such, neither the object nor its features can move out of the domain of embedded tensed clause to check the higher features.

63 I abstract away from the various functional material left in the array and focus only on the lexical material.

64 I have used AgrO for ease of exposition.

65 Bosković rules this out in terms of a uniformity condition defined over θ-versus non-θ-positions. This position cannot be maintained if the analysis of Control in chapter 2 is adopted. It is also not clear what would conceptually motivate this kind of uniformity condition.

66 The two arguments displayed here are different in one important metatheoretical respect. The first argument relies on the details of Chomsky's (1995) theory to generate the difficulty. The problem can be resolved once some of Chomsky's (1995) assumptions are revised. For example, his (1998) theory also prevents the derivation considered given that phases prevent the indicated movements that save the derivation. It is unclear whether phases are conceptually well motivated. However, they have some empirically interesting properties and perhaps need to be adopted. If so, the first argument is inconclusive.

The second argument is more interesting as it is generated directly by the assumptions adopted in earlier chapters, particularly the idea that nominals can bear multiple theta-roles. The structures considered in (53) and (54) do not induce new phases and so the problem is real even given a theory that adopts phases. In effect, the argument is that once one drops the bi-uniqueness condition on theta-role/nominal pairs, it becomes very useful to assume that expletive *it* is an "elsewhere" expression.

67 It is interesting to note that (53), were it acceptable, is intended to mean what (55) does mean. Thus one could also rule this out by only allowing pronoun use where they "make a difference" to interpretation. Chomsky (1995) makes this assumption citing Reinhart and Fox. See Hornstein (1999) and Lasnik (1999) for criticism of this assumption.

68 Note that the Chomsky–Reinhart–Fox assumption can be exploited here to allow deictic pronouns. Chomsky (1995: 294, (76)) follows Reinhart in suggesting that an expression can be part of the numeration iff it affects the output. Say that we adopt this for the use of pronouns and we say that the relevant effect is at the CI interface. Then we can use pronouns if they alter the thematic structure of the sentence. In the case of deictic pronouns in place of local reflexives this will indeed be the case. In the other cases discussed above this is not the case.

Observe that the use of the "Affect Output" principle is different here than in Chomsky (1995). First, it is not sensitive to PF output. Second, it is not used to evaluate arrays of lexical items but is used to determine whether the use of a pronoun is licit. One might be able to *locally* determine whether or not the use of a pronoun at a given point in the derivation would affect interpretation. In other words, this use of the principle might not be burdened with the kinds of global computational decisions that Chomsky's use of the principle suffers from. Whether this is indeed the case awaits further investigation.

69 This section leaves many facts relating to WCO unaddressed. The hope is to sketch a different way of looking at the effect. Current approaches, even where empirically rich, leave it unclear why WCO effects should exist at all. What follows tries to sketch a story. Filling in the details is for future work.

70 Or convergence under thematic identity, see note 74.

71 This is reminiscent of Aoun's (1982) idea that bound pronouns are spell out versions of traces.

72 The ideas developed here clearly derive from Chomsky's (1981) Avoid Pronoun Principle. The aim is to show how to implement this idea within a broadly minimalist framework.

73 See Chomsky 1995: 263 for discussion. This may also violate case theory as the DP that is moving has checked genitive case and so cannot move to another case position.

74 This likely needs to be tempered to only compare derivations which are thematically identical, i.e. pronoun using derivations are compared with those that do not use pronouns and would result in thematically identical structures.

75 The Left Branch Condition has been analyzed in Chomsky (1995) as the attempted movement of a non-constituent. For current purposes, this serves equally well to block the movement derivation.

76 The logic is rather similar to that outlined in Chomsky (1986b) with respect to the Binding Theory. He introduced the notion of BT compatibility which resulted in the evaluation of a possible binding configuration with respect to alternative permissible configurations.

77 I assume that demerging an expression consists of copying it back into the array/numeration. I also assume that the operation of inserting the pronoun is actually an operation that replaces all copies of the element that is demerged. There is no doubt that this sort of operation is very cumbersome. However, this is not obviously a problem in the current context as it is intended to be far less economical than movement.

78 Observe that both approaches are variants of the old rule of pronominalization but defined to "change" copies rather than terminals introduced from the lexicon. This earlier theory, like the present one, was essentially a theory of bound pronouns, not deictic pronouns. It also saw pronouns as grammatical rather than lexical formatives. Lastly, it construed pronoun use as more costly than use of anaphors by ordering pronominalization after reflexivization. In this sense, both implementations suggested here reflect a return to earlier views about the grammar of pronouns.

79 This is the bound pronoun condition discussed in Higginbotham (1980). See Reinhart (1983) for further discussion. It is well known that there are configurations where bound pronouns are possible despite the fact that the pronouns are not c-commanded by their antecedents. See Hornstein and Weinberg (1990) and Hornstein (1995) for discussion. We return to discuss some of these below.

80 *Trace* is used here descriptively. I assume that movement leaves copies not traces. Note that the first implementation in terms of the MLC as a BOC is virtually identical to Aoun's (1982) suggestion.

81 There is another derivation that should be considered for completeness. Following Nunes (1995) I have assumed that sidewards movement is a licit operation. The question then arises what is wrong with the following derivation.

(i) Form 'everyone's mother'

(ii) remove 'loves' from the array and sidewards move 'everyone' and merge it with 'loves'

(iii) Merge 'everyone's mother' into the Spec vP of 'loves'

This derivation is illicit because (ii) is. It violates the Left Branch Condition. However the NMA of this step does not. In (iv) 'his' subs for the "moved" copy and merges sidewards with 'loves'.

(iv)   'love everyone' 'his mother'

However, (iv) is also illicit as it violates economy. It is cheaper at this step to merge 'everyone's mother' with 'loves' than it is to copy 'everyone' and merge it. So (iv) is less economical at this step than (v).

(v)   loves MERGE everyone's mother

This then blocks the otherwise acceptable derivation in (iv). Note further that merging 'everyone's mother' into Spec vP rather than with 'loves' is fine.

(vi)   'everyone's mother' MERGE 'v loves'

This yields 'everyone's mother loves' considered in the text.

82   There is another case to consider. What accounts for (i).

(i)   *Who$_i$ does his$_i$ mother love t$_i$

If 'who' must merge to its θ-position prior to raising to Spec CP (see Chomsky 1998) then (i) just reduces to (66).

  I have argued in Hornstein (1998) that an expression need not merge into its θ-position but can merge into its case position and lower to its θ-position at LF. The analysis in Hornstein (1998) does not consider what happens in cases of A'-movement. One possible way of distinguishing these cases from others is to assume that (in the unmarked case) an expression can be interpreted as a binder for a pronoun if and only if it is θ-marked. This would force the copy that binds a pronoun to be θ-marked and so force the movement urged by Chomsky. However, first merge is required into a θ-position only if pronoun binding is required. Otherwise one can merge into a non-θ-position and lower (see Hornstein 1998).

  One further point. This must be a markedness notion as it is possible to get pronouns that are resumed by WHs generated in Spec CP. If these WHs are not independently θ-marked, which seems reasonable, then the prohibition against binding a pronoun by a non-θ-marked expression must be tempered.

83   Reinhart (1983) claims that they are ill-formed. Hornstein and Weinberg (1990) suggest that LF movement allows these constructions by altering the c-command relations of the antecedent via LF movement.

84   It should also be possible to find cases of overt movement to non-c-commanding positions. It is interesting to consider Chomsky (1995) and Cardinaletti's (1997) examples of adjunct control in this light.

(i)   There arrrived several men without PRO introducing themselves

Here 'several men' controls PRO though it does not c-command it. This should, in principle, be a fine binding configuration if sidewards movement is allowed. More needs to be said about these cases. The facts as described by Chomsky and Cardinaletti requires further analysis as they tie the possibility of control to agreement phenomena. See Chomsky (1995) and Cardinaletti (1997) for discussion.

85   This derivation will also eventually violate principle C. See discussion in chapter 3. The movement of a case marked/checked DP results eventually in an unchecked case.

86   There are other derivations that need to be considered and eliminated. For example, why is there no superior derivation involving a reflexive? In the case in the text this alternative does not exist due to the absence of nominative reflexives (see below for some discussion). However, the same argument can be made for examples like (ii).

(ii)   I will drink no wine before Fred tastes itself

This example will be blocked by minimality, i.e. the Shortest Move Condition. See chapter 3 for discussion of how to state the condition.

Observe that this has as a consequence the conclusion that the pronoun in (iii) is not a bound variable.

(iii)   What did John read t after Fred reviewed it

This is not implausible. Note that, in contrast to (iv), (iii) strongly invites only a single answer, e.g. Moby Dick. (iv) allows a list of books e.g. Moby Dick, Pride and Prejudice, War and Peace.

(iv)   What did John read after Fred reviewed

87   This reasoning is likely incorrect for it relies too heavily on the assumption that case quality is derivationally relevant, contrary to Chomsky (1998). I currently have no other reason to offer for why movement is blocked. Perhaps what is at issue in these cases is not so much the contrasting case quality (genitive versus accusative) as the kind of case marking. Genitive case is a property of a whole DP not just the head, in contrast to other structural cases that appear as head features. Perhaps this makes it impossible for the second kind of case feature to check the first kind. If so, the problem here is case incompatibility though not of the kind mooted in the text. These speculations are the best that I can offer at the moment. It would be nice if some other movement requirement that is unfulfilled and thereby licenses the indicated NMA.

88   Audrey Li (p.c.) asked the following question: what prevents (i):

(i)   Nobody's mother loves himself

This derivation should be preferred if, as argued above, reflexives are the residues of movement and bound pronouns are only viable if movement fails. The question is what kills the derivation in (i)?

The most plausible answer is that what kills (i) is the incompatibility of genitive case and 'self'. There are several reasons for thinking that this is the source of the problems here. First, there are no genitive reflexives in English.

(ii)   himself's picture

Second, there appear to be languages in which examples similar to (i) are well formed.

(iii) ? meigeren de shu dou xie (ta)ziji
       everyone book   describe self
       "Everyone's book describes himself"

Thus in Chinese one can have sentences with structures similar to (i). Furthermore, the equivalent of (iv) is actually ill-formed (see Aoun and Li (1993a: 24, ex. 34b))

(iv) *Meigeren de   shu$_i$ dou xie ta$_i$
      everyone book all describe him
      "Everyone's book describes him"

This is what we would expect if examples like (iv) were well-formed in Chinese.

    This is suggestive material given the current analysis but more remains to be said. The equivalent of (i) in Chinese is unacceptable with the reflexive targeting the DP in the determiner. It is only when the containing DP would make no sense as the antecedent that the determiner DP can be antecedent for the reflexive. At present it is unclear to me why this restriction should hold. However, it is interesting that when reflexives are possible they block bound pronouns even in cases without c-command.

    Last of all, we do find cases in English in which the indicated anaphoric binding in (i) seems fine. 'Each other' is compatible with genitive case.

(v) Each other's books

Moreover the binding in examples like (vi) seems quite acceptable with the reading that A's book criticized B and B's criticized A.

(vi) The men's books attacked/defamed/criticized each other

    Consider another example from Holmes (1995: 13):

(vii) Their epistemologies and metaphysical beliefs were . . . opposed to each other's

Here *each other* is understood as having *their* as antecedent.

89 Just how adjunct PPs assign case and θ-roles is unclear even within GB. That they assign θ-roles of some sort seems reasonable given the semantic differences among the various prepositions, e.g. 'from' does not mean 'against'. Moreover, it is likely that adjunct PPs do not assign θ-roles in concert with other expressions the way complement PPs might.

90 This presupposes that adjunction is regulated by Extension as argued for in chapter 3.

91 See chapter 3 for some discussion of DP/NP structure as applied to relative clauses. For a fuller discussion see Kim (1998) where these structures are motivated. Kim assumes that strong DPs begin with the quantifier inside the NP. It then raises to Spec DP. The resulting structure is similar to the one in (82).

92 See, for example, Lees and Klima (1963).

93 David Lightfoot (p.c.) observes that this makes sense in a language like English in which there is no verb raising to Infl.

94 Speakers produce examples like this one too often for comfort. It is possible that nominative reciprocals are acceptable. See note 107 for some discussion. I assume the standard judgments here.

95   This follows the work of Salmon (1992) who argues for this sort of semantic treatment of reflexives.

96   A similar structure has recently been proposed by Dalrymple et al. (1998). They argue that propositions that contain reciprocals contain polyadic predicates (in the simple case a relation) and that reciprocals are polyadic quantifiers that map sets and binary relations into truth values (pp. 182–3).

97   I treat X as a variable over plural expressions. Plurals have a very complex semantics. For current purposes I assume that the plural "antecedent" of the reciprocal has a pair of theta roles that it satisfies. The satisfiers for the predicate $\lambda X[P(X,X)]$ come from the antecedent. The predicate is satisfied just in case elements drawn from the antecedent stand in the relation P reciprocally. See below for further details.

98   Dalrymple et al. (1998) treat 'each other' as a polyadic quantifier that takes the set specified by the plural and the polyadic predicate as arguments. Though I pursue a slightly different approach in the text, my main point, i.e. that reciprocals are formed by movement via multiple θ-positions and this is what yields complex/polyadic predicates, is compatible with this analysis. It is also compatible with their analysis that 'each other' be an adverb so long as it bear quantificational force. Adverbs of quantification are known to behave in this manner.

99   The full interpretive procedure relies on features of the interpretation of plurals, in particular the sum of plurals reading. Thus, function of the plural subject in (i) is like the plural DPs in (ii).

(i)   The kids saw each other
(ii)   The kids saw the dogs

(ii) has a reading in which the kids collectively saw all the dogs. So, say there were 5 dogs and 3 kids then when one adds up all of the dog sightings by the 3 kids one gets a total of 5. So, a total of 3 kids saw a total of 5 dogs. (i) can be read similarly but this time the set satisfying both the subject and object thematic positions is the same one, the one designated by 'the kids'. Thus, the reciprocal can be paraphrased as (iii):

(iii)   The kids saw the kids reciprocally

This will be true just in case members of the group of kids saw members of the group of kids and at least one of these seeings is non-reflexive. Note that on the sum of plurals reading it need not be the case that all the kids are involved, though they can be.

For further discussion of plurals see Schein (1993).

100   The complexities mainly revolve around how strong a reciprocity condition these constructions impose. All now agree that reciprocals need not involve full reciprocity, as is required in constructions like (i).

(i)   Each of the men likes the others

However, what is less clear is whether more than weak reciprocity is ever required except pragmatically. For recent discussion see Dalrymple et al. (1998).

101   There is some additional evidence in support of this treatment of reflexives and reciprocals as both involving complex monadic predicates. It is well known that auxiliary selection in some languages treats reflexives and reciprocals identically. In Italian they both require a 'be' rather than a 'have' auxiliary. Other constructions that do the same are passives and unaccusative constructions.

These four construction types form a natural kind once one analyzes reflexives and reciprocals as leading to the construction of complex monadic predicates. In all four cases the 'be' auxiliary "selects" a monadic predicate. Passives and unaccusatives involve simple monadic predicates while reflexives and reciprocals involve constructed (by movement) monadic predicates.

One last point. There is an important difference between a monadic predicate and a transitive predicate. I use the latter term to indicate the θ-structure of a predicate. The sentences in (i) are all transitive in this sense.

(i)   a.   John likes Mary
       b.   John likes himself
       c.   The men like each other

However, (ia) differs from (ib) and (ic) in that in the latter two the predicate is monadic while in (ia) it is dyadic. This means that the transitive predicate in (ia) has the (logical) structure in (iia) while those in (ib,c) have the (logical) structure in (iib).

(ii)   a. $\lambda x\,\lambda y\,(x \text{ likes } y)$
      b. $\lambda xy\,(x \text{ likes } y)$

102   For example, it is better to check all the features it is possible to check from any given source rather than checking one feature from one source and another feature from another.

103   Kjartan Ottósson (p.c.) has informed me of an interesting fact. In quirky case constructions such as (i), there is an obviation effect when a pronoun is substituted for the reflexive.

(i)   a.   John$_i$ V [[pronoun$_i$/self$_i$ Quirky Case] T . . .]

In other words, there is a strong preference to interpret the pronoun as disjoint in reference from the matrix subject *John*. This effect goes away when the embedded clause is nominatively marked. In this case, the subject can easily antecede the pronoun.

This is precisely what is expected given the current analysis as movement is possible in the first case but not the second. As movement blocks bound pronominalization, we expect obviation in the case where it is possible but not otherwise.

104   See p. 148, example (29), in Chomsky (1995), a reprint of Chomsky (1991).

105   See Woolford (1999: 277ff) for a review of the kinds of accounts offered.

106   Reciprocals seem considerably freer than reflexives in being licensed in the subject position of finite clauses:

(i)   The men don't ask where each other were parked
(ii)   John and Bill don't believe that each other were at the party

If reciprocals differed from reflexives in being able to bear phi-features, then it should be possible to derive these sorts of structures given the analysis above coupled with a treatment of reciprocals similar to the one in appendix 1.

107   This assumes that *self* is an item that needs to be linearized even though it is not part of the array/numeration.

108   If checking it permits convergence. Note that if more than just case needs checking then *John* might have to check case. See Appendix 2.

6

Case, C-Command, and Modularity

Introduction

This chapter aims to consider what the proposals in the earlier chapters tell us about the contours of Universal Grammar on the assumption that they are essentially correct. The theoretical setting of the discussions above has been broadly minimalist in nature. This is so in two senses.

First, I have adopted the methodological assumptions of the program. A recurrent theme of the earlier chapters has been to find ways of reducing the complexity of UG by eliminating rule types, modules, types of empty categories, and various redundancies. In addition, the analyses have exploited various kinds of least effort reasoning. For example, economy considerations lie at the center of the account for why PROs in adjuncts are generally controlled by subjects and least effort considerations are adduced in reducing the Minimal Distance Principle to the Shortest Move Condition.

Second, the analyses presented above have been cast in the technical idiom of current minimalist theorizing. For example, the Bare Phrase Structure approach to constituency has been exploited, as has case checking, greedy movement, the copy theory of movement, the LCA, the Extension Condition and more. These are standard tools in a minimalist's technical tool box and feature regularly in current minimalist practice.

In these two senses then, the analyses presented above are "minimalist" in spirit and detail. However, certain features of the analyses are, to some degree, non-conventional. Let me mention some of these here.

The analyses of control and Principle A have critically assumed that movement via theta-positions is licit. In effect, the analyses are based on the assumption that theta-roles are grammatically "featural" in the same way that case and phi-features are in the specific sense that all three can license greedy movement.[1]

A second assumption is that the grammar allows sidewards movement. Sidewards movement features prominently in the analyses of adjunct control, parasitic gaps, and the host of A'-movement operations discussed in chapter 3.[2]

A third distinctive feature is the assumption that Move is a complex operation, COPY and MERGE (but *not* ATTRACT), and that copies are no different from "originals" in their grammatical powers. They can block movement, they can themselves be copied etc. In effect, the analyses above adopt a strong version of the copy theory of movement and dispense with virtually all residues of trace theory. Following Nunes (1995), I have assumed that traces per se do not exist, viz. the grammar contains no expression akin to [$_{xp}$ e], and so require no special licensing conditions (such as the ECP). I have assumed that there is no interesting theoretical distinction between heads and tails of chains. All copies are on an equal footing. All copies must meet the interpretive demands of the interfaces. The fact that only one generally will lies behind the observation that movement does not generally result in a spate of copies sprinkled throughout the sentence. Ill formed copies must delete or there is no convergence.

This brings us to a last distinctive assumption of the foregoing analyses: all deletion operations are deterministic in the sense that they can only apply to "defective" expressions. Put another way, the proposals have crucially assumed that copies that meet all their grammatical requirements cannot be optionally eliminated even if this deletion serves to permit convergence. If a copy has all of its relevant features checked, then no grammatical operations can apply to remove it.

These assumptions, both the idiosyncratic and the more conventional, have all been put to the service of one big end: the elimination of construal rules from the grammar. The common denominator of the analyses above is the substitution of relations established by movement for ones established by construal. The big claim embodied in these proposals boils down to the following: the only way to establish a grammatical relation between two XPs is via movement. Thus, for example, a DP controls a PRO iff the DP has moved from the position occupied by PRO, a DP binds a reflexive iff the DP has moved from the position occupied by the reflexive, two gaps are in a real gap/parasitic gap relationship iff there has been movement from one to the other, etc. In all cases where GB has suggested an indexing relation established via a rule of construal, the analyses above substitute a set of movements relating the two expressions. This is an informal description, of course. For strictly speaking, if the foregoing is correct, there is no PRO and reflexives have no antecedents etc. However, viewed from the perspective of GB, the above can be seen as claiming that construal operations do not exist and that all inter-phrasal relations whose establishment was the grammatical province of construal processes are actually the result of various (more or less exotic) applications of MOVE.

Three big conclusions result if this is correct. First, movement is far more ubiquitous than heretofore assumed. Second, that construal operations are either very costly or non-existent. Third, the conditions used to define the structures for licit construal (e.g. c-command as part of the binding theory) are plausibly eliminable as grammatical primitives. All three of these conclusions have interesting implications for the character and structure of UG. We turn to some of these now.

1   The Place of MOVE in UG

The fact that natural languages manifest displacement is uncontroversial. But, *why* they do so is much less clear. The earliest minimalist musings on this topic regarded displacement (and the movement operations thought to underlie these) as a conceptually unnatural phenomenon. In contrast to MERGE, a "virtually conceptually necessary" operation, MOVE has been regarded as very problematic with little to conceptually recommend it. In fact, Chomsky (1995) exploits this difference to ground an economy distinction between MERGE and MOVE in which applications of the former are more economical than applications of the latter precisely because MERGE is conceptually natural while MOVE is not.

In more recent thinking on this topic, it is still assumed that there is something contrived about MOVE. However, now reasons are provided for why such an odd operation must nonetheless exist in the best of all possible grammars (see Chomsky 1998). The reasoning goes as follows. The objects produced by the grammar are handed over to the interfaces for interpretation. It is a feature of the interfaces that peripheral positions (viz. positions on the left or right edge of the clause) are the locus of certain kinds of information that the interfaces "care" about, e.g. theme/rheme, topic/comment, old/new information. If we assume that the grammar is optimal then it produces objects designed to be perfectly "legible" at the interfaces. Thus, the displacements that exist are not odd excrescences reflecting poor design but are required to meet the informational demands the interfaces impose. The grammar with its attendant MOVE operations is computationally optimal for it perfectly meets these interface requirements. In short, given this picture, the best grammatical design involves movement because of interfaces demands.

This approach still leaves it unclear why the interface has the properties it does or why these demands require movement to peripheral positions in order to be satisfied. It is conceivable that these exigencies could have been met in some other way, one that did not require displacement, e.g. different intonations on the relevant words or distinctive morphology or accompanying hand gestures. At any rate, this is the current favored story for why displacement exists.[3]

It is interesting to observe that MOVE is standardly contrasted with MERGE. Its relative standing with respect to rules of construal has yet to be addressed.[4] In the analyses developed in the earlier chapters of this book the standard rules of construal have been eliminated. In place of construal for the interpretation of (obligatory) control, we have movement. Substituting for anaphor binding, there is movement. In place of 0-operator identification/predication, there is movement. Even bound pronouns are taken to be related to their antecedents indirectly via movement, i.e. in terms of their NMAs which are defined in terms of possible MOVE. Assume that this is roughly correct. It raises an interesting question: are there rules of construal at all? Note, if they do exist then they must be more costly to use than MOVE for otherwise we should find construal operations substituting for movement processes. After all, construal does not seem to manifest displacement and so, if displacement is bad *ceteris paribus* then we should see intraclausal dependencies grammatically determined in terms of relations between expressions established by construal rules rather than via movement. In short, we expect the opposite of what earlier chapters have argued is actually the case.

This then raises another question: if there are no rules of construal, why not? One possible answer is that the preferred mode of coding grammatical dependencies in a phrase marker is via MOVE.[5] This suggests that MOVE is not a grammatically awkward process, contrary to the line of thinking surveyed above, but the optimal way of coding dependencies between non-sisters. In what follows, I would like to suggest a way of thinking about MOVE that makes its grammatical presence virtually ineluctable.

As a first step, consider why MERGE is considered conceptually unavoidable. It starts from the observation that there are at least two kinds of grammatical objects: words, the atomic units, and phrases (including sentences, i.e. Inflection/Complementizer phrases), complex composite units made up of words. It is a truism that natural languages distinguish between atoms/words on the one hand and phrases/complexes on the other. The "infinity" of natural languages depends on this as does the clear competence native speakers have in dealing with previously unencountered sentences. It is also obvious that these facts demand that words be combinable into larger units (i.e. that something like recursion characterize grammatical competence). The simplest mode of combination is MERGE, i.e. take two units and put them together. So, the source of MERGE's conceptual necessity is the fact that natural languages are compositional and this is just another way of saying that sentences are composed of words/units in various combinations.

The distinction between words versus phrases/sentences is standardly reflected in the distinction between the lexicon on the one hand and the computational system, i.e. grammar, on the other. The lexicon is (at the very least) the repository of lexical exceptions and idiosyncratic information. Virtually every system of grammar posits a lexicon which contains the units that the grammar manipulates.

In minimalist theories one begins a derivation by assembling an array of lexical items culled from the lexicon. One ends a derivation when all members of this set have been combined to form a larger unit. What does this process of accessing the lexicon consist in? What, in other words, does the operation of "taking an item from the lexicon" amount to? Clearly, it is not the same as taking a ball from an urn or Santa taking a present from his bag. In the latter cases once taken from the urn or the bag the urn/bag contains one less item than it contained prior to the removal of the item. In contrast, when the lexicon is accessed it does *not* reduce in size. This tells us a bit about what accessing the lexicon amounts to. It is the process of copying an item from the lexicon to the array/numeration.[6] In other words, selecting atomic units from the lexicon for computational manipulation by the syntax involves the COPY operation. In effect, the distinction between words and phrases, the idea that phrases are made up of words and the notion that there is a distinction between the lexicon and the grammatical system requires an operation like COPY. In this sense, one is tempted to say that the distinction between words and sentences conceptually requires the operation of COPY no less than it requires the operation of MERGE. However, if this is correct, then MOVE which just is the complex operation COPY and MERGE (at least on the Copy theory of movement adopted here) is a conceptually costless operation in that the sub-operations that comprise it are conceptually necessary. Thus, MOVE must be an available grammatical option once one distinguishes words from phrases and considers what the conceptually minimum operations required to relate them are.

Let me put this one other way. Compositionality requires MERGE. It also requires a distinction between atoms and complexes and a "place" to store the atoms (viz. a lexicon). In the domain of language, when words are used, they can be used again. Thus, selecting words from storage involves copying them. So compositionality in the linguistic domain requires COPY. But MOVE just is COPY and MERGE so the most basic facts about natural language render MOVE conceptually natural. If one further assumes that one uses the operations that one naturally has to do whatever work needs doing, then MOVE, which is capable of coding an expression's interphrasal dependencies, will be the preferred grammatical method for establishing such relations. In short, displacement, on this view of things, is expected to be a standard feature of natural languages since such languages encode intrasentential dependencies.

One important consequence of this is that construal processes should be less preferred than movement if the aim is to establish intraclausal dependencies. The reason is that MOVE is "virtually conceptually necessary" while construal isn't.

A second consequence of this is that we retain a principled account for why MERGE is preferred to MOVE despite the fact that both operations are conceptually required. The reason is that MOVE is a composite operation whose subparts are MERGE and COPY. This makes MERGE a subpart of MOVE and so a simpler operation than MOVE. For this reason the local application of MERGE is preferred to that of MOVE. We discussed various issues that arise if MOVE is thought of in this way in chapter 3. What is relevant here is the point that we need not abandon the position that MERGE is more economical than MOVE *even if both are conceptually necessary operations.*[7]

2   Why Case?

Case and movement are intimately related through the notion of least effort. Movement can be greedy by resulting in a checked case feature.[8] Just what is case? It is the paradigmatic *non*-interpretable feature, a feature with no interpretation at the LF interface.[9] In a minimalist context, the existence of such features is a real puzzle. Why should they exist? More particularly, given that the aim of grammatical manipulations is to produce objects "legible" at the interfaces, why should expressions begin their computational lives covered with uninterpretable features like case. Note the question is not *if* features like case are grammatically important but *why* a system that is conceptually elegant (even optimal) would contain such a feature. Wouldn't things be easier (and more elegant, economical etc.) if the grammar simply eschewed the use of such features? Put more baldly: how elegant and optimal can grammars be if they include features (like case) whose sole import in the system is to be eliminated?

This puzzle concerning case has motivated Chomsky's various attempts to link case with displacement. As noted above, his story ultimately sees displacement as the result of various interface requirements. This also motivates the existence of case features. They are required to drive movement and movement is required by the legibility conditions of the interface. Hence case is required for grammars to optimally meet interface conditions.

This line of reasoning may well be correct. However, it leaves some questions unanswered. For example, to date we have no very compelling account of the informational properties that (structural) case serves. As a result, we have little reason for thinking that the use of uninterpretable features to drive movement is the optimal mechanism for meeting the interpretive requirements of the interfaces. Moreover, it is not particularly clear how covert movement to check case fits into this picture of things.[10] In fact, as it is standardly assumed that case can be discharged without displacement, it is unclear how its existence is explained by the need for displacement.[11] Whatever the virtues of this approach to case, in what follows I would like to sketch another account of how case and movement might be related.

Since the early 1980s case and movement have been intimately linked through the notion of a chain. In GB terms (A-)chains are well formed only if the head of the (A-)chain is a case marked position. In minimalist writings this requirement on chains translates into the requirement that MOVE be greedy. Given conventional assumptions, theta-roles are not features that can license greedy movement. This basically leaves case and phi-features as the primary spurs to greedy movement.[12] In the analyses above, I have in addition assumed that movement can be driven by the requirement to check theta-roles. This addition complicates the question of why case exists for with the assumption that theta-roles suffice to license movement, it is logically possible to have displacement without an uninterpretable feature like case driving the movement. In short, the (already tenuous) connection between case and MOVE becomes further strained. In what follows I outline a line of reasoning that shows that a feature like case, a feature that is *necessarily* uninterpretable, is required by a well designed grammar with the range of properties characteristic of natural languages.

A wedge into this discussion is provided by thinking about what we would lose if displacement were removed from the grammar. Consider what falls under A-movement in the present account. Reflexivization, reciprocals, control, and pronoun binding all ultimately rely on MOVE.[13] Thus, if this is roughly correct, without MOVE natural languages would not have these construction types. More generally, without MOVE intrasentential dependencies would not be optimally statable (see section 2). How is case related to MOVE? In the present system, uninterpretable features are not required for MOVE, e.g. movement from one theta-position to another is legitimate. Given that this is so, how is MOVE tied to case in the present system (if at all)?

Movement and case relate as follows. MOVE is just COPY and MERGE. Consequently, when there is movement there are necessarily multiple copies. When MOVE has applied to a DP, for example, a structure like (1) with multiple DP copies results.

(1) [... DP .... DP .... DP ...]

In order to get an interpretable object from (1) the phrase marker must be linearized. I have argued that a form of linearization was required both in overt syntax and LF.[14] However, multiple copies prevent linearization and so, convergence. In order to converge deletion must apply so that all copies but one are eliminated. But, deletion, I have argued, is deterministic. In other words, copies cannot freely delete. Determinism only allows the deletion of copies that are in some way defective. This implies that all the copies in (1) but one are in some way defective at one of the interfaces. What makes an expression defective at the interface? Possessing an uninterpretable feature. This amounts to saying that all but one of the DPs in (1) bear an uninterpretable feature, i.e. a feature akin to case.

Let me put this another way. In an optimal grammar, intersentential dependencies are coded via MOVE (see section 2). Thus in any natural language with reflexives or reciprocals or control etc. the optimal representation of these relations will involve MOVE. Movement necessarily produces copies. Copies prevent linearization. Deletion is thus required for convergence if there is movement. If deletion is deterministic then we need features to cripple all copies but one. Case, a non-interpretable formal feature, fits this bill perfectly. Only one copy is case checked in an (A-)chain. Thus all copies but one can (and must) deterministically delete.

Observe that case has been motivated here from rather general requirements internal to the operations of the grammar. The key assumptions are (i) the idea that the optimal way to code intra-sentential dependencies is via MOVE, (ii) the need to "order" linguistic expressions prior to interface interpretation (e.g. the LCA) and (iii) the requirement that deletion operations be deterministic, viz. forced rather than free.[15] These desiderata require a formal feature to doom most copies. In effect, they require a feature like case. If this is correct, then we have just deduced the necessity of case features as part of optimal grammatical systems for languages that code intra-sentential dependencies.

This still leaves many issues about case unresolved. For example, why are there only three or four structural cases; nominative, accusative, dative (and possibly genitive)? Why is case sometimes covertly and sometimes overtly checked? However, we have provided an answer to the question of why does case, an uninterpretable formal feature, exist at all. It is required by the optimal kind of grammar needed to code intra-sentential relations.[16]

This story echoes a classical GB theme.[17] It essentially restates the GB Visibility Hypothesis in minimalist terms, the requirement that DPs need case in order to be visible at LF.[18] Here we have the flip side of this. To be interpretable, all copies but one must retain case. This ties case to interpretability just as the Visibility Hypothesis does. Given that there is very little distinction between checking versus assigning case, the difference between these two ways of construing the role of case are very very close. In effect, visibility is plausibly required on minimalist grounds.

Two last points of interest. Note that if this is correct, it suggests that deletion may be unnecessary. What I mean is that deletion might not be part of the inventory of grammatical operations. There is no operation DELETE akin to MERGE and COPY. Rather deletion is just the absence of interpretability at an interface. Interpretable objects are interpreted. Those with non-interpretable features are ignored. With this understanding of deletion there is no clear advantage to postulating a rule like DELETE to the grammar.[19]

Second, this entire rationalization of case features relies on MOVE being the favored method of coding intra-sentential dependencies. If construal were an available option then this argument would collapse. This can be viewed as another reason for thinking that construal processes, if they exist at all, are grammatically marginal.[20]

3   Modularity

It has been proposed that the language faculty is modular in two senses of the term. The first is that the language system as a whole is informationally distinct from other cognitive systems. The second is that the language faculty is itself composed of separate modules. The first sense of modularity is uncontroversial and is adopted without comment here. The discussion that follows is entirely directed to the second of these modularity claims; call it "internal modularity" (I-modularity)

One of the distinctive properties of GB style theories of UG is their highly I-modular construction. Chomsky (1981), for example, distinguishes various independent modules including subsystems of principles for bounding, government (ECP), theta-properties, binding, Case and control. In conjunction with the principles and parameters architecture, this modular view of UG's internal construction is one of the salient characteristics of the GB view.

The claim that UG is I-modular has been neither endorsed nor repudiated by the Minimalist Program. However, if one applies the standard measures of theory evaluation characteristic of minimalism it quickly becomes clear that adopting internal modularity requires substantial independent evidence. The reasons for this are the familiar methodological ones enumerated in chapter 1: all things being equal, it is better to have fewer modules to more. Just like it is better to have fewer levels, fewer grammar internal primitives, fewer rule types etc. Indeed, this sort of reasoning has been used to motivate the specific reanalyses outlined above. So, on general methodological grounds, internal modularity must be vigorously defended on empirical grounds if it is to be accepted.

One of the consequences of the proposals set forth here is that they remove much of the empirical motivation for adopting internal modularity as a feature of UG. In short, if the analyses presented here are roughly correct, then there is little reason for distinguishing separate modules internal to the grammar. In place of the various modules, the analyses above substitute extensive movement greedily checking a variety of features. Let me elaborate.

Chapters 2 and 5 aimed at the elimination of the control and binding modules. Chapter 3 aims to remove predication processes from the grammar.

The claim was that the general principles regulating control, binding and predication are more adequately construed in terms of MOVE. Technically, this requires permitting movement between theta-positions and this, in turn, technically requires treating theta-roles as features just like case and phi-features, in the sense of being able to license greedy movement. Once this is allowed, the various locality restrictions and interpretive properties characteristic of control and binding can be deduced. Or so it was argued above. *If* this is correct, then at least two modules (and whatever is responsible for predication) can be removed from the grammar and relegated to the properties of movement.

One might object to this conclusion as follows: the elimination of the modules requires a proliferation of features. The current account has not really done away with the case module. Rather it has repackaged the properties of the module in the case features that have been exploited. Similarly, considerations apply to theta-features. So the elimination of modules has proceeded via the proliferation of features and this is not obviously a step forward.

This objection, however, misses the point. An analogy will help. One feature of earlier work leading up to GB was the elimination of construction specific movement processes such as Raising and Passivization in favor of the general process of Move-alpha. In effect, the construction specific processes were reanalyzed as manifestations of a much more general process of movement. As a consequence of this, subject to subject movement (Raising) and object to subject movement (Passivization) were no longer considered separate operations. This, in turn, allowed an explanation for why the properties of these two types of movement were so similar; e.g. why they had similar locality restrictions.

Minimalist analyses have adopted more or less the same attitude towards movement to check case and phi-features. Virtually all minimalist analyses assume that movement must be greedy, i.e. that movement must be licensed by feature checking. Moreover, it is generally assumed that movement that results in checking a case feature is similar to movement that results in the checking of phi-features (see Chomsky 1995). In other words, the kinds of features that are checked do not necessarily individuate the kinds of movements that occur.[21] This is analogous to the GB contention that the fact that the targets (or origins) of movement might differ in two applications of Move-alpha does not suffice to distinguish two kinds of movement operations. Now for the punchline: adding theta-roles to the inventory of features does not surreptitiously add a new kind of Move operation. Rather, it simply says that there are various kinds of grammatical "features" and *all* can be checked in the same way, viz. by MOVE, and all function in the same way, viz. to license greedy movement.

If this is correct, then the picture of UG that emerges from the earlier chapters is one considerably less modular than the one featured in GB based theories. In fact, I believe that the evidence for a variety of modules is very thin. Consider the inventory of I-modules one ends up with if one adds the present suggestions to the other standard minimalist proposals.

In place of an X′-module, minimalists have Bare Phrase Structure. This latter theory attempts to reduce virtually all of the standard properties of phrases to the MERGE operation. Given that MERGE is not only a feature of phrase structure but also part of movement processes, the contention that phrases have properties traceable to a separate X′ module evaporates.

Case theory similarly reduces to the theory of movement, case just being another feature. The case filter reduces to the observation that case is uninterpretable at the C-I interface and so must be eliminated. The domains for checking case are functional domains for functional heads are the sorts of expressions that also bear case features. Section 2 above tries to explain why there should be a feature with the uninterpretability that is characteristic of case features. If successful then there is nothing special about case that requires a separate subsystem of principles.

The control modules and binding modules are gone.

Much of the theta-module can be similarly eliminated. Consider the theta-criterion. It falls into three parts. The first is that all theta-roles of a predicate must be assigned. The second is that every nominal must have a theta-role. The third is that theta-role assignment is one-to-one, i.e. a nominal can have at most one theta-role. It is plausible to interpret the first two parts of the theta-criterion as instances of the Principle of Full Interpretation (PFI) which in turn is the expression of the idea that all expressions must be legible (i.e. provided with an interpretation) at the C-I interface.[22] If this is correct, then the first two parts of the theta-criterion simply amount to saying that predicates and arguments must be interpretable to be legitimate.

The conceptually problematic part of the theta-criterion is the third bi-uniqueness condition. This follows from nothing and is a grammar internal condition not an interface requirement. Note that this conceptually problematic part of the theta-criterion has been dumped in the analyses above and crucially so. Thus, if we accept that the proposals outlined above are roughly correct then most of theta-theory follows from properties of the interface and so requires no separate grammar internal module.[23]

This leaves bounding theory and the ECP. Note that both characterize MOVE. I argued in Hornstein (1995) that the ECP fits poorly with minimalist sensibilities. The fit is poorer still in the present context given the adoption of a strong version of the copy theory of movement. The ECP has been viewed as a trace licensing condition. This makes sense in a theoretical context in which traces are formatives with distinctive properties which make them liable to licensing. However, if traces are simply copies (as assumed here) with no special characteristics then it is unclear what makes them problematic and why they should be required to meet special conditions. One *can* add ECP requirements to any theory. However, the copy theory of movement makes the addition of ECP licensing requirements conceptually unwelcome.

Fortunately, many of the facts that rely on the ECP for explanation have been reanalyzed in non-ECP terms. For example, the unacceptability of (2a) can be seen as a violation of greed rather than the ECP and (2b) can be analyzed in terms of the Shortest Move Condition.[24]

(2)   a.   *John seems [t was here yesterday]
      b.   *John seems that it was told that Bill left

It seems reasonable to hope that the other empirical supports for the ECP
will be similarly reanalyzed. There are minimalist proposals for many of these.
The ECP has been used to account for a variety of restrictions in multiple
WH questions, pair-list constructions, quantifier scope, antecedent contained
deletion constructions and movement of adjuncts out of islands. These are
all discussed in non-ECP terms in Hornstein (1995) and (1999). See chapter 4
as well. Kitahara (1999) also proposes various non-ECP based approaches to
adjunct/argument asymmetries.[25]

As for bounding, chapter 3 exploits a plausible analysis of island effects
proposed by Uriagereka (1999). This essentially renders all adjuncts islands
the by-product of LCA requirements.[26]

It is surely the case that some of these recent proposals will themselves be
reanalyzed. However, if they are roughly on the right track they support the
conclusion that internal modularity is *not* a property of UG, contrary to the
standard assumptions made within GB.

4   C-Command

An aim of the Minimalist Program is to construct theories using natural predicates and relations. One GB casualty of this pursuit has been the government
relation, which, it has been forcefully argued, is neither natural nor desired
(see Chomsky 1993). Chapter 1 reviews the thinking that leads to the repudiation
of government as a proper conceptual building block for minimalist theories.
This section considers the status of c-command from a similar perspective.

Like government, c-command is everywhere. Within GB it is required for
the proper formulation of antecedent government, the binding principles, the
bound pronoun condition, the chain condition and the theory of control.
Minimalist theories that adopt some version of the LCA also use (asymmetric)
c-command to define the linearization algorithm.[27] Despite its ubiquity, however, it is not conceptually clear why c-command should be so important.
Among all the possible relations that one can define over phrase markers why
is c-command the one that the grammar exploits?

This question has been most directly tackled in Epstein (1999).[28] The tack
that Epstein's work takes is to rationalize c-command. He argues that the
properties of c-command can be largely accounted for by seeing it as the
relation that tracks the MERGE operation. If so, it is a relation that the grammar
naturally makes available by being an offshoot of its (virtually conceptually
necessary) computational properties. Little wonder, then, that when a relation
is called for it is c-command that is used.[29]

Note that Epstein (1999) does not aim to remove c-command as a grammatically primitive relation. Rather his work argues that c-command is a natural
relation given a minimalist conception of the grammar. Consequently, the

omnipresence of the relation in various aspects of the grammar is not a cause for conceptual concern.[30]

This attitude towards c-command is in striking contrast to the one recommended for government. There have been no attempts to rationalize government in ways analogous to Epstein's work on c-command. Rather the assumption has been that government is an unnatural relation that should be dispensed with. In what follows I consider whether c-command might not be similarly treated.

It is taken as obvious that c-command governs grammatical interactions. Where is it critical? It is clearly required to define the notion "binding," which is relevant within the binding theory as well as for the proper treatment of control, and the correct definitions of antecedent government and chain. This suggests that reanalyzing the binding theory, control and movement should have consequences for the status of c-command. It does.

Assume that the analyses in chapters 2 and 5 are correct. If they are then binding relations are established under MOVE. In effect, μ is interpreted as binding β just in case μ has moved from β, i.e. μ and β are copies formed as a result of MOVE. Now consider the different ways that MOVE applies.

Consider first movement within a single subtree. Here (overt) movement must proceed to a c-commanding position. The reason is that any other kind of movement will violate the Extension Condition. In other words, if MOVE must obey Extension then for cases of MOVE within a single subtree the only legitimate applications of MOVE to an expression E will be to move E to a c-commanding position. Note that this is not due to some fact about chains, i.e. the object created, but the fact that operations must extend the subtrees they manipulate. Recall that the analyses of control and binding outlined above assumed that the relevant movements take place overtly. As such, we expect the relevant movements to conform to c-command.

Consider now sidewards movement. Here things are quite different. In some cases c-command will result. However, there are cases where we find control and binding but where c-command does not seem to hold. For example, we discussed cases of binding reciprocals from determiner positions in chapter 5.

(3)   the men's books viciously attacked each other

There are also many instances of pronoun binding without c-command. For example, (4).[31]

(4)   a.   Nobody's$_i$ mother loves him$_i$
       b.   Mary talked to nobody$_i$ before being formally introduced to him$_i$

Lastly, the analysis of parasitic gaps (and other 0-operator constructions) requires movement to non-c-commanding positions. Thus, in the present context, it is false that *all* movement is to c-commanding positions. If chains are simply objects formed by MOVE then not all chains require their links to be in c-command configurations.[32]

(5)　Which book did you read t before Frank reviewed t

This holds for A-movement as well. Chomsky (1995) and Cardinaletti (1997) provide examples of control without apparent c-command.

(6)　There arrived many men without PRO introducing each other

So, in the standard cases of movement we expect c-command to obtain and in cases of sidewards movement we expect cases that violate it. Both expectations have empirical support. What does this imply for the status of c-command? It suggests that it is eliminable. In other words, if the analyses outlined above are correct then it suggests that c-command is superflous in stating binding conditions, control configurations or movement requirements. All of these follow on more general grounds having to do with how trees are constructed. In many cases, these result in c-command configurations *but not because movement structures must meet a c-command requirement.* Rather that's just the way things generally turn out in simple cases. In more complex cases this need not hold and there is evidence to suggest that it does not.

So here is a tentative conclusion: the characterization of binding, control, and predication configurations does not require the use of the c-command as a primitive relation of UG.[33]

Let's now turn to LCA issues. This is a very large topic and I cannot do it justice here. My remarks are merely intended to be suggestive. The standard procedure for linearization takes a fully formed phrase marker and converts it into a linearization by an algorithm something like (7).[34]

(7)　μ precedes β iff μ asymmetrically c-commands β

What work does c-command do in (7)? It does the following. A linearization of expressions is an asymmetric ordering, i.e. if T^1 precedes T^2 then T^2 does not precede T^1. To linearize a phrase marker requires finding some asymmetric relational property of the phrase marker which can be used to map expressions (in the phrase marker) that are not linearly ordered into a linearization of these expressions. C-command provides a very convenient (generally) asymmetric relation which can be so used. For example, subjects generally c-command everything else in the clause. They also precede everything in the clause. One can relate these two facts by keying the precedence of the subject to the fact that it asymmetrically c-commands everything else in the phrase marker. In effect, one defines a linearization function that maps expressions that are ordered by (asymmetric) c-command into a set of expressions ordered by precedence.

Is c-command the only way of getting the required asymmetry on which we can hang the linearization function? Perhaps not. C-command is useful because the other relations that minimalist grammars have had at their disposal until now are not suitably asymmetric. For example, two expressions can be related via MERGE. However, MERGE has generally been taken to be a symmetric operation in the sense that merging μ with β is the same as merging β with μ. In effect MERGE(μ,β) = MERGE(β,μ). However, more recently it has been suggested that MERGE is inherently asymmetric (at least for substitution operations).[35] Thus, when μ and β merge it is predictable which will project its label; the one that checks a feature as a result of the MERGE operation. This fact suggests that MERGE is asymmetric with μ merging with β if β projects and β merging with μ if μ projects.

If we accept this, then tree building provides an asymmetric relation in terms of which we might be able to define linearization. Something like (8) perhaps.

(8)   μ precedes β iff μ merged with β

(8) works adequately for a range of cases. For example, when DP subjects MERGE with I^0, I^0 projects. Say this is because the DP checks features of I^0 such as case and phi-features. Following (8) this requires that DP subjects precede the I-projection they have adjoined to. If we assume that μ precedes β if and only if all parts of μ precede all parts of β, then MERGE will induce a linear ordering.[36]

There are two features of this approach worth noting. First, the linearization operation is not restricted to terminals. Every MERGE operation has a corresponding linearization. This is so even if the elements that MERGE are complexes composed of terminals. This goes against a common assumption that it is only terminals that enter into linearization. This, perhaps, indicates a failing of this particular version of the LCA.[37] Second, the definition of precedence stipulates that constituents are prohibited from overlapping. This stipulation is well supported empirically but it is a stipulation, though, to my mind, a reasonable one. Once again, this may indicate that this way of proceeding is incorrect.

Assume, nonetheless, that these possible objections are not fatal. What we end up with is (perhaps) a way of defining a linearization operation without adverting to c-command. The asymmetry of the MERGE operation provides a sufficient fulcrum for hoisting a phrase marker into a linearly ordered expression. C-command may not be required.[38]

To sum up. There are two places where c-command has been thought to be necessary within current minimalist approaches to grammar: in defining conditions for binding, control, chains etc. and for the LCA. The analyses provided in earlier chapters suggest that c-command is not needed to code the dependencies evident in binding, control etc. These can be established entirely via MOVE. Moreover, MOVE, if it includes sidewards movement, need not result in chains whose links are in a c-command configuration. I have also lightly sketched a way in which linearization might be statable without using c-command. If these twin suggestions prove successful, it allows us to remove c-command entirely from the inventory of basic grammatical relations. This simplifies the grammar in ways that are minimalistically pleasing. Instead of rationalizing an otherwise unwelcome relation, it appears possible that we could simply dump it.

5   Conclusion

I noted at the outset that minimalism is less a theory than a program. This said, the program will be successful to the degree that theories based on its major precepts are developed and shown to have theoretical virtues and broad empirical support. It is likely that many mutually incompatible theories can be built on equally adequate minimalist bases. The development of these alternatives is to be welcomed for it will enable us to sharpen the issues and questions that minimalism has raised. My aim in this book has been to develop one such minimalist theory in some detail. The main features of the present proposal make MOVE, interpreted as COPY and MERGE, the primary vehicle for coding intra-sentential dependencies. This large idea has been serviced by several technical assumptions including the idea that theta-roles are feature like, that copies are indistinguishable grammatically from "originals," that sidewards movement is possible, that pronouns are last resort expressions and more. It would be great if the theory here outlined proved to be (more or less) true. This, however, is unlikely to be the case. A second best would be if the analyses presented here proved to be firm stepping stones to deeper and empirically richer future accounts.

Notes

1   Others have made a similar assumption so this departure from conventionality is not a lonely one. As noted in the chapters above, Bosković and Lasnik, in particular, have similarly explored the possibility of movement to theta-positions.
2   This second assumption is less unconventional in some quarters than in others. See Bobaljik and Brown (1997), Nunes (1995), and Uriagereka (1998).
3   It is a story rather than a theory for all we really have at present are these sorts of informal comments. The details have yet to be fleshed out.
4   The reason for this might be the tacit belief that binding and control are not part of the core grammatical system. Suggestions to this effect occur in Chomsky (1998: note 45).
5   Actually, head to head dependencies will be coded by MERGE of sisters while longer distance interphrasal dependencies will exploit MOVE.
6   I mention array/numeration for concreteness. It is not required that this be the actual technology.
7   Chomsky 1995 suggests that the expense of MOVE with respect to MERGE is due to the superior conceptual status of MERGE over MOVE. In particular, whereas MERGE is conceptually necessary, MOVE isn't. The point in the text is that one can adopt the view that MERGE is more economical than MOVE without conceding that MOVE is less conceptually natural than MERGE.
   Note that the proposal to distinguish MOVE from Merge in terms of economy rests on empirical, not conceptual, grounds. There is empirical evidence that this is the case. Assume for a minute that this evidence was reanalyzed so that there was no reason to consider MOVE as more costly (see Castillo, Drury and Grohmann (1999) for the beginnings of such an argument). What would this do to the present proposals? Not much. If this turned out to be so we could derive the result simply

by assuming that there is no numeration/array but that lexical items are directly accessed from the lexicon rather than being culled into a numeration/array prior to the operations of the computational system. If this step were eliminated then there would be no conceptual reason for thinking that movements were more costly than mergers at any given point in a derivation. In both cases, the only question would be whether to copy an item in the derivation and merge it or copy an item from the lexicon and merge it. Thus, we see that the main reason for postulating an array rests on the empirical evidence (such as it is) that economy plays a role in derivations. Observe, that economy might be critical in distinguishing pronoun use from movement even if there is no array/numeration. I hope to flesh out these cryptic remarks in future work. I would like to thank Barry Schein for comments that stimulated this note.

8   Chomsky (1998) has argued that it is agreement features rather than case features that act in this way. In what follows this is not particularly important. The focus is on the existence of uninterpretable features whatever their other formal properties.

9   In many languages, structural case does receive a phonetic interpretation. Thus, case is plausibly interpretable at the PF interface. To be non-interpretable (in the present context) it suffices that a formal feature have no LF interpretation.

10   By "covert" I simply mean movement that does not result in manifest displacement. In this sense, checking case via feature movement is "covert."

11   In Chomsky's various versions of this story things can be more elaborate. What ultimately drives displacement in Chomsky (1995) and (1998) is morphology rather than case. Displacement is due to (implicit) pied piping requirements rather than the need to check case. It is unclear to me how these morphological requirements are motivated by interface conditions.

12   D-features have also been employed but what these are is very unclear and invoking them is seldom theoretically satisfactory. Chomsky (1998) appears to have dropped reference to D-features, at least for purposes of modelling the EPP. Earlier chapters (following arguments in Castillo, Drury and Grohmann (1999)) have suggested dropping the EPP in non-finite clauses. If so, D-features can be dispensed with as well.

13   Hornstein (1995, 1998, 1999) argue that relative quantifier scope also is related to A-chain movements.

14   In the latter case a scope order was required rather than a linear order. See chapter 3. That there is a form of linearization at both PF and LF was proposed in Kayne (1994) and early drafts of what became Nunes (1995). For recent discussion see Nunes (1999).

15   (iii) can be seen as a generalization of least effort notions to all operations. Deletion, like all other operations, can only apply if it must. Note that Chomsky (1998) suggests that even Merge is greedy. This extends least effort thinking quite generally to the grammar.

16   Note, I have assumed that once required for some function case becomes generalized throughout the grammar. In other words, there is now a policy that case is always required whether there is a coded dependency or not.

17   I owe the following observations to Paul Pietroski.

18   This hypothesis is attributed to Joseph Aoun in Chomsky (1986).

19   See Nunes (1995) for arguments against having both delete and erase as grammatical operations. If Nunes is correct, then deletion can be interpreted to mean invisible at the interface.

Technically, in the context of the present proposals, there remains the issue of how to state pronominal insertion without an operation similar to delete. It is possible that deletion (or something similar such as demerge) exists though it is not required to delete copies at LF.

20 Chapter 3 (appendix) examines a way of treating WH features like case features. If this is successful then the argument above, which is confined to A-dependencies, can be restated for A'-dependencies as well.

21 I am being careful here for we have seen in chapter 3 that the distinction between A and A' movement must be retained.

22 A similar point is made in Brody (1993).

23 There remain some features of theta-theory that we have not addressed, in particular UTAH based generalizations.

24 Chapter 4 proposes that (2b) be seen as a violation of economy. In effect, it prematurely uses a pronoun in the derivation.

25 The head government part of the ECP has, to date, resisted minimalist analysis. For an attempt to bring these into line with minimalist sentiments see Hornstein and Lightfoot (2000).

26 Chomsky (1998) proposes yet another approach in terms of "phases" and cyclic access to numerations. This approach is largely compatible with what has been proposed here though the details will have to be changed in various respects to fit the two sets of proposals together. For example, to allow a movement analysis of control to combine with Chomsky's conception about phases would require moving via Spec CP in OC constructions. Something like this was already proposed in a GB framework in Clark (1985).

27 See Chomsky (1995) and Uriagereka (1999).

28 See also Chametzky (1996).

29 Chomsky (1998) offers another example of this sort of reasoning.

30 Chomsky (1998) argues to the same conclusion: c-command is a very natural relation given the basic operations of the grammar and certain reasonable generalizations of these.

31 These are more fully discussed in chapter 5.

32 It might be that chains are the objects that the C-I interface can "read." This might then require an operation like FORM CHAIN (Nunes 1995). I have assumed in chapter 3 that this sort of rule is not required. I have argued against A-chains as desirable grammatical formatives in Hornstein (1998).

33 This conclusion should be tempered. The analyses above regulate movement via the Shortest Move Condition. In chapter 4, I interpreted this condition in terms of minimality. In particular, an XP cannot move over a position where it could have moved to on its way to another position. The relevant notion of a possible landing site might require the notion c-command. I say *might* for it is possible that the notion path suffices and that c-command is unnecessary. I leave full consideration of this issue to future work.

34 Different approaches to linearization exploit slightly different sets of definitions. For example, Kayne (1994) requires that there be a total ordering of terminals in terms of asymmetric c-command for a linear order to get imposed. Chomsky (1995) uses the definition provided in (7). Uriagereka (1999) considers a two-step algorithm that is only defined over terminals but has a process for forming "complex" terminals by the application of Spell-Out.

35 See Chomsky (1998).

36 This, in effect, requires that a linearization necessarily be non-overlapping.

37 However, it is unclear why the LCA should be restricted to terminals. Kayne (1994) concentrates on terminals as he requires that the LCA induce a total ordering on terminals so that he can use this to derive the X' properties of phrases.

However, if these are independently derived from Bare Phrase Structure considerations (Chomsky 1995) then it is unclear that a total ordering of terminals is necessary or desirable. Whether the LCA applies to non-terminals may be more an empirical question than a conceptual one. If it can, then the proposal above has some hope of being on the right track.

38   To go beyond these very speculative remarks will require considerable work. The biggest issue will likely involve figuring out what relation obtains between functional and lexical categories when they merge. If it is the standard one, then it would seem that all languages should be like Japanese, head final. Clearly more needs to be said. It is not impossible that a residue of the head parameter will have to be retained in fixing the order of complements to functional categories. This is just one of, no doubt, many problems that will require solution to make this elimination of c-command viable in the context of LCA issues.

Bibliography

Abney, S.: 1987, "The English Noun Phrase in Its Sentential Aspect," Ph.D. dissertation, MIT, Cambridge, MA.

Aoun, J.: 1982, "On the Logical Nature of the Binding Principles: Quantifier Lowering, Double Raising of *there* and the Notion Empty Element," in J. Pustejovski and P. Sells (eds.) *Proceedings of NELS 12*, GLSA, University of Massachusetts, Amherst, 16–35.

Aoun, J.: 1986, *Generalized Binding*, Foris, Dordrecht.

Aoun, J. L. Choueiri, and N. Hornstein: 1999, "Bound Pronominals," MS, University of Southern California, Los Angeles and University of Maryland, College Park.

Aoun, J. and R. Clark: 1985, "On Non-Overt Operators," *Southern California Occasional Papers in Linguistics* 10: 17–36.

Aoun, J., N. Hornstein, D. Lightfoot, and A. Weinberg: 1987, "Two Types of Locality," *Linguistic Inquiry* 18: 537–77.

Aoun, J., N. Hornstein, and D. Sportiche: 1981, "Some Aspects of Wide Scope Quantification," *The Linguistic Review* 2: 211–36.

Aoun, J. and A. Li: 1993a, *Syntax of Scope*, MIT Press, Cambridge, MA.

Aoun, J. and A. Li: 1993b, "Wh-Elements in Situ: Syntax or LF," *Linguistic Inquiry* 24: 199–238.

Arnold, M. D.: 1995, "Case, Periphrastic *Do* and the Loss of Verb Movement in English," Ph.D. dissertation, University of Maryland, College Park.

Authier, J.-M.: 1992, "A Parametric Account of V-Governed Arbitrary Null Arguments," *Natural Language and Linguistic Theory* 10: 345–74.

Bach, E.: 1979, "Control in Montague Grammar," *Linguistic Inquiry* 10: 515–31.

Bates, E. and J. Elman: 1996, "Learning Rediscovered," *Science* 274: 1849–50.

Bobaljik, J. D. and S. Brown: 1997, "Interarboreal Operations: Head Movement and the Extension Requirement," *Linguistic Inquiry* 28: 345–56.

Boeckx, C.: 2000, "A Note on Contraction," *Linguistic Inquiry* 31: 357–66.

Bosković, Z.: 1994, "D-Structure, Theta-Criterion, and Movement into Theta-Positions," *Linguistic Analysis* 24: 247–86.

Boskovic, Z.: 1995, "Principles of Economy in Nonfinite Complementation," Ph.D. Dissertation, Storrs, University of Connecticut.

Boskovic, Z.: 1999, "On Multiple Feature Checking: Multiple Wh-Fronting and Multiple Head Movement," in S. D. Epstein and N. Hornstein (eds.) *Working Minimalism*, MIT Press, Cambridge, MA, 159–87.

Boskovic, Z. and D. Takahashi: 1998, "Scrambling and Last Resort," *Linguistic Inquiry* 29: 347–66.

Bouchard, D.: 1984, *On the Content of Empty Categories*, Foris, Dordrecht.

Brody, M.: 1993, θ-Theory and Arguments, *Linguistic Inquiry* 24: 1–24.

Brody, M.: 1995, *Lexico-Logical Form*, MIT Press, Cambridge, MA.

Burzio, L.: 1986, *Italian Syntax*, Reidel, Dordrecht.

Cardinaletti, A.: 1997, "Agreement and Control in Expletive Constructions," *Linguistic Inquiry* 28: 521–33.

Castillo, J. C., J. E. Drury, and K. K. Grohmann: 1999, "Merge Over Move and the Extended Projection Principle," *University of Maryland Working Papers in Linguistics* 8: 63–103.

Chametzky, R.: 1996, *A Theory of Phrase Markers and the Extended Base*, State University of New York Press, Albany, NY.

Chierchia, G.: 1992, "Functional Wh and Weak Crossover," in D. Bates (ed.) *Proceedings of WCCFL 10*, CSLI, Stanford, CA, 75–90.

Chomsky, C.: 1969, *The Acquisition of Syntax in Children from 5 to 10*, MIT Press, Cambridge, MA.

Chomsky, N.: 1957, *Syntactic Structures*, Mouton, The Hague.

Chomsky, N.: 1964, *Current Issues in Linguistic Theory*, Mouton, The Hague.

Chomsky, N.: 1965, *Aspects of the Theory of Syntax*, MIT Press, Cambridge, MA.

Chomsky, N.: 1973, "Conditions on Transformations," in S. R. Anderson and P. Kiparsky (eds.) *A Festschrift for Morris Halle*, Holt, Rinehart and Winston, New York, 232–86.

Chomsky, N.: 1977, "On Wh-Movement," in P. W. Culicover, T. Wasow, and A. Akmajian (eds.) *Formal Syntax*, Academic Press, New York, 71–132.

Chomsky, N.: 1981, *Lectures on Government and Binding*, Foris, Dordrecht.

Chomsky, N.: 1982, *Some Concepts and Consequences of the Theory of Government and Binding*, MIT Press, Cambridge, MA.

Chomsky, N.: 1983, "Some Conceptual Shifts in the Study of Language," in L. S. Cauman, I. Levi, C. D. Parsons, and R. Schwartz (eds.) *How Many Questions? Essays in Honor of Sidney Morgenbesser*, Hachet Publications, Indianapolis, IN, 154–69.

Chomsky, N.: 1986a, *Barriers*, MIT Press, Cambridge, MA.

Chomsky, N.: 1986b, *Knowledge of Language*, Praeger, New York.

Chomsky, N.: 1991, "Some Notes on Economy of Derivation and Representation," in R. Freidin (ed.) *Principles and Parameters in Comparative Grammar*, MIT Press, Cambridge, MA, 417–54. Reprinted in Chomsky (1995), 129–66.

Chomsky, N.: 1993, "A Minimalist Program for Linguistic Theory," in K. Hale and S. J. Keyser (eds.) *The View from Building 20. Essays in Honor of Sylvain Bromberger*, MIT Press, Cambridge, MA.

Chomsky, N.: 1995, *The Minimalist Program*, MIT Press, Cambridge, MA.

Chomsky, N.: 1998, "Minimalist Inquiries: The Framework," *MIT Occasional Papers in Linguistics* 15, MITWPL, Cambridge, MA. To appear in R. Martin, D. Michaels, and J. Uriagereka (eds.) *Step by Step*, MIT Press, Cambridge, MA.

Chomsky, N. and M. Lasnik: 1977, "Filters and Control," *Linguistic Inquiry*, 8, 425–504.

Chomsky, N. and H. Lasnik: 1993, "The Theory of Principles and Parameters," in J. Jacobs, A. von Stechow, W. Sternefeld, and T. Vennemann (eds.) *Syntax: An International Handbook of Contemporary Research*, de Gruyter, Berlin, 506–70.

Chuang, L. L.: 1997, "Long Distance Anaphora and Multiple Feature Checking: A Minimalist Approach," Ph.D. dissertation, University of Maryland, College Park.

Cinque, G.: 1990, *Types of A'-Dependencies*, MIT Press, Cambridge, MA.

Clark, R.: 1985, "Boundaries and the Treatment of Control," Ph.D. dissertation, University of California, Los Angeles.

Comorovski, I.: 1996, *Interrogative Phrases and the Syntax-Semantics Interface*, Kluwer, Dordrecht.

Cowie, F.: 1999, *What's Within: Nativism Reconsidered*, Oxford University Press, Oxford.

Crain, S. and P. Pietroski: 1999, "Nature, Nurture and Universal Grammar," *University of Maryland Working Papers in Linguistics* 8: 118–63.

Culicover, P. and R. Jackendoff: Forthcoming, "Control Is Mostly Semantic," *Linguistic Inquiry*.

Dalrymple, M., M. Kanazawa, Y. Kim, S. Mchombo, and S. Peters: 1998, "Reciprocal Expressions and the Concept of Reciprocity," *Linguistics and Philosophy* 21: 159–210.

Diesing, M.: 1992, *Indefinites*, MIT Press, Cambridge, MA.

Dowty, D.: 1989, "On the Semantic Content of the Notion of 'Thematic Role'," in G. Chierchia, B. H. Partee and R. Turner (eds.) *Properties, Types and Meaning. Volume II: Semantic Issues*, Kluwer, Dordrecht, 69–129.

Dresher, B. E.: 1998, "Charting the Learning Path: Cues to Parameter Setting," *Linguistic Inquiry* 30: 27–67.

Dresher, E. and J. D. Kaye: 1990, "A Computational Learning Model for Metrical Phonology," *Cognition* 34: 137–95.

Epstein, S. D.: 1999, "Un-Principled Syntax: The Derivation of Syntactic Relations," in S. D. Epstein and N. Hornstein (eds.) *Working Minimalism*, MIT Press, Cambridge, MA, 317–45.

Epstein, S. D., E. M. Groat, R. Kawashima, and H. Kitahara: 1998, *A Derivational Approach to Syntactic Relations*, Oxford University Press, Oxford.

Etxepare, R.: 1998, "Minimalist Perspectives on Pied-Piping," paper presented at the *17th Summer Courses*, University of the Basque Country, San Sebastian/Donostia (July).

Fodor, J.: 1975, *The Language of Thought*, Thomas Y. Crowell, New York.

Fox, D.: 1998, "Economy and Scope," *Natural Language Semantics* 3: 283–341.

Fox, D.: 1999, "Reconstruction, Binding Theory and the Interpretation of Chains," *Linguistic Inquiry* 30: 147–96.

Grimshaw, J.: 1990, *Extended Projections*, MIT Press, Cambridge, MA.

Grohmann, K. K.: 1998, "Syntactic Inquiries into Discourse Requirements on Multiple Interrogatives," *Groninger Arbeiten zur germanistischen Linguistik* 42: 1–60.

Helke, M.: 1970, "The Grammar of English Reflexives," Ph.D. dissertation, MIT, Cambridge, MA.

Higginbotham, J.: 1980, "Pronouns and Bound Variables," *Linguistic Inquiry* 11: 679–708.

Higginbotham, J.: 1983, "Logical Form, Binding and Nominals," *Linguistic Inquiry* 14: 395–420.

Higginbotham, J.: 1992, "Reference and Control," in R. Larson, S. Iatridou, U. Lahiri, and J. Higginbotham (eds.) *Control and Grammar*, Kluwer, Dordrecht, 79–108.

Higgins, R.: 1973, "The Pseudocleft Construction in English," Ph.D. dissertation, MIT, Cambridge, MA.

Hornstein, N.: 1995, *Logical Form. From GB to Minimalism*, Blackwell, Oxford.

Hornstein, N.: 1998, "Movement and Chains," *Syntax*, 1, 99–127.

Hornstein, N.: 1999, "Movement and Control," *Linguistic Inquiry*, 30, 69–96.

Hornstein, N. and D. Lightfoot: 1981, "Introduction," in N. Hornstein and D. Lightfoot (eds.) *Explanation in Linguistics: The Logical Problem of Language Acquisition*, Longman, London, 9–31.

Hornstein, N. and D. Lightfoot: 1987, "Predication and PRO," *Language* 63: 23–52.

Hornstein, N. and D. Lightfoot: 2000, "Minimizing Government," MS, University of Maryland, College Park.

Hornstein, N. and A. Weinberg: 1990, 'The Necessity of LF," *The Linguistic Review* 7: 129–67.

Huang, C.-T. J.: 1983, "A Note on the Binding Theory," *Linguistic Inquiry* 14: 554–61.

Jackendoff, R.: 1992, *Languages of the Mind: Essays on Mental Representation*, MIT Press, Cambridge, MA.

Jaeggli, O.: 1980, "On Some Phonologically Null Elements in Syntax," Ph.D. dissertation, MIT, Cambridge.

Jones, C.: 1985, "Syntax and Thematics of Infinitival Adjuncts," Ph.D. dissertation, University of Massachusetts, Amherst.

Jones, C.: 1991, "Decapitation (or Some So-Called 'Null Operator' Constructions)," in A. L. Halpern (ed.) *Proceedings of WCCFL 9*, CSLI, Stanford, 317–29.

Kajita, M.: 1967, *A Generative-Transformational Study of Semi-Auxiliaries in Present-Day American English*, Ph.D. dissertation, Princeton University.

Kato, M. and J. Nunes: 1998, "Two Sources for Relative Clause Formation in Brazilian Portuguese," paper presented at the *Eighth Collquium on Generative Grammar*, Universidade de Lisboa, Palmela (April).

Kawashima, R. and H. Kitahara: 1996, "Strict Cyclicity, Linear Ordering and Derivational C-Command," in J. Camacho, L. Choueiri, and M. Watanabe (eds.) *Proceedings of WCCFL 14*, CSLI, Stanford, CA, 255–69.

Kayne, R. S.: 1981, "ECP Extensions," *Linguistic Inquiry* 12: 93–133.

Kayne, R. S.: 1984, *Connectedness and Binary Branching*, Foris, Dordrecht.

Kayne, R. S.: 1989, "Facets of Romance Past Participle Agreement," in P. Benincà (ed.) *Dialect Variation and the Theory of Grammar*, Foris, Dordrecht, 85–104.

Kayne, R. S.: 1991, "Romance Clitics, Verb Movement, and PRO," *Linguistic Inquiry* 22: 647–86.

Kayne, R. S.: 1994, *The Antisymmetry of Syntax*, MIT Press, Cambridge, MA.

Keenan, E.: 1994, "Creating Anaphors: An Historical Study of the English Reflexive Pronouns," MS, University of California, Los Angeles.

Kennedy, C.: 1997, "Antecedent-Contained Deletion and the Syntax of Quantification," *Linguistic Inquiry* 28: 662–88.

Kim, K.: 1998, "(Anti)-Connectivity," Ph.D. dissertation, University of Maryland, College Park.

Kitahara, H.: 1999, "Eliminating* as a Feature (of Traces)," in S. D. Epstein and N. Hornstein (eds.) *Working Minimalism*, MIT Press, Cambridge, MA, 77–93.

Koizumi, M.: 1995, "Phrase Structure in Minimalist Syntax," Ph.D. dissertation, MIT, Cambridge, MA.

Koopman, H.: 1984, *The Syntax of Verbs: From Verb Movement Rules in the Kru Languages to Universal Grammar*, Foris, Dordrecht.

Koopman, H. and D. Sportiche: 1991, "The Position of Subjects," *Lingua* 85: 211–59.

Koster, J.: 1978, *Locality Principles in Syntax*, Foris, Dordrecht.

Koster, J.: 1984, "On Binding and Control," *Linguistic Inquiry* 15: 417–59.

Kuroda, S.-Y.: 1988, "Whether We Agree or Not: A Comparative Syntax of English and Japanese," *Lingvisticae Investigationes* 12: 1–47.

Larson, R. K.: 1988, "On the Double Object Construction," *Linguistic Inquiry* 19: 335–91.

Lasnik, H.: 1981, "Restricting the Theory of Transformations," in N. Hornstein and D. Lightfoot (eds.) *Explanation in Linguistics: The Logical Problem of Language Acquisition*, Longman, London, 152–73.

Lasnik, H.: 1992, "Two Notes on Control and Binding," in R. Larson, S. Iatridou, U. Lahiri, and J. Higginbotham (eds.) *Control and Grammar*, Kluwer, Dordrecht, 235–51.

Lasnik, H.: 1995a, "Last Resort," in S. Haraguchi and M. Funaki (eds.) *Minimalism and Linguistic Theory*, Hituzi Syobo, Tokyo, 1–32.

Lasnik, H.: 1995b, "Last Resort and Attract F," in *Proceedings of FLSM 6*, Indiana University Linguistics Club, Bloomington, IN, 62–81.

Lasnik, H.: 1995c, "Verbal Morphology: *Syntactic Structures* Meets the Minimalist Program," in P. Kempchinsky and H. Campos (eds.) *Evolution and Revolution in Linguistic Theory*, Georgetown University Press, Washington, DC, 251–75.

Lasnik, H.: 1995d, "A Note on Pseudogapping," in R. Pensalfini and H. Ura (eds.) *Papers on Minimalist Syntax, MIT Working Papers in Linguistics* 27: 143–63. Reprinted in H. Lasnik (1999) *Minimalist Analyses*, Blackwell, Oxford (not otherwise quoted in this bibliography).

Lasnik, H.: 1999, "Chains of arguments," in S. D. Epstein and N. Hornstein (eds.) *Working Minimalism*, MIT Press, Cambridge, MA, 189–215.

Lasnik, H. and M. Saito: 1992, *Move α: Conditions on Its Application and Output*, MIT Press, Cambridge, MA.

Lasnik, H. and M. Saito: 1993, "On the Subject of Infinitives," in L. K. Dobrin, L. Nichols and R. M. Rodriguez (eds.) *Papers from the 27th Regional Meeting of the Chicago Linguistic Society 1991. Part 1: The General Session*, Chicago Linguistics Society, University of Chicago, 324–43.

Lasnik, H. and J. Uriagereka: 1988, *A Course in GB Syntax*, MIT Press, Cambridge, MA.

Lebeaux, D.: 1983, "A Distributional Difference between Reciprocals and Reflexives," *Linguistic Inquiry* 14: 723–30.

Lebeaux, D.: 1984–5, "Locality and Anaphoric Binding," *The Linguistic Review* 343–63.

Lees, R. and E. Klima: 1963, "Rules for English Pronominalization," *Language* 39: 17–28.

Lidz, J.: 1997, "When Is a Reflexive Not a Reflexive? Near-Reflexivity and Condition R," in K. Kusomoto (ed.) *Proceedings of NELS 27*, GLSA, University of Massachusetts, Amherst, 251–61.

Lidz, J. and W. J. Idsardi: 1997, "Chains and Phono-Logical Form," in A. Dimitriadis, H. Lee, C. Moisset and A. Williams (eds.), *Proceedings of the 22nd Annual Penn Linguistics Colloquium. University of Pennsylvania Working Papers in Linguistics* 8, 109–25.

Lightfoot, D.: 1976, "Trace Theory and Twice Moved NPs," *Linguistic Inquiry* 7: 559–82.

Lightfoot, D.: 1982, *The Language Lottery: Toward a Biology of Grammars*, MIT Press, Cambridge, MA.

Lightfoot, D.: 1989, "The Child's Trigger Experience: Degree-0 Learnability," *Behavioural and Brain Sciences* 12: 321–34.

Lightfoot, D.: 1991, *How To Set Parameters: Arguments from Language Change*, MIT Press, Cambridge, MA.

Lightfoot, D.: 1999, *The Development of Language: Acquisition, Change and Evolution*, Blackwell, Oxford.

Longobardi, G.: 1994, "Reference and Proper Names: A Theory of N-Movement in Syntax and Logical Form," *Linguistic Inquiry* 25: 609–65.

Manzini, M. R.: 1983, "On Control and Control Theory," *Linguistic Inquiry* 14: 421–46.

Manzini, M. R. and A. Roussou: Forthcoming, "A Minimalist Theory of A-Movement and Control," *Lingua*.

Martin, R.: 1996, "A Minimalist Theory of PRO and Control," Ph.D. dissertation, University of Connecticut, Storrs.

Martin, R.: 1999, "Case, the Extended Projection Principle, and Minimalism," in S. D. Epstein and N. Hornstein (eds.) *Working Minimalism*, MIT Press, Cambridge, MA, 1–25.

Martin, R. and J. Uriagereka: 2000, "Introduction: Some Possible Foundations of the Minimalist Program," in R. Martin, D. Michaels and J. Uriagereka (eds.) *Step by Step*, MIT Press, Cambridge, MA.

May, R.: 1977, "The Grammar of Quantification," Ph.D. dissertation, MIT, Cambridge, MA.

May, R.: 1983, "Autonomy, Case and Variables," *Linguistic Inquiry* 13: 162–8.

May, R.: 1985, *Longical Form. Its Structure and Derivation*, MIT Press, Cambridge, MA.

Milsark, G.: 1974, "Existential Sentences in English," Ph.D. dissertation, MIT, Cambridge, MA.

O'Neill, J.: 1995, "Out of Control," in J. N. Beckman (ed.) *Proceedings of NELS 25*, GLSA, University of Massachusetts, Amherst, 361–71.

Nunes, J.: 1995, "The Copy Theory of Movement and Linearization of Chains in the Minimalist Program," Ph.D. dissertation, University of Maryland, College Park.

Nunes, J.: 1999, "Linearization of Chains and Phonetic Realization of Chain Links," in S. D. Epstein and N. Hornstein (eds.) *Working Minimalism*, MIT Press, Cambridge, MA, 217–49.

Nunes, J. and J. Uriagereka: Forthcoming, "Cyclicity and Extraction Domains," *Syntax*.

Pesetsky, D.: 1991, "Zero Syntax II: An Essay on Infinitives," MS, MIT, Cambridge, MA.

Postal, P.: 1971, *Cross-Over Phenomena*, Holt, Rinehart and Winston, New York.

Postal, P.: 1974, *On Raising: One Rule of English Grammar and Its Theoretical Implications*, MIT Press, Cambridge, MA.

Reinhart, T.: 1983, *Anaphora and Semantic Interpretation*, Croom Helm, London.

Reinhart, T.: 1995, "Interface Strategies," OTS Working Papers, Utrecht University.

Reinhart, T. and E. Reuland: 1993, "Reflexivity," *Linguistic Inquiry* 24: 657–720.

Reuland, E. 1996, "Pronouns and Features," *Proceedings of NELs 26*, K. Kusumoto ed., Amherst, MA.

Richards, N.: 1997, "What Moves Where When in Which Language?," Ph.D. dissertation, MIT, Cambridge, MA.

Richards, N.: 1999, "Featural Cyclicity and the Ordering of Multiple Specifiers," in S. D. Epstein and N. Hornstein (eds.) *Working Minimalism*, MIT Press, Cambridge, MA, 127–58.

Rizzi, L.: 1986, "Null Objects in Italian and the Theory of *pro*," *Linguistic Inquiry* 17: 501–57.

Rizzi, L.: 1990, *Relativized Minimality*, MIT Press, Cambridge, MA.

Rosenbaum, P.: 1967, *The Grammar of English Predicate Complement Constructions*, MIT Press, Cambridge, MA.

Rosenbaum, P.: 1970, "A Principle Governing Deletion in English Sentential Complementations," in R. Jacobs and P. Rosenbaum (eds.) *Readings in English Transformational Grammar*, Ginn, Waltham, MA, 20–9.

Rudin, C.: 1988, "On Multiple Questions and Multiple Wh-Fronting," *Natural Language and Linguistic Theory* 6: 445–501.

Safir, K.: 1997, "Symmetry and Unity in the Theory of Anaphora," in H. Bennis, P. Pica and J. Rooryck (eds.) *Atomism and Binding*, Foris, Dordrecht, 341–79.

Sag, I.: 1976, "Deletion and Logical Form," Ph.D. dissertation, MIT, Cambridge, MA.

Salmon, N.: 1986, "Reflexivity," *Notre Dame Journal of Formal Logic* 27: 401–29.

Salmon, N.: 1992, "Reflections on Reflexivity," *Linguistics and Philosophy* 15: 53–63.

Schein, B.: 1993, *Plurals and Events*, MIT Press, Cambridge, MA.

Soames, S.: 1989/90, "Pronouns and Propositional Attitudes," *Proceedings of the Aristotelian Society* XC, Part 3, 191–212.

Sportiche, D.: 1988, "A Theory of Floating Quantifiers and Its Corollaries for Constituent Structure," *Linguistic Inquiry* 19: 425–49.

Stjepanović, S.: 1995, "Short-Distance Movement of Wh-Phrases in Serbo-Croatian Matrix Clauses," MS, University of Connecticut, Storrs.

Stowell, T.: 1981, "The Origins of Phrase Structure," Ph.D. dissertation, MIT, Cambridge, MA.

Stowell, T.: 1982, "The Tense of Infinitives," *Linguistic Inquiry* 13: 561–70.

Tsai, W.-T. D.: 1994, "On Economizing A-Bar Dependencies," Ph.D. dissertation, MIT, Cambridge, MA.

Uriagereka, J.: 1988, "On Government," Ph.D. dissertation, University of Connecticut, Storrs.

Uriagereka, J.: 1998, *Rhyme and Reason*, MIT Press, Cambridge, MA.

Uriagereka, J.: 1999, "Multiple Spell Out," in S. D. Epstein and N. Hornstein (eds.) *Working Minimalism*, MIT Press, Cambridge, MA, 251–82.

Vergnaud, J.-R.: 1974, "French Relative Clauses," Ph.D. dissertation, MIT, Cambridge, Mass.

Watanabe, A.: 1992, "Wh-In-Situ, Subjacency, and Chain Formation," *MIT Occasional Papers in Linguistics* 2, MITWPL, Cambridge, MA.

Weinberg, A.: 1988, "Locality Principles in Syntax and Parsing," Ph.D. dissertation, MIT, Cambridge, MA.

Williams, E.: 1977, "Discourse and Logical Form," *Linguistic Inquiry* 8: 101–39.

Williams, E.: 1980, "Predication," *Linguistic Inquiry* 11: 203–38.

Williams, E.: 1982, "The NP Cycle," *Linguistic Inquiry* 13: 277–96.

Williams, E.: 1983, "Syntactic vs. Semantic Categories," *Linguistics and Philosophy* 6: 423–46.

Woolford, E.: 1999, "More on the Anaphor Agreement Effect," *Linguistic Inquiry* 30: 257–87.

Wu, J.: 1999, "A Minimalist Account of Quantification in Chinese," Ph.D. dissertation, University of Maryland, College Park.

vanden Wyngaerd, G.: 1994, *PRO-legomena: Distribution and Reference of Infinitival Subjects*, Mouton de Gruyter, Berlin.

Zubizarreta, M.-L.: 1987, *Levels of Representation in the Lexicon and in the Syntax*, MIT Press, Cambridge, MA.

Index

Abney, S., 92
abstract level, 3, 5, 7, 8–10, 78, 125
  see also levels of representation;
    D-Structure; S-Structure
acquisition, 2, 35, 64 n.19
adjectives, 109–10, 112, 131 n.76, 197 n.31
  see also adverbs
adjunct clauses, 36, 46–9, 56, 60, 64 n.23,
    65 n.58, 72–4, 77–9, 81–4
Adjunct Control (AC), 18, 28, 36, 46–9,
    56, 60–1, 64 n.23, 67 n.50, 68 nn.58
    and 63, 72–137, 144, 181, 203 n.84,
    208
  see also adjuncts; control; movement,
    sidewards
adjunction, 20, 66 n.37, 74, 90, 96, 99,
    102, 105, 114, 121, 121 n.1, 126 n.37,
    128 n.44, 128 n.49, 130 n.67,
    131 nn.70 and 72, 134 n.99, 183,
    197 n.27, 198 n.42, 205 n.90
  see also adjuncts; adverbs; phrase
    marker; phrase structure; movement,
    sidewards
adjuncts, 66 n.37, 67 nn. 52 and 55,
    68 n.59, 78–9, 97, 99, 116, 121 n.1,
    123 n.11, 126 n.39, 128 nn.49 and 50,
    130 n.67, 131 n.72, 181, 183, 197 n.31,
    198 n.42, 218
  attachment of, 90–1, 97, 99, 102,
    114–15, 121, 122 n.7, 126 n.38,
    127 n.40, 128 n.44, 132 n.83
  vs. complements, 78, 95, 127 n.43,
    128 n.46, 199 n.47, 218
  and extension, 20, 74, 130 n.66, 183,
    205 n.90
  head of, 108, 117, 124 n.20, 197 n.27
  infinitival, 110, 128 n.43
  and selection, 95–6, 123 n.12,
    134 n.99

see also Adjunct Control; movement,
    sidewards; phrases; self, as an
    adjunct; specifiers; X'-structure
adverbs, 99, 111, 128 n.50, 187, 206 n.98
  circumstantial, 111
  manner, 128 n.50
  presentential/scene-setting, 111
  pronominal, 139
  of quantification, 206 n.98
  sentential, 132 n.83
  temporal, 128 n.50
  see also adjectives; adjunction; adjuncts;
    movement, sidewards
Affect Output Principle, 201
agreement, 11–12, 16, 29, 50–1, 69 n.65,
    74, 76, 118–19, 123 n.16, 132 n.79,
    161, 174, 188–90, 195 n.24, 197 n.31,
    203 n.84, 223 n.8
  see also configurations; features;
    movement
A-movement, 39, 42, 60, 66 n.39, 82, 90,
    98, 103, 118–19, 127 n.40, 152, 156,
    166, 168, 181, 188, 213, 220
  overt vs. covert, 8, 22 n.13, 39, 51,
    70 n.72, 80, 152, 155–62, 161, 165–6,
    170, 172, 175, 184–5, 188, 191,
    193 n.7, 195 n.24, 196 n.25, 197 n.28,
    223 n.10
  see also case, copies; control; features;
    movement; NP-movement;
    pronouns; raising; reflexives; self;
    traces
A'-movement, 76–7, 80, 81–2, 85, 103,
    107, 118, 203 n.82, 208
  covert vs. overt, 79, 81, 107, 111, 119,
    124 n.17, 125 n.34
  multiple, 142
  see also Adjunct Control; movement;
    WH movement